ORIGINS OF THE RUSSIAN INTELLIGENTSIA

BY MARC RAEFF:

Siberia and the Reforms of 1822

*Michael Speransky: Statesman of Imperial
Russia, 1772–1839*

*Russian Intellectual History:
An Anthology*

*Origins of the Russian Intelligentsia:
The Eighteenth-Century Nobility*

TRANSLATIONS:

The Decembrist Movement

*Plans for Political Reform
in Imperial Russia*

Origins of the Russian Intelligentsia

The Eighteenth-Century Nobility

MARC RAEFF

An Original Harbinger Book

HARCOURT, BRACE & WORLD, INC.

New York

ACKNOWLEDGMENTS

The research for this book was carried on at various stages through the generosity of the following institutions:

John Simon Guggenheim Memorial Foundation
American Philosophical Society
Social Science Research Council
Inter-University Committee on Travel Grants
American Council of Learned Societies
Russian Research Center, Harvard University
Clark University
Russian Institute, Columbia University

The help and encouragement of these institutions are gratefully acknowledged, but they are absolved from any responsibility for the ideas and opinions—as well as the shortcomings—of this book.

TO THE MEMORY OF MY FRIEND
Alexander Wittenberg
(*1926–1965*)

Contents

Contents

ORIGINS OF THE RUSSIAN INTELLIGENTSIA

ONE

Introduction

Two major themes, it can be said fairly, dominated the history of Imperial Russia from the reign of Peter the Great to the Revolution of 1917:[1] westernization (or modernization) and revolutionary ferment. These two developments had been brought about by small leadership groups, the nobility and the intelligentsia. Like westernization and revolutionary agitation, the nobility and the intelligentsia were related genetically, for the former was the seedbed of the latter. In the case of both trends, moreover, the state played a paramount role: actively participating in the process of westernization, consistently repressive and negatively conservative in its reaction to progressive aspirations. And so it was that the character and role of the nobility and intelligentsia were largely determined by their members' relationship to the state that had issued from the reforms of Peter the Great. But the actions of the two élite

3

groups were aimed at improving the lot of the entire Russian nation as well. Both the nobility and the intelligentsia, therefore, had to work out their attitude and relationship to the Russian people, mainly the peasantry. This process was not a smooth one, and it reflected the way in which the upper classes as well as the mass of peasants subjectively interpreted their relationship.

In recent years the intelligentsia has received much attention from historians, in the Soviet Union as well as in the West.[2] Much remains to be done still, of course. In particular, it seems to us, in order to understand fully the evolution and actions of a social group, we ought to have a good idea of its institutional and intellectual roots. As we lack a clear and full picture of the Russian nobleman in the eighteenth century, we are handicapped in our understanding of the characteristic traits of the nineteenth-century Russian intelligentsia who came out of the nobility. At the same time it is more difficult to appreciate and assess the process of westernization that—as far as the cultural life of the upper class is concerned—was virtually complete at the moment the intelligentsia made its appearance in the first quarter of the nineteenth century. The relationship between westernization and Russia's ideological development on the one hand, and between the élite and the state on the other, are of importance in understanding the dynamic forces that moved individual members of the intelligentsia. We are not forgetting, of course, that the men we count among the first Russian intelligentsia—Herzen, Bakunin, Stankevich, Khomiakov, for instance—were unusual personalities. All were near geniuses with very individual personalities and minds.[3] Yet what has sometimes seemed the personal fate and particular trait of a single individual actually proves to have been the effect of a whole group's experiences and attitudes.[4]

Unlike the intelligentsia, the nobility has received relatively little attention from modern historians. A few studies of a purely descriptive institutional type were published at the end of the nineteenth and the beginning of the twentieth centuries, but nothing substantive has been added since. The scholars who studied the nobility before 1917 were mainly historians of law and jurists, and they focused their attention almost exclusively on the juridical status of the nobles as a class and on their legal relationships to other classes and to the government. Left out of the picture were those institutional elements that shaped the life of the nobleman—his family, his education, his relations to other individuals, and his experiences as an active member of Russian society. Equally neglected was the meaning of the intellectual experiences a nobleman might acquire within the framework of this institutional pattern. Our study focuses, therefore, on these relatively neglected aspects of the life of the nobility in the eighteenth century, in the hope that our observations will throw useful light on the nature of the intelligentsia in the nineteenth century.

Undertaking the historical description and analysis of a social group is, at best, a most hazardous enterprise. In a sense, such an undertaking may perhaps never be successfully completed, for not only can we not take into account all the evidence but it is well nigh impossible to make due allowance for the many particulars that enter into the group and class. (And who can say that a specific fact or situation is exceptional rather than typical?) Incomplete as his results may be, in order to understand the nature and role of a group in the life of a people, the historian must try to make the available evidence meaningful. To come to grips with the history and character of a social group, three paths are open to him. The first approach is to make a detailed statistical investigation of a chronologically and geographically well-defined group, usually on the basis of documents recording its members' economic activities.[5] Not only is this a most difficult and tedious process, but its results are meager in comparison to the effort expended, for the picture that emerges is partial and static. In the case of the Russian nobility (as of most nobilities) the lack of documentation comparable to the notary records of the Parisian bourgeoisie makes such an approach even less profitable if one's prime interest is attitudes and frames of mind.

A second approach is to study one or several individual cases for which the records are fairly complete. But our most complete records usually relate to individuals or families that may not be considered typical in any significant way, and it may not be possible to make meaningful conclusions from the experiences of an individual (or a selected number of individuals).

The third approach—which we have followed—is to forgo the detailed monograph based on exhaustive documentation and try to sketch the main lines, convey the dynamics of a process, and interpret the forces and attitudes that have determined the history and role of the particular social group. Admittedly this approach harbors the danger of impressionistic judgments. But with care, constant reference to the sources, and the checking of intuitive conclusions against the hard facts of individual fates and events, the approach may yield meaningful observations. The results of such an undertaking are best presented in essay form, for it is the general trends and synthesis that matter, not the detailed facts and figures.

As a perusal of the footnotes will show, our sources fall into four major categories. First are official government sources, which contain many revealing details on individual situations and cases as well as evidence for broader trends. Curiously enough, we are better off for the first half of the eighteenth century than for the second. Interested in distilling some basic trends and broad patterns, we could easily discount the official bias of these documents and accept the accuracy of the concrete details. As the questions we addressed to these documents were quite different from those of their original authors, the latter's subjective bias could easily be disregarded.

Probably the most important second group consists of memoirs, diaries, and letters of contemporaries. Unfortunately the memoirs predominate, but used with caution they proved very revealing despite their obvious subjectivity and retrospectiveness. What we were interested in was so much taken for granted by eighteenth-century noblemen that they could not disguise it; but instead we were faced with the fact that the information and attitudes we sought were not explicitly stated, and had to be ferreted out from casual remarks and ordinary as well as unusual occurrences. Because of its chronological scope and variety of subject matter, the most voluminous and important memoir is that of A. T. Bolotov. And while Bolotov himself was an unusual figure, he described events he witnessed and contemporaries he met that were very ordinary and typical; this is true of much of the other memoir literature we used. We are also fortunate in having the reminiscences or diaries of rank-and-file members of the nobility, as well as those of eminent and exceptional figures.

The third kind of source consisted of contemporary literature, periodicals, pamphlets, and books, as well as Russian belles-lettres. These sources raise the very important question of the modes of expression as reflecting the cast of mind of eighteenth-century men, the use of symbols and metaphor as a key to the prevalent way of thought. But the problem proved too large for inclusion in this essay, and will have to be the subject of a later, separate study. It is these contemporary literary documents that provide the most important evidence on the intellectual life of the nobility. Much work has already been done on the various Western influences on Russian thought and culture in the eighteenth century, mainly by literary historians.[6] It was not necessary to go over the same ground. What we were concerned with in the last part of the essay was to determine the effect of these influences on the cast of mind of the Russian élite. We tried to find out what impact these cultural elements had in directing the attention of the educated Russians to the reality surrounding them and in showing them where to look for the solution of the problems they had come upon.[7]

Lastly, available biographies and monographs were consulted. The former are few in number, and in using the latter, which deal primarily with legal institutional aspects, it was possible to avoid going too much into the detail of legislative and formal institutional details.[8] We were interested in legislative and institutional regulations only in terms of their contribution to the noblemen's outlook, attitudes, and ideas. In this connection, too, we tried to indicate elements of comparison and contrast with the Western situation and tradition. But as these comparisons are by no means final or exhaustive, they have often been relegated to the notes.

Finally, we must turn to the always tricky problem of terminology, for Russian reality and concepts have no obvious equivalents in the West. Our study concerns the *dvorianstvo*[9] of the eighteenth century (or *shliakhetstvo*, as it was known in the first half of the century). We might have used the Russian term throughout, but it is cumbersome and not terribly helpful to the non-Russian-speaking reader. How, then, is one to translate this term? We have chosen to render it as "nobility." In British usage, "nobility" denotes titled persons of the realm. Such a restricted meaning would not be appropriate for eighteenth-century Russia, as there were few titled persons and they did not constitute a separate legal or social group. *Dvorianstvo* could be rendered as "gentry," as some English-speaking writers have it. Superficially this term corresponds rather well to Russian reality in the eighteenth century, except that in English historical literature "gentry" implies ownership of land and participation in local affairs. The Russian *dvorianstvo*, on the other hand, included all titled persons, serf owners, officers, officials, professional people, whether they owned land or not. The one thing they had in common—and which had no equivalent in the West—was that they held a specified rank in the Table of Ranks (or, at any rate, that they were children of a father who had held such a rank). As our exposition will hopefully make clear, the definition of the *dvorianstvo* remained vague in Russia throughout the period under consideration. No clear juridical definition was ever made, nor did the privileges enjoyed by noblemen in themselves define the nobility unambiguously.[10] The vagueness of the legal and social definition of the *dvorianstvo* reminds one of the French situation at the end of the eighteenth century, when the nobility had lost much of its original homogeneity and feudal *raison d'être*.

--- ◆ ---

The social and cultural preeminence of the nobility in Russia in the period from Peter the Great to the Emancipation needs no elaborate proof or illustration. Anyone acquainted with the essentials of the history of this period, and certainly anyone familiar with the major Russian writers of the nineteenth century, has been well aware of the nobility's paramount role in society, letters, government—in short, in the destinies of the country's élite. Far more controversial has been the question of the role played by the nobility in Russia's economic and political development—specifically, its impact on the modernization of Russia's economy on the one hand and on the administration and autocracy on the other. Of these two facets, it was the latter that was of prime importance in the formation of the patterns of thought and behavior characteristic of the intelligentsia that emerged in the first half of the nineteenth century. The fact that the first generation of the Russian intelligentsia stemmed largely from the nobility (though there were exceptions, of course) is well known.[11] But how did membership in this privileged class—which served the sovereign in return for economic and social advantages such as the right to own serfs and enjoyed virtual monopoly of all the benefits the system could offer—become transformed into membership in an "order" devoted to the overthrow of this system? This is the basic question we shall endeavor to answer as we examine the main features of the nobility's way of life and thought in eighteenth-century Russia. Inasmuch as the role of the intelligentsia was characterized by its ideological orientation and its political commitment (or attempt at action), it might be profitable to look for clues in the nature of the institutional relationships that determined the position of the nobility in eighteenth-century Russian society and helped to shape the cultural experience of its members.

The traditional view of the history of the Russian nobility in the eighteenth century can be summarized fairly as follows: Peter the Great subjected the nobility to compulsory state service, a service that was difficult, harsh, and very much hated by the nobles. After his death, profiting from the weakness of his successors, the confusion created by the absence of a clear law of succession, and the military power concentrated in the noble guard regiments, the nobility strove relentlessly for its "liberation" from compulsory service and the securing of its position as a privileged class or estate, with complete mastery over the serf population. Freedom from service was achieved in 1762; privileged corporate status and absolute control over the serfs was established by 1785. Thus, the argument goes, the eighteenth century saw the gradual satisfaction of all the nobility's demands, the victory of the nobility over the resistance of the state.

But if this was the case, one may well ask, why did Russia not evolve into an aristocratic society and oligarchic state? Why did the nobility not further exploit its "victory" over the state politically? After all, in spite of the favor shown the nobility by Catherine the Great (whose reign seems in retrospect to have been the golden age of the nobility), Russia did remain an autocracy. The absolute power of the emperor was not whittled down, the nobility did not cease to be a service class, and its political and economic role in the country did not become fully secure. This paradoxical outcome of the nobility's "victory" is usually explained by the "alliance" struck between the nobility and the autocracy in order to preserve serfdom. But this explanation does not seem quite convincing. It fails to account for the serious frictions between the autocracy and nobility—frictions that contributed to the emergence of the intelligentsia from among the ranks of the nobility; nor does the explanation fully account for the radical ideology and orientation of the members of the intelligentsia and for the profound, and eventually irreconcilable, opposition between the state ("they") and society ("we"). The thesis also suffers from an inability to explain satisfactorily why it was the state, the autocracy, that initiated emancipation at the expense of the nobility and why it failed to take the nobility into its political confidence. Finally, the traditional interpretation fails completely in accounting for the suspicion with which the state viewed all efforts of the nobility to consolidate and implement the rights granted to it in 1785 and to develop a more active, responsible role as the first "estate" of the realm. Eventually, the government (or the bureaucracy) was to become completely alienated from the nobility (or vice versa) from which it had originally issued.

Can we, therefore, not account more adequately for the situation of the Russian élite around, say, 1820? Around 1820 the autocracy was in full command, and the nobility suffered from a great deal of social and political insecurity. We can abandon the traditional emphasis on the striving for liberation from state service as the major driving force in the political life of the nobility in the eighteenth century without denying that state service was both onerous and frequently resented, or that many noblemen did everything in their power to avoid it. But service did remain an obligation until 1762, and even under the weak rulers who occupied the throne between 1725 and 1762 no attempt was made to completely eliminate state service as the principal duty and occupation of the nobleman. Nor did Peter III's "freeing" of the nobility, incidentally, save his crown and life. Even after the abolition of its compulsory character, state service remained the most popular way of life for the nobility, and the ranks obtained through state service remained the prime factor in defining the status of members of the upper class in the Russian Empire.

The present essay will attempt to determine the meaning of state service in Russia in the eighteenth century, its requirements, and—most important of all—its influence and role in shaping the nobleman's outlook on himself and his society. We shall therefore stress the positive effects (without any value judgment) of service on the nobility. Of course, this does not mean that the negative features that have been pointed out in the historical literature did not play a role too. Nor does it mean that other factors, such as the economic effects of serfdom, for example, were not significant as well. The contribution of such factors to the formation and character of the Russian élite will certainly be touched upon in these pages, and obviously, the same material might be used to illustrate other aspects of the nobleman's life as well. But we have fastened on what seemed to us the one experience that largely determined all other facets of his thinking and feeling, for it is these latter that he transmitted to his "children," the first generation of the intelligentsia.

Although we are dealing with a social class that was numerically small (between .5 and 1 per cent of the total population in the eighteenth century), we have focused on only those elements that participated actively in the cultural and institutional life of the country. Indeed it is from their ranks that came both the creators of modern Russian culture and the critics of its conditions—in short, the élite of Russian society. For this reason we have stressed the factors that actively shaped their points of view and patterns of behavior, and largely left out of the picture the life patterns and experiences of inert members of the ruling class.

In short, this essay describes a set of concentric circles.

The reader will be led from the widest to the narrowest—in terms of both activities and members involved. In the widest circle we shall discover the pattern of service and its effects on all members of the nobility. In the second circle we shall focus on the educational experiences of a broad élite from among the nobility. Finally, in the smallest circle we shall observe the currents that agitated the most sophisticated and enlightened members of Russia's leading class.

TWO

The Noble Serviceman
in Muscovite Russia

A T T H E beginning of the sixteenth century, Muscovy hardly knew a homogeneous and well-defined social class.[1] The nobility was no exception, and it too was composed of a large number of disparate and variegated groups, some of which survived even into the period of our concern. Two major groups constituted the nobility of Muscovy: the class of the old servants of the Grand Duke of Moscow, the boyars, and the formerly appanaged (*udel'nyi*) princes.[2] The latter usually did carry the title of "prince" (*kniaz'*), the only title (as opposed to service rank) known in Muscovy. According to Russian custom, the title was inherited by all male members of the family. As a result, some of these appanaged families sprouted into large trees with many branches, that varied greatly in wealth and importance, depending on accidents of succession and good or bad fortunes in the service of the Grand Duke of Moscow. By the beginning of the seventeenth century, however, the old service boyars and those former appanaged princes who had preserved a high social and economic status had merged into a single class. The appanaged princes had completely lost their connection with the region they had formerly ruled as independent sovereigns. They were now owners of large estates in other areas of Muscovy (the process of dispersion had been much accelerated by the policies of Ivan the Terrible), and except for name and title they were identical with the Moscow boyars. While the princes claimed precedence over the boyars, they could make this claim stick only on grounds of service function and the favor bestowed upon them by the Tsar of Moscow.[3]

Beginning late in the fifteenth century, and more particularly throughout the sixteenth century, there arose a new group of noblemen: the service nobles of the Grand Duke and Tsar, the *dvoriane* (sing. *dvorianin*). Originally they had been ordinary servants and lowly military retainers of the grand dukes, attached to the latter's household and court.[4] The *dvoriane* rose in importance as a consequence of the growing need for a large-scale military establishment, the increasing complexity of administering an expanding empire, and the relative decline of the old boyar and appanaged group whose loyalty the Tsars, especially Ivan the Terrible, felt justified in questioning.[5] During the sixteenth and seventeenth centuries these new service nobles bore a variety of names, depending on their functions and service status: *boiarskie deti, moskovskie dvoriane, gorodskie,* etc., and they were referred to collectively as *sluzhilye liudi* (service people). They were given means of support for themselves and their squires or servants and rewarded for loyal and long service by the granting of estates—*pomestie* (hence also their name *pomeshchik,* possessor of an estate; later the word came to signify land and serf owner). Theoretically, the serviceman retained the *pomestie* and his economic and social status only on condition that he remain in the Tsar's service, and upon the serviceman's retirement or death the estate reverted to the state, unless the serviceman's children took over his service obligations.[6] But over a period of several generations, the status in effect became hereditary. The noble's service status did not prevent him from acquiring land in his own right through purchase, marriage, or inheritance; such lands were owned permanently on a personal basis and called "patrimony" (*votchina*). Quite naturally, the serving nobleman aimed at obtaining similar right of permanent personal ownership of his granted *pomestie*. But by the end of the seventeenth century this permanence had not been granted to him by law, though in the majority of cases it was so in fact. Even the lowliest serviceman could rise to the status of the upper nobility by dint of great effort, ability, and luck. He might be able to obtain a high rank (*chin*) at court and even become a member of the boyar duma (as did Ordyn-Nashchokin, for instance). Usually, however, such progress was very slow and extended over several generations, the role of family status being the major handicap that had to be overcome, as we shall see shortly.[7]

As the preceding summary has brought out, the status of a person within the nobility depended mainly on his service functions and rank. This was equally true of the old Muscovite boyar, the newly created *dvorianin,* and of the formerly appanaged prince. Members of princely families or of old boyar houses who did not take up or continue active service for the Tsar saw their status decline very rapidly. Their children fell to the rank of ordinary nobles, and sometimes their descendants would be lost altogether among the tax-paying commoners. This process was called *zakhudenie* —that is, "growing wan"—a picturesque description of the social reality involved.[8] There was also an economic reason for the widespread character of this process in Muscovite Russia: the absence of primogeniture and entail. Inheritances, including patrimonies of boyars and formerly appanaged princes, were split up among all children, so that within a few generations even the largest patrimony was fragmented into parcels barely large enough to support an average family adequately.[9] One way of counteracting the effect of this practice was to enter the service of the Tsar so as to receive new grants of land and valuable gifts. Thus service became the most natural way of retaining wealth and acquiring status, for in the final analysis nobility depended on service in the military and administrative concerns of the Tsar. So strong was service as a means to economic, social, and political status that even the appanaged princes, who theoretically could have been independent of service, were drawn into it.

Whatever the origins of the first boyars in the Kievan state, the noblemen in Muscovy were creatures of the sovereign, the nobility a by-product, or result, of the service system. Naturally this situation affected the relationship between noblemen and Tsar. The elements of a feudal order —with its autonomy for social classes and hierarchy of mutual obligations and rights—may have existed in the fourteenth and fifteenth centuries in Russia. But whatever there was of a feudal system—and there is even question of the very existence of its embryonic elements—did not survive the radical policies of Ivan the Terrible and the upheavals of the Times of Troubles.[10] In the seventeenth century, therefore, the relationship between nobles and Tsar was simple and one-sided. The noble was in complete subjugation to the Tsar, at least in law. The relationship, of course, might be attenuated and varied, depending on personalities and circumstances, but the basic fact remains that the nobleman felt that all he had—name, position, wealth—depended on his service to the Tsar. It was no accident that to the Tsar any noble, however high his status, was nothing but a servant (*kholop*).[11] The nobleman used only deprecatory diminutives for his own name when addressing the Tsar, while public ceremonial and court etiquette emphasized the subservient, humble status of the nobleman.[12] Muscovy knew nothing that even remotely resembled the independence and pride of a Western feudal noble vis à vis his lord and king.[13]

Of course, in speaking of seventeenth-century Russia we are speaking of a society that was still very much family oriented, whose legal and social outlook was largely determined by clan ties and loyalties (although Solov'ev and other historians have certainly exaggerated the role of clan organization (*rodovoi byt*) as a determining factor in pre-Petrine Moscow). In addition, the respect in which certain traditional values and institutions were held precluded even the most absolute and powerful rulers from readily flouting them. (Ivan the Terrible did, but few of his successors would be tempted to follow his example.) Kliuchevskii grasped the essence of the situation when he wrote with his usual felicity of expression that "the lord of Muscovy had wide power over the individual, but not over the institutions." While most of these institutions had arisen out of the service needs of the state, they had by the seventeenth century acquired some autonomy by force of prescription. The Tsar could violate these patterns openly and freely, but without urgent necessity he preferred not to do so. Could it have been otherwise in a relatively primitive and simple rural society that had not yet turned to modern technology and rationalism? We should think of seventeenth-century Russia, not in terms of contemporary France, England, or Sweden, but in terms of fifteenth-century Western Europe before the triumph of the modern absolute state.

These circumstances explain the role played by the family —or clan, to give the literal translation of the Russian term *rod*—in Muscovite Russia. The assertion that the Slavs had always possessed a stronger notion of family and group solidarity than did any other peasant society is questionable. The legacy of migration, colonization, and mobility over the vastness of the Russian plain, as well as the individual's consequent feeling of insecurity, would sufficiently account for the dominant role played by family ties. The family was the only institution that could counteract the individual's sense of isolation in space and his insecurity with respect to his neighbors and to his political overlord (be he a Mongol khan or a Russian grand duke). Family solidarity also waxed strong as a means of countering the individual nobleman's complete dependence on the prince's favor and the splintering tendencies of the inheritance system. It was also used to perpetuate, or at least safeguard, for more than one generation the gains and advantages acquired by a single individual or generation. How else could status, wealth, and privilege acquired through service be preserved and transmitted to successive generations?

In the West the nobleman's status rested on his power as a local lord and only secondarily on his function in the royal service (an exception, and only a partial one at that, was the courtier at Versailles under Louis XIV).[14] In Russia, on the other hand, only the advantages and status acquired by service to the state were of value. This was the origin of the peculiar system of precedence, *mestnichestvo,* which was current in Muscovy from about the end of the fifteenth century until 1682. The immediate cause for its development was the effort made by the Moscow boyars to protect their status against the influx of formerly appanaged princes and their retainers. The system sank roots also because it played into the hands of the grand dukes (as a means of keeping the former independent princes from gaining the upper hand) and—paradoxically—into the hands of those formerly independent princes who had risen to high posts in Moscow and wanted to safeguard their new gains against newcomers.[15]

The *mestnichestvo* system defined the status of a family on the basis of the service rank attained by its head; furthermore, it stipulated that subsequent members of the family —provided they served—be appointed only to those functions that in dignity and status were not below the rank attained by their forebear. It also meant in practice that the

Tsar could not appoint anyone he wished if such appointment meant subordinating an official whose family status was
high to someone whose family status was lower. Of course,
the Tsar was free to raise any of his servants to whatever
rank he wished, but the custom developed that such promotions could not come too rapidly and in complete disregard
of the claims of status seniority that other families made.
Conversely, and it serves to underline the service nature of
the nobility, a family's high status was easily lost if its members either did not serve or served so little and poorly that
they could not possibly be appointed to positions commensu-
rate with their family's status.[16] We are not concerned here
with the practical consequences of the system on the efficiency of military and administrative institutions. The main
handicaps of the system with respect to military operations
had been removed in the middle of the sixteenth century
when appointments to commands in the field were exempted
from *mestnichestvo* considerations. The main sources of dis-
putes and conflicts about precedence arose primarily in cases
of appointments to high court functions and did not affect
the average nobleman's service career.

Quite obviously, the *mestnichestvo* was designed to balance
the exclusive dependence on service as a source of status
and wealth. It provided some security and continuity for the
status of a family, even if it did not enhance the personal
security of a particular individual. The system might also be
construed as limiting the Tsar's absolute freedom of action,
for he could only confer ranks on individuals, not give status
to families.[17] ("The Tsar grants rank, not family status." [18])
But to interpret this restriction as a real limitation on the
autocracy does not seem very convincing. In the final analysis, even family status was dependent on service. True, the
mestnichestvo might conceivably have provided the basis for
the transformation of the Muscovite service nobility into a
genuine "estate" with an autonomous existence not completely dependent on the arbitrary will of the autocratic

Tsar. But instead of becoming the foundation for a genuine aristocracy or "noble estate," the *mestnichestvo* handicapped good administration and leadership and developed into a source of insoluble conflicts that rent the ranks of the nobility.

On one hand, well-established families, whose members had distinguished themselves in the past and held high functions for several generations, were eager to preserve a system that perpetuated their status automatically. In Max Weber's terminology, these nobles claimed that their ancestors had displayed charismatic talents in the service of Tsar and country and that this charisma, transmitted through inheritance, justified their present high status. Looking to conditions prevailing abroad, especially in Poland and Sweden (with whom Muscovy had frequent, if not always friendly, contacts), they wanted to make use of the *mestnichestvo* to create a true aristocratic, hereditary privileged estate.

On the other hand, the same reasons that made the old and important families defend the *mestnichestvo* system led the run-of-the-mill noble servicemen to oppose it. Indeed, the *dvorianin* could expect promotions and eventually high social status only by dint of his merits in service. Perpetuation of high status and preference in appointments reserved for some families were a barrier to his own rise. Sometimes he too referred to the example of Poland, but it was to stress the equality under law of all members of the nobility (*szlachta*).[19]

The Russian nobility of the seventeenth century (as of the sixteenth) was a deeply divided class. It was composed of at least two main groups whose interests diverged radically; their strength was rather evenly balanced, for the advantage one held in terms of numbers, the other made up by wealth and status. In the seventeenth century, therefore, we note the continuing basic conflict between the principles of family and merit. The former was facing an uphill struggle, as it was opposed by the monarchs as well as by the rank-and-file service noblemen. In the final analysis, the conflict between service and family, *sluzhba* and *rod,* had become the dominant element in the historical condition and destiny of the Russian nobility.

If everything about the nobility hinged on service, what was the nature of this important element, what were its institutional and cultural manifestations?

The rules of service were uniform for all members of the nobility. Yet, in practice, a distinction can be made between those who served at the Tsar's court in Moscow and the ordinary servicemen in the provinces and in the field. For the holders of *pomestie,* service was compulsory, as usufruct[20] and possession of land and peasants hinged on performance of service. As the seventeenth century drew to a close, however, many service nobles also acquired patrimonial holdings in full ownership and began to consider their *pomestie* as part of their patrimony.[21] It is not surprising that these noblemen did not recognize the absolute necessity to serve the state as a condition for possession of their estates. They endeavored, more or less successfully, to evade their service obligations without forfeiting their economic privileges. Since the country was vast and the Tsar's law enforcement staff was small (and not infrequently reluctant to exercise its power against fellow noblemen), avoidance of service was possible, at least for a while. Much has been made of the known cases of evasion and resistance through flight, bribery, or outright disobedience. Many historians have seen in these instances evidence of a very widespread situation and have argued that evasion of service was attempted by almost everybody, though not always successfully. But the fact remains that the Tsar did always manage to staff his armies and administration quite adequately for his needs as they were conceived at the time. Admittedly, evasion of service was not uncommon, but it was the exception, while the performance of service obligations was still the prevailing norm.

In principle, the serviceman was subjected to call to service from the moment he was capable of bearing arms—usually at the age of fifteen—and he was expected to remain at the call of the Tsar until old age or infirmities had rendered him useless in the field. But even then he could still be called upon to take on assignments in the administration. This life-long service, however, was "seasonal." In time of war the nobleman was called to his regiment or unit when the campaign opened (usually in spring), and he went home in winter when the operations came to a standstill. He was called only when a war was planned or actually declared, or in those rare instances when his unit was ordered to special maneuvers or given special assignments (usually of a ceremonial nature). For the remainder of his time the nobleman stayed home and managed his estate. With the development and increase in numbers of professional troops and foreign regiments, the petty country nobleman was called only when he was needed for serious military efforts. The corps of average small servicemen became more like a militia than a regular military force.

From the somewhat limited evidence available, it would appear that in the course of the seventeenth century the practice had developed for the provincial nobility to serve in units along territorial (geographic) lines. Nobles from the same area formed a regiment, company, or whatever.[22] Service in common and the resulting social and psychological closeness gave rise to a sense of group solidarity, almost to an *esprit de corps*. This novel development also found expression in the fact that these territorial units tended to elect their officers and commanders from those in their own midst and decided on the distribution of duties and burdens in common. In some cases this corporate approach was transferred to the domain of local administration and these same nobles elected their local judicial and administrative officials. This trend was particularly noticeable in the long-settled and rather homogeneous areas of northeastern European Russia.[23] It was a situation that permitted the survival of local differences and the perpetuation of special customs, rights, and privileges within certain groups of the nobility. Besides the Cossack Host, which does not belong to our story, this was the case of the service nobility in several border areas, the best documented example being that of Bielorussia. There the local nobility managed to preserve its militia features and shreds of corporate autonomy until the middle of the eighteenth century.[24]

The situation of the upper nobility and of servicemen attached to the court and central offices in Moscow differed mainly in that their service was truly permanent. In a sense, officials of the Tsar's court and of central administrative institutions, the officers of the military establishment in Moscow, were regular career service people who only rarely visited their estates or spent any significant amount of time on them. Promotion and rewards depended entirely on the good graces of the Tsar (or of his favorites and close counselors), and it was essential for the serviceman to remain close to the Tsar so as not to be forgotten and by-passed. Life was highly competitive and thus very insecure. Much depended on accident and personal favor or caprice, and absence or withdrawal from the limelight often resulted in the ruining of a career or of hopefully nursed plans. In a way, the situation was reminiscent of the court of Louis XIV at Versailles, except that in the French case the nobles' presence had a mainly decorative function, while in Moscow the noblemen in residence did actually perform a vital service for the ruler.

The permanent service in Moscow was in effect also compulsory. Membership in the boyar duma and tenure of court ranks carried with them the obligation of being at the beck and call of the Tsar at every moment of one's active life, which in the case of the highest dignitaries lasted until death or disgrace. The military service personnel in Moscow served on a permanent basis in part because they performed regular garrison duty in the capital and in part because they were also constantly used for special assignments of a diplomatic or administrative nature. As chances for rapid advancement and opportunities for rewards and gifts were greatest in the proximity of the Tsar, those who could be in Moscow endeavored to do so. Transfer from the nobility's rolls (*razriad*) in some provincial town or unit to those of Moscow was considered a desirable promotion. Servicemen on the rolls of Moscow were considered a privileged group of the Russian service nobility.

Service had a very personal character, both for the petty provincial noblemen and for the high dignitaries in Moscow: the Russian nobleman served not so much the state or even the country as the sovereign. Truly a servant of the Tsar, he had no existence and rights independent of the good will and favor of his sovereign.[25] His very person and property were at the complete mercy of the Tsar, who could deprive him not only of his *pomestie* (which was held temporarily on condition of service), but even of his patrimony. In practice, of course, except in relatively rare dramatic cases of sudden disgrace or the suspicion of treason, the average nobleman was secure in the possession of his patrimony. But the slightest suspicion of disloyalty, of a connection with someone out of favor, might bring about disgrace, confiscation of all goods and property, exile, and even death. Pushkin, with his usual keen sense for historical reality, discerned it very well when he made Shuiskii say to Boris Godunov, "Not torture but your disfavor frightens me." [26] Under weak rulers, changes at court among the camarilla, the loss or gain of influence by a family or clique, were accompanied by wholesale reprisals against the fallen favorites and their clients.[27] Such was also the fate of those who failed in performing to the Tsar's satisfaction or were convicted of some misdeed.

The personal relationship between the service nobleman and the Tsar was only the manifestation of the basically patrimonial nature of the Tsar's power; Russian people believed that the sovereign was the lord of the country, which was his patrimony. This belief had evolved during the Middle Ages (the thirteenth to the fifteenth centuries), when the independent and appanaged princelings were the patrimonial lords (*votchinik*) of their small territories or appanages (*udel*) and administered them as if they were their personal estates. It was under this condition of splintered sovereignty in Russia that the Church worked out the official theory of kingship. This theory emphasized the moral and social responsibility of the prince toward his people, equating it with the responsibilities of a father for the good conduct, moral life, and religious orthodoxy of his children. Toward the end of the seventeenth century, despite the development of a genuine state and the growth of a relatively complex system of administrative institutions, it was the personal element that still determined the relations beween noblemen and Tsar.

For the very same reasons there was no comprehensive, formal system of hierarchy or career pattern. The documents of the period convey the impression that there was no institutional system for rising through the ranks; every step up seemed to be the result of direct and personal intervention by the Tsar. Naturally, this was not quite so in practice, for many promotions and rewards were recommended—and at times even given out—by high officials. Yet in every case the promotion was considered to have been a favor of the Tsar, a direct grant or gift of the monarch. The special assignments given to Muscovite servicemen and the missions entrusted to high officials were all termed the Tsar's personal errands (*posylka*). It was the Tsar's business—not the state's or country's—that the serviceman took care of.

The sense of loyalty and obligation to the Tsar's person played an important role in Muscovite Russia (such a personal relationship had, of course, also been the case in Western Europe before the formation of the large centralized absolute monarchies),[28] and it mitigated somewhat the sense of insecurity and dependence on the Tsar's own arbitrary decisions and whims. In the final analysis, one had recourse to the personal mercy and justice of the Tsar: if only the Tsar could be informed of the true state of affairs, if the appeal for mercy or justice would reach his ears, if one could only approach, see, and speak to the Tsar, the injustice would be redressed, the merited punishment mitigated. In spite of the Tsar's absolute and arbitrary rule, even his cruel tyranny, the belief in the personal and patriarchal nature of the relationship between Tsar and subjects, the feeling of a family bond between the monarch and his servants, did not weaken. It helped to cement the unity of the country and maintain the loyalty of the subjects, even in the face of the greatest provocation of autocratic and arbitrary rule.[29]

Historians have noted the growing "rationalization" and complexity of the administrative, institutional, and social patterns in seventeenth-century Muscovy.[30] The variety and multiplicity of informal and patriarchal relationships were gradually giving way to greater uniformity and rigidity; and effort was made to increase the rational efficiency of the institutions. The trend toward rationalization found its reflection in the destinies of the service nobility. In the first place, the government of Moscow made a conscious effort to introduce greater uniformity, and greater efficiency in particular, into the military and administrative establishments. In the military realm it meant greater reliance on professionals and foreigners, as well as a conscious striving toward regular and permanent service. Noblemen who knew only how to handle the simple old-fashioned weapons (sword, pike, etc.) were called upon less and less frequently. An effort was made to compel the nobility to acquire more technical skills, to learn the use of more intricate weapons, and to gain familiarity with modern combat formations. As the role of active military service became more and more complex, it led to longer and more frequent periods of active duty. At the same time, similar pressures for technical modernization and rational efficiency in the administration were putting a premium on ability and training, which consequently fostered the decline of the role of birth and family status. This alone contributed greatly to the doom of the *mestnichestvo* system.

As a result, the government came to put more emphasis on the quality of performance and to pay greater attention to merit. The natural tendency of noblemen to consolidate their gains and privileges by strengthening the elements of family status and heredity met with increasing opposition from both the government and the lower nobility, and the situation led to the emergence of two paradoxical and contradictory trends, neither of which was allowed to reach its logical conclusion.

First, the age-old, natural drive on the part of the nobility to transform their precarious position into a permanent, hereditary, and stable one stimulated imitation of neighboring nobilities—the Swedish to some extent but more particularly the Polish. (One result of this imitation was the development of the fashion of designing and sporting coats of arms and coining slogans and mottoes for the family.) While the more westernized and sophisticated upper nobility of Moscow (the "aristocracy," so to speak) took the lead in imitating the Polish magnates and Swedish aristocrats, the average nobleman stressed the legal equality, special status, and rights of the Polish *szlachta*. But while there were some differences on details between the "higher" and "lower" rungs of servicemen, both groups were essentially striving for the same goal. More specifically, they were both making efforts to obtain security of person and property against arbitrary action by the administration, as well as a clear definition of their status and privileges to set them apart from commoners. Thus it would appear that a good basis existed for a common front—one that would enable all noblemen to unite against the autocracy and the state and secure the advantages everybody craved.

Such a common front, however, was precluded by the second trend. For the emphasis on the hereditary element (implicit in a recognition of the privileges noted above), conflicted with the needs of rational efficiency (that is, a pattern of action designed to attain specific goals). The latter was of concern to the nobility, as well as to the state, for it increased the advantages that might accrue from a system based entirely on rewards proportionate to service performance. To abandon the service pattern would be to change completely the institutional framework of the Russian nobility. It would also mean recognizing the split of the nobility into two groups, causing the lower to lose forever the hope of attaining the status of the upper. In the minds of seventeenth-century Russians there even was serious doubt that the nobility's economic status, *i.e.* the right to possess and own settled estates, could be preserved without a *quid pro quo* in the form of state service. Lastly, the rank-and-file noble servicemen harbored a great deal of distrust toward the big families, as well as a fear that the latter might gain control of the government. The lingering memory of the period of splinter principalities led to the ever-present fear that the unity of sovereignty, forged at such great cost by the princes of Moscow, might be lost, that Russia might again be split up and thus invite foreign conquest and the loss of religious, cultural, and national independence.[31] Naturally, the ordinary nobleman did not relish the idea of finding himself in the position of retainer to a magnate, as was the fate of the poor *szlachtic* in Poland. Indeed, however powerful and rich a magnate was, he could never provide the opportunities and rewards that the autocratic Tsar of Moscow and of All Russia could dispense.

Primarily engaged in the service of the Tsar, the nobleman was not strongly bound to any specific locality or region. Whatever signs of developing local and corporate solidarities might be observed in the seventeenth century on the basis of common service activities were the exception rather than the rule. Most nobles received estates wherever the Tsar deemed it was convenient or wherever free land was available for grants. The sixteenth century had seen mass transfers of noblemen from one area to another, and long-established groupings and solidarities had been broken. And while the drastic measures of Ivan the Terrible had not been renewed after his death, the dislocation of the Times of Troubles completed what he had begun. Nor did the system of inheritance and the serviceman's dependence on the Tsar's discretion for land grants give the Russian nobleman much of a feeling of being tied to his *terroir,* a feeling that played such an important role in the life and outlook of the Western nobleman. It was precisely this attachment to a specific locality, and the bonds of group and corporate loyalty it nourished, that had paved the way for the formation of estates in the West and given them a solid foundation for their privileged political role.[32] Russia had either missed this development completely or experienced it in a very atrophied form.

Was service the Russian nobleman's only occupation in the seventeenth century? What life did he lead as a private individual and what role did he have as an owner of estates and serfs? Economic life in Muscovite Russia was still quite primitive, much closer to a natural agrarian economy than to one based on money or trading. Very few estates produced for the market, and almost none produced for a foreign market. The average nobleman derived from his estate only those products necessary for his upkeep—items that were sent to him at his place of service, or else consumed on the spot. And in the majority of cases, the bulk of the household consumption in foodstuffs and other articles of daily use came from the noblemen's suburban estates, although the generosity of the Tsar provided them with some rare luxury items and the hard cash with which to purchase the things that were not produced on the estate. For the military, war spoils and booty played a similar important role in diversifying and increasing revenues. But on the whole, economic activities, specifically the management of his estate, took little attention and time out of the average nobleman's life.[33]

Such a situation should not be surprising. For how could the serviceman manage and care for his estates during his lengthy absences on campaigns and other "errands" for the Tsar? Of course, other members of his family—his old father or an energetic mother or wife—might on occasion take over active management. But the absence of the real master and owner nonetheless affected operations on the estate. One result was that the village commune, the peasant *mir*, often played the role of day-to-day manager and supervisor, a function that dovetailed with the performance of public duties with which the state also entrusted the village commune. In this way the estate developed a life pattern of its own: the villagers automatically took care of routine operations (and in a relatively primitive agrarian economy, with a tradition-conscious population, little was not a matter of routine). As long as the master was kept supplied with the essentials, he did not need to (and did not) interfere. Even when in residence on the estate between his tours of duty the landowner had little to do, unless he wanted to transform things radically and take matters in his own hands for the sake of implementing innovations of his own. But this almost never occurred, for the wisdom of the average Muscovite serviceman consisted in doing as his ancestors had done.

Away from service, life on the estate was one of relative leisure, of lazy enjoyment of the few pleasures and little entertainment that the Russian countryside could offer in the seventeenth century. In fact, service noblemen spent much of their time at home eating and sleeping, disciplining their household serfs, hunting, visiting and entertaining neighbors on occasional outings, and taking part in church festivities. It was a life entirely centered on the satisfaction of the simplest, even the grossest, personal pleasures; it was a life without meaning, without purposeful activity or energy-

absorbing concerns. Since illiteracy among the service nobility was still the rule rather than the exception, there was
little scope for intellectual or spiritual life. At best the nobleman could on occasion watch the performance of some clown
or traveling mountebanks in his courtyard, or listen to the
stories, romances, or epic poetry recited or read by a more
educated traveler or neighbor.[34]

Since only the wealthier nobles could afford to live in
cities with their families, retainers, and servants, the choice
of a way of life was limited for the average nobleman: he
could serve the Tsar or do nothing on his estate. In going
away to serve, the noble left behind him a life of inactivity,
a life without any serious responsibility or concern. In spite
of the very shallow existence at home—nay, because of it—
the serviceman resented the necessity of leaving his warm
nest, where he had nothing to do but indulge his personal
whims and cater to his physical comfort, for the labors, hardships, and dangers of military campaigns and other government missions. When regular professional and foreign regiments became the mainstay of Muscovite military power,
fewer demands were made on his services and the serviceman
grew even more reluctant to serve. Secure in the possession
of his estates, no longer called upon to serve frequently, the
nobleman came to believe that his way of life was free of any
obligation to the state—political, economic, social, or cultural.
At the same time this introduced an element of "alienation"
into his existence: he was threatened with becoming useless
to his monarch and to his society, yet he could not fall back
on any other activities—spiritual or economic—to preserve a
meaningful relationship with his world. He seemed on the
way to becoming a "superfluous man" *avant la lettre*.

For those who would not remain content with their modest
condition the only means for fulfillment of their aspirations
was service. Service led to travel, residence in bigger centers,
perhaps a permanent stay in Moscow, and even—on occasion
—to a mission abroad. In the seventeenth century opportuni-

ties for better education, more sophisticated entertainment, and a richer spiritual life were available practically nowhere but in Moscow. But in order to be able to live in the capital, the nobleman had to be in service there. It was only regular service in the capital that gave access to those positions of responsibility that imbued the nobleman with a sense of individual worth and usefulness to society.

During the seventeenth century the notion was established that avoidance of state service implied absence of purposeful occupation and meaningful concerns. Indeed, despite its hardships and risks, service was the surest way of leading a richer life, of participating in the affairs of the world, and of acquiring habits of social responsibility. A life of vegetation and isolation at home on the estate as against a life of activity and potential growth and development in service—such was the dilemma faced by the Russian nobleman. It was a limited choice, indeed, quite a way from the variety of opportunities and interests available to the West European nobleman on the eve of modern times. In short, so far as the nobility was concerned, the basic fact of Muscovite reality was that, in the absence of a genuinely worthwhile personal life and corporate solidarities, everything was focused on Moscow and contained within the framework of service to the Tsar.

THREE

The State and Service
in the Eighteenth Century

THE REIGN of Peter the Great, which revolutionized the Muscovite pattern of existence, marks a radical break in the history of Russia. It is quite true, as many distinguished historians have pointed out, that the transformations wrought by Peter did not come unexpectedly, that they had antecedents in Muscovite times. Yet Peter helped to transform the political and cultural life of Russia so drastically and thoroughly that we can in truth speak of it as a revolution, at least in the accepted eighteenth-century meaning of the term, *i.e.* turning away from a previously established course.[1] In this study we shall be concerned only with those of Peter's activities—and their results—that affected the pattern of the nobleman's life and the institutional framework of his service obligations. Moreover, we shall disregard the details of the emperor's wavering and changing policies to consider only the final outcome of his measures.

The deepest and most fateful transformation wrought by Peter the Great was his introduction of an entirely new conception of the role of government and political power; he put an end to the personal character of authority current in Muscovy. Those elements of this transformation that had made their appearance before his time had not developed enough to play a dynamic and active role in the life and political consciousness of seventeenth-century Russia. Peter's predecessors had conceived of the political entity over which they reigned as an amalgam of monarch, Church, land, and people. The Russia over which they ruled, and which they defended against foreign enemies, was a geographic, ethnographic, and—most frequently, although not always explicitly —religious entity. The Grand Dukes of Moscow and later the Tsars of All Russia conceived it as their task to protect the Russian people—the orthodox men and women—against the infidel and to defend their land's security against foreign invaders.[2] Implicit in this task was the protection of the Russian Christian people as they moved into new lands and forests, onto new pastures and rivers. On the rare occasions that the Tsars and their counselors reflected on their political task in a general way, they thought of "state" and "country" only as signs standing for a vivid and complex human and geographic reality.

Not so with Peter and his companions in reform. For them "state" or "country"[3] were more than mere signs, and even more than symbols; they had a life and reality of their own. From the creative turmoil of Peter's reign there emerged a new notion of the relationship between monarch and subject. Peter the Great ultimately created the Russian state as an institution and as a concept. And the ruling class accepted the new creation and endowed it with an existence and purpose independent of the life and striving of the "people."[4]

Of course, Peter too believed in the real existence of the Russian land and people underlying the state. But like most modern men he had not only transformed the sign into a symbol, he had endowed the symbol with an autonomous existence. And having been endowed with some of the characteristics of "real life," the symbol acquired a purpose of its own and a pattern of action, or behavior, consonant with its purpose; it came to exist independently of the men and land that in fact were Russia. For Peter, Russia had become the Russian state, and to his mind the interests of this abstraction were identical with the interests of Russia's land and people. As in the West with the triumph of absolute monarchies, the state—as an institution and idea—had achieved an autonomous existence and acquired its own self-perpetuating interests, goals, and concerns.[5] Those who ran the state were only its servants (as Frederick the Great of Prussia was to put it) and the dictum *l'état, c'est moi* was only a personalized expression of the same point of view.[6] The interests, personal concerns, desires, and conveniences of individuals—whether officials of the government or merely private subjects—were to be subordinated to those of the state; they were to have no existence or status outside the purposes and needs (real or imaginary) of the state. The state alone had a policy, a goal, an interest, a commitment—the people were only the passive objects of these larger considerations, and the tools for their realization. True, the happiness and welfare of the people (conceived as an abstraction somewhat lacking in content) were also the state's concern, but they were a concern only because their fulfillment maximized the power of the state.[7] Not until the nineteenth century, and reluctantly at that, did the "happiness" and "welfare" of the concrete, living, individual member of society become the goal of, as well as justification for, the state's existence.

After he had organized the institutions and machinery of the modern Russian state and set its goals, Peter the Great had to fashion the personnel necessary for running them. He himself became the first servant of the state, the first *kholop* of Russia. His personal fate or life had no meaning or importance; only his work and role in the state mattered.[8] And what he expected of himself, Peter demanded of others. The individuals he selected to assist him had also to think of themselves as the servants of the state, not of Peter. An individual's usefulness in furthering the interests of the state was alone to provide the basis for his position in society. To reach the higher rungs of society, to obtain status and material rewards from the monarch, one had to be of more than average usefulness to the state and the nation.

But old habits and traditional ways of viewing social relationships do not die easily. Under great stress they outwardly adjust to new conditions and begin to play a new role. This outward adjustment may, in turn, gradually bring about the complete transformation of the traditional structure, while preserving the old forms. Like a shell, the old forms may only hide the new life inside them; sooner or later the new life will break the shell that has not grown apace with the living organism inside it. The *homines novi* drawn into state service by Peter and his successors thought of themselves primarily as servants of the state, whose task and duty consisted in promoting the interests of the new Russia founded by Peter the Great. Members of the old nobility, however, while serving in the newly created institutions, still retained the feeling that they were serving the Tsar, albeit under the new title of Emperor. The new rules and institutional patterns imposed on their service might belie this relationship, but the individual serviceman clung to it because it was the intellectual tradition that defined his self image in society and— in his own eyes at least—justified his privileges and status.

The first reaction of the nobility to Peter's policies was also a very personal one. Those who were converted to Peter's ideas, involved in his interest and enthusiasm for the westernization of Russia, saw him as an almost superhuman hero, whom they worshiped as a person as much as Tsar and master. They considered themselves only his humble retainers, pupils, and helpmates. They believed that they were

Peter's creation, as well as his creatures, in a very literal sense—or, as Pushkin perceptively put it, "the fledglings of Peter's nest." No wonder that the Emperor's sudden and early death produced such an acute sense of loss, the feeling of having been left orphaned.[9]

On the other hand, those who rejected or criticized Peter's work also did so in very personal terms. They blamed his idiosyncrasies for the evil they believed was done to Russia. In more extreme cases, avoiding the obligations Peter wanted to impose on them, they justified their disobedience by the argument that Peter was not the lawful monarch of Russia, that he himself had betrayed his duties and responsibilities to the Russian people.[10]

The changes wrought by Peter in the concept and very nature of political authority and administration directly affected the pattern of state service. State service became the only activity that gave one a right to social and economic privileges and rewards. Even before the service pattern had been given its permanent forms, a decree had made explicit that status in society and personal rights were dependent on the performance of service obligations to the state; without such performance the wealthiest and best-born individual was to count for nothing.[11] Performance in service naturally became the basis for differentiating between members of the service class, the source of special distinction and rewards. In principle, merit became the only publicly recognized foundation for the hierarchical structure of the service class and of Russian society. The Muscovite nobility had not known any differentiating titles (except for the empty title of *kniaz'*). Whatever distinctions existed were those of function, and this applied primarily to nobles residing and serving at court. Peter the Great introduced a regular hierarchy, the fourteen grades of the Table of Ranks.[12] Originally these grades connoted duties as well, but very soon they functioned mainly as titles and marked distinctions of status. In addition, the formal equality of the Russian nobility was broken by the introduction of titles that the monarch alone could bestow: "count" and "baron," in addition to the already existing "prince." In fact, however, in the absence of a service rank, these titles proved to be as meaningless as the title of prince had been in seventeenth-century Muscovy.[13]

The service grades of the Table of Ranks were not hereditary. In theory, therefore, the status of ancestors and service distinctions of past members of the family did not play a direct role in determining an individual's position in Russian society after Peter the Great. Only economic status was hereditary, at least to the extent that the practice of equal inheritance permitted it. In principle every man started at the bottom of the hierarchical ladder of the Table of Ranks (or even below it), and normally he was expected to go through all the lower rungs in order to reach the highest. Membership in a prominent family did not confer any special privileges. Ideally, Peter the Great hoped, the individual who was born noble would not receive public recognition of his noble status until he had obtained a service rank that in itself conferred nobility. At all times a person's status would depend exclusively on his position in the hierarchy of the Table of Ranks. A person in service, whatever his rank, always had precedence over any person not in service (unless retired for good cause), whatever the latter's title, wealth, or ancestry.

Peter the Great's reforms reopened, in a new form, the perennial debate between heredity and service as basis for defining the nobility. We have seen what a divisive issue this had been for the Muscovite nobility. The Table of Ranks sharpened the conflict, for not only did it provide for a hierarchical scale of ranks on the basis of service performance, it also specified that noble status itself was to be given to the individual who had attained in service a rank equivalent to that of a full commissioned officer. Noble status became hereditary from the eighth rank on.

Peter's newly modernized state (especially its military establishment) had great need for capable and technically trained officers and administrators. This led, albeit not on a mass scale, to the admission to state service of those who were taxable commoners; and a commoner capable enough to merit a high position could join the nobility through a successful service career.[14] The old established noble families resented this, of course.[15] Promotion and eventual ennoblement of the commoner for high deeds in the field and on the seas, requiring easily discernible talent and courage, was accepted by the hereditary nobility as a deserved reward. But when promotion did not come for publicly performed deeds of distinction, suspicion arose that the promotion had been the result of intrigue or bribery, or was a reward for winking at abuses by one's superiors. The promotions to high rank and nobility of non-combat personnel were particularly resented. The average nobleman (like all line troops and officers of all armies in all times) believed that the office staff and clerks engaged in dubious activities, made illicit gains at the expense of their fellow soldiers' welfare, and, consequently, should be ineligible for advancement that led to nobility.

On the other hand, those who had benefited from the new and relatively easy way in which one could accede to nobility and those who hoped to benefit from it in the future were naturally set in defense of Peter's policy. Predictably, the government took the side of this group, as it wanted to be free to secure the best qualified individuals without regard to anything but performance and merit. As a result, the old division within the ranks of the Russian nobility became complicated by the influx of a large number of *homines novi*.[16] And the influx of new men was not likely to stop so long as the basic rule of promotion to nobility through the Table of Ranks was preserved.

The principle of merit and the new practices in the organization, hierarchy, and rewards of the service system also affected the psychology and outlook of the nobility. Peter's institution of the Table of Ranks put an end to the aspirations to special privilege of old families, made impossible the perpetuation of special status through mere heredity, and precluded a return to the *mestnichestvo* system. It equalized ("democratized," as some historians have put it) the nobility and put exclusive stress on personal merit and talent. Above all, perhaps, the merit clause of the Table of Ranks provided both the stimulus and the foundation for the development of individualism. It was the first time, since the Times of Troubles at least, that an individual's worth was given public recognition and status in Russia; a definite end was put to the family orientation (*rodovoe nachalo*) of the upper class. But at the same time a new element of personal insecurity was introduced: no one could feel he had a place and role in society (and the state) until he had secured it by dint of his own efforts and work. Reinforced by social and political realities, the individual nobleman's sense of vagueness and insecurity as to his status played a significant part in fostering his transformation into a member of the intelligentsia.[17]

Peter the Great extended the service obligation to cover administrative as well as military (and naval) duty. An individual incapacitated or incapable of military service was expected to do his bit in the local or central administration of the empire. Service had become the unavoidable, compulsory, and universal activity of the Russian nobility. There had, of course, been compulsory service in Muscovy for all those who had held a *pomestie* and wished to preserve it, as we have seen. But avoidance of service, whatever other punishment it might lead to, had not resulted in the offender losing his status and privileges. The government had sought out delinquent nobles (*netchik* or *v netiakh*), hauled them back to their units, and punished them, but their status as noblemen had not been put in jeopardy. Finally, there had always been the possibility of escaping service by entering the clergy. With Peter, however, service became the *sine qua non* of the nobility.[18]

Peter's changes in the character of the service obligation led to innumerable instances of evasion of service obligations. The government issued decree after decree and prosecuted individuals in order to compel obedience.[19] The severest measures were taken to track down and punish the recalcitrant noblemen: regular manhunts, confiscation of property, taking members of the family as hostages, and heavy fines and imprisonment for repeated violations.[20] While the attempts to escape service indicate its unpopularity, these examples do not prove that, in general, the rulers were unable to enforce their will. After all, cases of evasion and violation are best documented in the sources; the normal application of a law or rule never leaves as much of a trace in official documents as do the violations. Numerous as the cases of evasion were, the lack of statistical evidence to the contrary seems to indicate that they were exceptions rather than the rule.

Besides making it compulsory, Peter turned the obligation of service into a permanent one. The nobleman was no longer to serve merely in military campaigns or for the duration of a diplomatic or administrative "errand," but permanently in the empire's regular military establishment or offices of administration. The military was put on a permanent, professional basis, with regiments and units remaining on active status even in time of peace. For a short period there was even an attempt to entrust the local administration to the regiments that were garrisoned in the province or district in peacetime. For the nobleman it became difficult, if not altogether impossible, to return to his home estate between campaigns and assignments. As long as he served, he had to be away from his home, and only when on leave—or if allowed to retire because of old age or incurable illness—could he go back to his estate. Neither the principle of service itself nor even the modern forms of organization introduced by Peter proved as novel and irritating to the Russian nobleman as the compulsory and permanent character of the service obligation—an obligation that weighed without letup from the moment the young nobleman could be called to active duty (at about fifteen) until death or total incapacity.[21]

From a human point of view, the fate of some servicemen was truly pathetic. The heart-rending statements in support of requests and petitions for leaves and retirement found in the minutes of government departments should, naturally, not be taken at face value; they were, after all, written to soften the heart of the monarch or impress the officials in charge. Yet their relative truthfulness can be inferred from the wealth of circumstantial detail adduced, from the corroborating independent government reports that often were attached to these petitions, and by contemporary literature, memoirs, and letters. The average Russian nobleman in the first third of the eighteenth century personally experienced service life as a most difficult and unpleasant hardship because it took place within the strict framework of a modern regular army and administration, and there was no legal means of escaping from it. A let-up in the rigors of the system was expected first at the end of the Great Northern War, and then again after the death of Peter the Great. But instead of his freedom or the extended leave he had awaited, the nobleman in army and navy was shunted into the civil government, given various fiscal or judiciary assignments locally, or entrusted with the administration of faraway regions—a form of exile acutely resented by those who had had a taste of the stimulating and sophisticated (comparatively speaking) environment in St. Petersburg.[22]

The nobleman felt trapped, at the mercy of the state, a Moloch who was eating him up and was set to devour his children and family possessions as well. The frequent transfers from one place or assignment to another and from mili-

tary to civil duties (and back), the low salaries and the irreg-
ular payment of them, the seemingly arbitrary promotions
and appointments appeared especially tyrannical to men who
still lived in another age psychologically and who did not
fully understand or accept the new standards of performance
expected of them and the sacrifices they were required to
make. The nobleman felt strongly that he had been put into
the service of a machine—huge, callous, and impersonal. Yet
he could not give up the hope that a personal approach and
an appeal to the human feelings of the ruler (and his ministers) might alleviate his condition; hence the pathetic form
of the appeals and petitions. They are graphic illustration of
the nobility's desperate attempt at counteracting—nay, at
denying—the new relationship between serviceman and monarch. But they met with the working of bureaucratic routine
and mountains of papers. Little wonder that the nobleman's
resentment fastened not so much on the permanence and
regularity of service as on its depersonalization.

The changes introduced by Peter into the formal organization of state service furthered the central government's control over the individual nobleman's life; at the same time they
highlight the Emperor's desire to subordinate traditional personal relationships to considerations of functional efficiency.
In seventeenth-century Muscovy the roster of the nobles in
service and records of their assignments had been kept by
the central military administration, Department of the Rolls
(*razriadnyi prikaz* or *razriad*). With the abolition of the
prikazy, Peter the Great shifted their functions to other institutions. At first the Colleges of War and of the Admiralty
became the offices concerned with service matters. Then the
Senate, in its capacity of collective assistant to the Emperor,
was given an important voice in making assignments, examining the young nobles, and entering them on the service
rosters. Eventually, the office of the Master of the Heraldry
was set up under the Senate and given the responsibility of
keeping records of everything pertaining to the nobility, most

particularly the individuals' service careers. But the Master of the Heraldry only kept the records and made the routine assignments. All questions of policy, as well as initial and important service assignments, remained in the hands of the Emperor and the bodies of councilors that most directly assisted him in governing the empire (Senate, Supreme Privy Council, Cabinet of Ministers). As long as compulsory service lasted, *i.e.* until 1762, original enrollment into service, retirement, and promotion were prerogatives of the Emperor, and ones he delegated only to the most trusted and highest organs of the state. This indicates the importance attached to service and the ruler's determination to keep this instrument of power and control over the nobility firmly in his own hands.[23]

The policy of rigid central control of service pursued by the state until the last quarter of the eighteenth century resulted in the individual serviceman's being treated merely like a small cog in a huge machine. The relative primitivity of Russia's institutional life—its limited functional differentiation—meant that servicemen were frequently shunted from one assignment to another—especially from military to civilian posts and vice versa. The simplicity of the vast majority of service functions, coupled with a basic lack of personnel, precluded a thorough study of all relevant materials and dossiers in making assignments. This bureaucratization of state institutions further accentuated the tendency to ignore personal idiosyncrasies, talents, or needs of individual noblemen.

Centralization also implied that basic personnel decisions were taken on an Empire-wide (*vserossiiskii*) basis, with little regard for the nobleman's local or regional ties, circumstances, or tradition. The embryonic manifestations of regional solidarity that had appeared in the seventeenth century came to an abrupt end. There had been a good deal of geographic mobility in sixteenth- and seventeenth-century Russia, and the service nobility had not been excluded from it. But the transformation of service under Peter the Great brought even greater mobility to the nobleman, and with it a sense of rootlessness. Like a modern soldier, the nobleman was assigned, transferred, and promoted according to the Empire's needs of the moment. He was a small interchangeable tessera in a big mosaic whose pattern was determined by an autocratic designer. This mobility and rootlessness led to an atomization, a fragmentation of the nobility as a class. Ties and friendships formed in the service were at the mercy of frequent reassignments and transfers. The individual nobleman was on his own; he could not count on the help and support of either clan or neighbors, since he was frequently stationed in places quite remote from his home estate, and individuals from the same larger family or locality rarely remained together in service.[24] These factors prevented the cohesion brought about by lifelong membership in the corps and regiment, as in Western Europe, where modern institutions were built on an existing foundation of strong social loyalties and local solidarities.

Mobility among noblemen was encouraged by the state's practice of rewarding service by land grants, which were judiciously distributed widely throughout the Empire, although this factor played less of a role in the second half of the eighteenth century than previously.[25] As there was little attachment to a specific estate or region, estates were freely sold, exchanged, or even given away. Noblemen considered only what revenue could be derived from the estate; the rest counted for little.[26] What mattered was not land but serf labor and the money and produce that became available through the land—wealth was calculated in terms of ownership of souls. Rare indeed were genuine estate "collectors" and "builders" who spent their lives in rounding out their domains. There was none of what we find in the West—the slow accumulation and close calculation, over the span of several generations, involved in building up a valuable and important domain.[27] *Kopidomstvo* (saving up for the household) was strongly disparaged or made the butt of satire. A property that had been in the family for only one generation was considered the family estate.[28] Naturally, the Russian nobleman had none of the political influence that derived from being lord of a manor in the West.[29]

The nobleman's attachment to his home locale was further weakened by the opening up of the eastern and southern frontier areas in the second half of the eighteenth century; many noblemen moved into the new lands.[30] Frequently this entailed service in places quite remote from the home estate. Such service-connected residences frequently lasted a long time; the nobleman became accustomed to the new environment, made friends, and, by marrying a local girl, acquired new family connections. Upon retirement from service it was not unusual for him to settle in the region where he had seen service. Thus many a nobleman came to own land and serfs in widely separated regions. His children split the inheritance and sometimes found it convenient to divide their time among estates. Because service experiences led many nobles to prefer settling in cities, especially the capitals, they visited their widely scattered domains only infrequently.[31]

As the Russian population had spread rather uniformly over most of European Russia and had carried in its wake institutions that were similar to each other, adjustment to existence in any one region was easy enough on a superficial level. (In this sense, perhaps, there is some similarity with America: the American, too, is at home everywhere in the United States and yet rooted almost nowhere.) Nowhere did the nobleman have the deep and ineradicable roots that would have helped to determine his outlook and way of life, as was the case in Western Europe,[32] because he was constantly on the move, shunted about by the necessities of service or looking for better economic opportunities. Too, he frequently took extended trips to visit members of his family, and the visits were often very long (lasting from a few days to months, and even years).[33]

The bureaucratization and centralization of service under

Peter the Great was reflected in the psychological attitudes of noblemen in both the military and civilian branches. Peter had given preference to the military service (including the navy, of course) by allowing only one out of three noblemen to enter the civilian branch, and by giving the military precedence over the civilian within the same rank. Such a policy was dictated by military necessity, as the nobility was particularly reluctant to face the hardships, dangers, novelty, and permanence of army and navy service. Actually, of course, the military had always been the traditional type of service for the nobility,[34] and its essentials could be mastered without too much difficulty, in spite of its growing technicality and modernization. Until the last third of the eighteenth century—and in many cases even later—a sizeable proportion of the small, poor, provincial nobility received only the rudiments of education and were hardly capable of learning more than the manual of arms and the general orders—just enough to lead a small group of men in the field and on the parade grounds. The service allowed for free time that could be spent in idleness, gambling, or drinking with fellow officers. In times of peace, the officer's duties were quite limited, most of the actual routine being taken care of by experienced noncommissioned officers. In his dealings with the soldiers, the average officer did not need to display great qualities of leadership; the soldiers were peasant serfs who could be ordered about in the same way as domestic or village serfs on the estate. Of course, the requirements were higher in the technical branches and the navy, where, on the average, the officers were better educated and more experienced than in the infantry and cavalry.

Naturally, the officer assigned to a civilian administrative post brought to his new position the training and habits acquired in the military; and as his civilian assignment was only temporary, he did not try to change his military attitudes. Since there was little or no functional division of labor in service,[35] a nobleman could be asked to fill any kind of position and given a variety of assignments. As a result, he developed the point of view that the same rules and patterns were applicable to all areas of national life, both military and civil, and that a reasonably well-educated nobleman could perform well in any public institution. Service in the modernized rational and bureaucratic military establishment indoctrinated the nobleman with the idea that a clear chain of command, hierarchical subordination, and absolute obedience were the essence of good administration; it convinced him of the need to apply uniform rules to all, without brooking individual exceptions, to formulate orders and regulations in curt and precise form, and to set up tasks and problems in neat "military" fashion.[36]

Most significant, perhaps, was his propensity to solve human problems by a purely mechanical application of rules and through decisions automatically derived from properly processed papers. The population entrusted to the tender mercies of such an official was disciplined and ordered around like an army. In some instances the administrator took the military model quite literally;[37] Arakcheev's administration of the military colonies was an extreme, but, alas, not completely atypical illustration of the effects of the military mentality. The arrogance, brutality, and callousness of so many Russian administrators, as well as the rigidly bureaucratic character of the administration, owed much to the military background of the officials.[38]

His military background also predisposed the official to what might be called a "global" view with respect to problems of administration and political organization. The administrator believed that all civilian laws, decrees, and ordinances, like army regulations, should be couched in general terms and applied uniformly throughout the whole Empire, with little or no account taken of special conditions and local differences. If the army was a single body acting according to a single set of rigid and well-defined rules, so too was the Empire; its administrative divisions, which produced uniform units, were introduced for the sake of convenience.[39] The official was confirmed in this approach by the strong feeling that he was the servant of the Russian state, of the Empire. The dedicated, conscientious and efficient administrator always remembered that only the interests of the state as a whole mattered. In his scheme of things, regional and local interests or special rights and norms had almost no place.[40]

This frame of mind was encouraged by the government's policy of constantly shifting the officials from the central to local offices and back, and from one area of the Empire to another. Throughout the eighteenth century few of those holding positions of responsibility had made the administration of a single area their life work. Under the circumstances, an official hardly had a chance to develop profound knowledge of or genuine sympathy for the region entrusted to his care. He neither struck roots nor felt thoroughly at home in a specific region;[41] he never became thoroughly familiar with the problems and conditions of any one branch of the Empire's administration. The nobleman, we recall, had no strong roots in his native province; his administrative experience only contributed to his feeling of alienation from the population.

Since the administration of the Empire was highly centralized, little responsibility and authority was left to local officials. Yet at first glance it does seem strange that even over a period of several generations these officials failed to develop local *esprit de corps* or distinctive patterns of behavior, as had been the case in other countries, notably Prussia and Austria. Consciously or vicariously, they assimilated the militaristic, bureaucratic, and global point of view that dominated Russian public life. They did not easily tolerate exceptional situations that did not fit into the narrow framework of prescribed regulations. They were helpless in those cases that could not be satisfactorily resolved or implemented by merely processing the flow of official papers and reports issuing from and returning to the central bureaus in St. Petersburg.[42] Local officials, therefore, were nothing more than the loyal defenders of the state's interests, the obedient executors of the central government's will. They developed neither a sense of initiative nor a feeling of responsibility for the locality or population in their care.[43]

With the new administrative apparatus of Peter the Great came a pressing need for new, skilled manpower. An effort was made to run the new institutions on principles of rational efficiency for the sake of the state's interests. The methods of operation involved, therefore, the elaboration of regular and rational norms of procedure, the keeping of adequate records, the use of general political concepts and "statistical" evidence. The Muscovite clerks had operated in a manner that was rather pragmatic, personal, less rational, and less efficient. Of course, the old clerks could be retrained, and many of them were, but even at that there were too few to take care of the expanding machinery of government.[44] For this reason, under Peter the Great and thereafter, positions of administrative leadership and responsibility were usually given to officers of the military and naval establishments, individuals with a minimum of Western-type education and experience in managing men and things.[45] But in addition, many officials of all ranks and all levels of education were needed to run the new institutions adequately, to assist dignitaries drawn from the army and navy in an area where it was necessary to write and think in abstract concepts.

The nobility was not in a position to fill the state's needs adequately in this respect. At first there were not enough noblemen to staff both the military and the lower ranks of the administration. The nobles preferred to go into the new army and navy rather than into the administrative bureaus, and Peter was only too glad to encourage this trend, for military needs took precedence.[46] In the administration, a higher level of literacy was needed, even for the lower positions, while positions of responsibility and leadership required talents and knowledge that could not be acquired through apprenticeship and experience alone. It was not surprising, therefore, that the government also turned to social groups outside the nobility proper to staff the various offices created in the process of modernizing and westernizing the Russian state. The main source were the *raznochintsy—i.e.* children of the clergy, with a sprinkling of sons of merchants, soldiers, and other non-noble free men.[47]

The clergy were at an advantage because they alone possessed the tradition and opportunity for obtaining the minimum of literary education needed for administration. Sons of clergymen were accustomed to working with books and papers, thinking in abstract concepts, expressing ideas, and giving their findings a more or less readable written form. They were also readily available. Indeed, the clergy had become a closed caste, with children succeeding in the profession of their fathers. But since the number of full-time and full-paying positions in the Church were limited, sons of parish priests often became monks or peasants. Peter, however, made entrance into a monastery impossible for a young man, and to become a peasant after Peter's introduction of the capitation tax (*podushnaia*) meant to lose one's freedom, in fact become a serf. The administration of the state, on the other hand, now offered opportunities for the more ambitious, talented, and energetic products of the ecclesiastical schools, the more so since the government made their admission to state service relatively easy.

Better prepared than most noblemen, accustomed to the life and procedures of paperwork, the children of the clergy were quite successful in their new field of endeavor and could expect a better career than the ordinary nobleman. Hence the nobility's complaint against the apparent preference given in the administration to these commoners, children of clergy and merchants—*krapivoe semia,* as they were derisively called.[48] The dislike and resentment were caused not only by the better chances for promotion and good jobs that the *raznochintsy* appeared to have, but also by the fact that these non-noble officials came to symbolize the impersonal machine of the state.

——•◆•——

Throughout the eighteenth century—as a matter of fact well into the nineteenth—there was much confusion and a great deal of debate on the question of who belonged to the nobility. It is a curious fact that in none of the Codes is there a clear or satisfactory definition of the nobility and of the status of a nobleman. Nor have the historians of Russian law come forth with a clear definition; they usually skirt the issue by merely describing the origin, duties, privileges, and rights of servicemen.[49] The main reason for this state of affairs is that the Russian nobility does not lend itself to clear and univalent definition.

It appeared at first that Peter the Great had introduced clarity when in the legislation on the Table of Ranks (and a few earlier decrees) he openly proclaimed the principle of service the only basis for claim to nobility. But as a matter of fact he did not eliminate the ambiguity; his legislation may perhaps have even served to make it worse by drawing the verbal and legal screen of the Table of Ranks around the situation. For Peter the Great did not abolish the role of family status. He always preferred to see the leadership roles in the new state reserved to men born of noble families. But he also believed that to serve the state was the highest privilege an individual could enjoy, his most glorious role in society. The well-born (*blagorodnyi*), endowed with nobility of character and mind, should wish to serve, should deem it their duty and privilege to contribute to the nation's glory and welfare. A nobleman who did not serve, or who retired from service without good cause, in Peter's view, forfeited all claims to nobility and to the name and treatment befitting a "well-born." On the other hand, the individual who by dint of his exertions, sacrifices, and efforts in the service of the state had proven genuine nobility of character and mind should be given recognition by receiving noble status.

By stressing the psychological and moral aspects of service, *i.e.* the notion that nobility was a quality of character and mind, Peter the Great opened a wide field for debate and conflict, leading to confusion and insecurity among the nobility. On one hand, the old nobility argued that these traits were hereditary and could be cultivated only in "good" families; the new men obviously could not possess them. By accepting the obligation of service, the old nobility displayed the required qualities, whereas the newcomers who lacked these qualities debased the nobility.[50] To preserve the status of the nobility, argued the old nobility, either stop the access of commoners to service or eliminate the provisions for automatic promotion to nobility through the Table of Ranks. The new nobility, on the other hand, suggested that education and cultural leadership be the criteria for noble status, since the newcomers could expect to have better educations than either the traditional nobility or the rest of the population.

The government tended to agree with the position of the newcomers, as this viewpoint served its own purposes of westernization; the more public-minded, progressive members of the old nobility, like the brothers Dmitrii and Mikhail Golitsyn, also agreed. Even the traditionalists recognized the obligation to serve and accepted the notion that nobility had originally been conferred as a reward for extraordinary achievements in state service, and this forced them to accept qualifications that made it possible for servicemen of low birth to accede to the nobility. The more sophisticated among the old nobility perceived the inherent flaw of their argument, even if they did not acknowledge it openly, and this contributed to their insecurity and ultimately forced them to rely exclusively on the autocratic sovereign to obtain some measure of satisfaction. Nor could they prevent the rise of new men to the top. The Russian nobility (in contrast to the

nobility of continental Western Europe) remained a relatively open class based on service—a fact that helped to
cause the failure of any serious "aristocratic reaction," on
the lines suggested by Dmitrii Golitsyn, Nikita Panin, and
Alexander Vorontsov. A Western education became a characteristic mark of nobility. This established a precedent to
be followed later by the élite of the nobility and the intelligentsia: in the absence of formal legal definitions, the way
of life and cultural outlook of a person determined his affilia-
tion with a specific social class or group.

There was also confusion as to the actual procedures by
which noble status was acquired. At the bottom of the difficulty, it seems to us, lay the traditional psychological set
of the noblemen, which required that a noble rank or any
similar social and political distinction be conferred by the
autocrat alone. The Tsar's favor and will should be the only
source of all privileges and rights. In the minds of eighteenth-
century Russians, not much used to legal symbols and abstract concepts, Peter's legislation created confusion when
it provided that nobility was secured automatically upon
reaching a specified service rank. That nobility could be
granted in the name of the monarch, through the mere sig-
nature of some official, violated the notion that all privileges
stemmed from the sovereign; many interpreted the law to
mean that subordinate officials had now been given the
power to confer nobility by virtue of their right to make
promotions within the hierarchy of the Table of Ranks. At
the same time, the way the rules of the Table of Ranks were
applied seemed to eliminate the element of personal merit,
for promotions (and consequent ennoblement) were frequently obtained automatically, through mere seniority.

The absence of clear procedural forms confused people
still more. Did possession of the required rank in itself give
nobility, without any special patent or decree? Was the
"certificate" of promotion signed by subordinate officials
evidence enough to establish a claim to nobility in the

future? [51] In the final analysis, what did constitute proof of nobility? Such questions had also arisen in Western Europe, but there tradition, the ownership of certain categories of land, or the hereditary enjoyment of some rights and privileges had been considered adequate proof.[52] In Russia, the situation was quite different: possession of land alone did not provide evidence of nobility, and there were no special rights and privileges independent of service status. In truth, service had become the major criterion for legal and social status. But was mere attainment of a specific rank sufficient in itself? Should it not require special imperial sanction?

In fact, the crux of this debate over procedures lay in the basic change wrought by the reign of Peter the Great: he had brought into existence the Russian state, and the old personal relationship between subject and ruler was on the way to virtual disappearance. The very personal and intense relationship to Peter, however, could not long survive the Emperor's death—a fact clearly demonstrated by the short, weak reigns of Peter's immediate successors. There was no dominant personality on whom to transfer feelings for or against Peter, and the brevity of reigns precluded any individual from putting his stamp on the country. As a result, the state (embodied in Peter's new administrative institutions) became the principal basis for stability and imposed its goals and needs on the service classes. Only Catherine the Great (and in some measure Elizabeth) was to come close to reviving the old habits of personal loyalty by holding the center of the stage so effectively and for so long. That both women possessed great personal charm and seductive power was an important factor in their success, and it gave a slightly erotic tinge to the relationship between monarch and subject.[53] Needless to say, such a relationship could not have survived them, even if their successors had had more likable personalities than Peter III or Paul I.[54]

It was not easy for the noblemen to give up their traditional relationship to the ruler. Their reluctance was sustained by two developments. First, preservation of the full force of autocracy meant that ultimately the monarch was the sole source of rewards and promotions. Whatever the rules of service and the regular pattern of promotion, they could be disregarded by the sovereign. Strong, conscientious, and hard-working rulers like Peter the Great and Catherine the Great directly supervised much of the important work done for the state and could personally reward the most meritorious servants and officials. As awards and promotions given by the monarch himself were valued more than those obtained routinely on the basis of seniority, the sovereigns reserved for their own decision certain appointments, promotions, and rewards.[55]

In the second place, the development of the new pattern of the "interposition" of the state (*i.e.* government officials and bureaus) between the nobleman and the Emperor was never fully accepted. Objections were particularly strong and grounds for complaints especially numerous at periods when favorites dominated the monarch's will. As far as the majority of the nobility was concerned, these favorites were barriers standing between a nobleman's good performance of duty and its recognition by the sovereign. While facilitating the task for a very few, the favorite made this direct approach more difficult, if not outright impossible, for the majority.[56] The service nobleman needed to be able to rely on the sovereign's personal recognition and reward as a protection against the formal inflexibility of rules and statutes. It was his only way of preserving some elements of a personal relationship with his monarch. This bespoke the nobility's deep fear of alienation from the object of their service-based *raison d'être*. But, naturally, it was at the same time a denial of the norms of efficiency and rationality on their way to triumph in the Russian state, a desperate effort at salvaging some shreds of the personal and patriarchal character of kingship in Russia.[57]

For his part, the Russian monarch wanted to preserve the trappings of his traditional personal relationship to the service nobility in order to retain full autocratic power. This required that he be the sole source and dispenser of every significant benefaction to his subjects.[58] It was important that the regular bureaucracy and the automatic functioning of laws and rules did not displace his will. For part of the sovereign's autocratic power consisted, after all, in his ability to remove a case from the regular procedures of administrative law, in his power to supersede the requirements of the law in individual instances.[59] Of course, open access to the sovereign also provided the ruler with a countercheck on officials and favorites. Finally, the external trappings of a personal relationship between monarch and noble servicemen were a relatively easy and inexpensive way of maintaining the loyalty of the nobility at a high pitch, even in the face of the growing importance of the bureaucratic machine. As long as the feeling of personal loyalty was kept alive, it saved the majority of servicemen from feeling alienated from the bureaucratized state as well.[60]

With the consolidation of the new governmental apparatus, however, and with an increase in the complexity of political and administrative tasks, the personal system of rewards became increasingly inefficient and disruptive of orderly procedures. The monarch personally became the source of only the most extraordinary rewards, and occasions for such unusual recognition and reward became more and more rare, at least as far as the average serviceman was concerned. Ultimately the courtiers (in the broadest sense of the term) came to be their main, if not exclusive, beneficiaries. It is fair to add that whenever the monarch did distribute favors specially and on a personal basis, the reception and gratitude were more than normally enthusiastic. Catherine the Great and Elizabeth were particularly adept at using this technique by stressing their feminine charm. Alexander I soon grew tired of it, and Nicholas I always scorned it—little wonder that these two rulers enjoyed little popularity among the rank-and-file service nobility.

The weakening of the personal relationship, along with its increasingly empty manifestations, led to an interesting and, at first glance, paradoxical result. The monarch ceased to be the object of the efforts, concern, and loyalty of the service nobleman, but the alternative focus of the serviceman's loyalty, the state, which Peter the Great had created and endowed with a life and purpose of its own, was too much of an abstract concept to satisfy the personalized Russian way of thinking. The institution of the state did not inspire the necessary emotional response—partly because it was viewed as the sum total of government officials who were disliked and held in contempt. The state could not impart to the serviceman the *feeling* that his efforts, labors, and sacrifices were being appreciated and recognized as useful and valuable. This tendency was heightened by the tediousness of bureaucratic procedures and the formalism, dryness, and coldness of the service routine. No longer was administration felt to be work done for the sake of individual people; it had become a pushing around of papers in the hopeful belief—constantly belied by observation and experience— that this activity in itself would in some way ultimately benefit the country and the people.

The service pattern established by Peter the Great served the first emperor's purposes well: Russia became an important European power, obtained access to the Baltic Sea, and squarely entered the path of westernization and modernization.[61] It is futile to speculate as to whether the same result might have been accomplished by different means, at least with a different use of the "human material" at the disposal of the Russian Tsar. But there is little doubt that the service pattern devised by Peter did saddle the country —and more particularly the nobility and administration—

with serious problems that were to play a decisive role in Russia's further economic, social, and, above all, political development. The economic impact of Peter's service reforms can be easily traced. The strain imposed by the system on the economy was undoubtedly very great, and it seems fair to argue that its excessive burden handicapped for a long time the harmonious and balanced economic development of the country.[62]

The relationship that existed between the psychological reactions to the service pattern and the economic interests of the people emerged quite clearly in the early years of Imperial Russia. As we have seen, permanent and regular service forced the servicemen to be away from their estates for very long periods, if not practically their whole lives. The seventeenth-century nobleman, in spite of his limited talent or knowledge and his lazy inclination not to interfere in his peasants' work, had taken better care of his estate than his absentee heirs in the eighteenth century merely by residing on it a good part of his life. "Only the master's eye sees clearly" [63]—this truth of the fabulist's lesson was fully borne out by the economic situation of Russia in the second quarter of the eighteenth century.[64] Long absences, the necessity of relying on hired managers or on womenfolk, led to a decline in the productive capacity of the estates, to the nobleman's impoverishment, and, through the deterioration of the peasant's condition, to an impoverishment of the state's treasury as well.[65]

The plight of individual noblemen is documented in the numerous petitions for leave or retirement we have already discussed. The motive given is always the economic ruin and financial decline resulting (or threatening to result) from the lack of supervision of the estates.[66] The petty noblemen were naturally most affected: those noblemen who had only a small estate with a few peasant families could ill afford draining its produce for consumption in faraway towns or garrisons, nor could they afford hiring a manager to supervise the serfs and to protect the land from the encroachments of neighbors.[67]

Peter the Great, it is true, had instituted a system of regular salaries as the principal form of compensation for service. But the salaries were quite small, and all too often they were not even paid out regularly or in full, the Treasury itself being completely depleted. Neither was it unusual for the government to pay part of the salary in kind—in "Siberian goods" (*i.e.* furs) or grain—leaving to the nobleman the task of marketing the goods, not always at a fair price.[68] While in theory the salary might be barely adequate to maintain a single nobleman in service (with cheap lodgings and food provided by the State) it did not suffice to take care of his family and the serf servants who accompanied him. It was not uncommon for a nobleman in service to rely on his valet's or orderly's extra earnings in a craft or business.[69]

In the years following Peter's death both government and nobility struggled hard to solve the economic consequences of the new service pattern. But neither looked for a solution outside the service framework, such as, for example, freeing the nobility from service to allow it to become an economically productive class and making it possible for those remaining in service to live on adequate regular salaries. The government could not afford it and the nobility did not care to give up service because they had no other ties or concerns —service had always been their only *raison d'être*, the basis of their privileged status. In addition, since Peter the Great, service had also become the source of modernization, culture, and a more interesting way of life.[70] The path of compromise was, therefore, taken.

Under Catherine I and Peter II, since peace had returned to Russia, it was not necessary to maintain full military and naval establishments. Year-long leaves of absence would be granted in rotation to one-third of the officers in active service. The nobles would be able to return to their estates, bring them into good order, and improve their (and their peasants') economic circumstances. At the same time, they would not receive any salaries, making for a saving to the Treasury. It was hoped, peace lasting, that the leaves could be rotated in such a manner that every serviceman would spend one year out of three on his estates. In a sense the plan amounted to a partial return to the Muscovite pattern, except that permanence of service had now become the norm and home leave the mark of a special state favor. It may be worth noting that the plan did not come about as a result of pressure put by the nobility, though the rate of desertions and avoidances of service was rather high. In fact, the proposal was put forth and the decision made by high government officials who in other circumstances had not displayed great concern for the welfare or interests of the nobility. The step was suggested at a moment when the military servicemen were not much needed, while members of the civil administration, who could not be so easily spared, were not affected by the proposed plan.[71]

During Anne's reign, the economic needs of the service nobility were dealt with, partly at the suggestion of the nobles, by permitting one member in every family to remain at home to manage the estate, so that the others could devote their energies to the service. But this solution did not prove very successful: it did not help families with only one adult male, and relations among members of the same family deteriorated, as the traditional system of inheritance did not fit the new situation easily.[72] The most satisfactory solution seemed to be restriction of the form of service, so that the nobleman could retire in the prime of life to attend to his economic affairs, provide for his children about to enter service, and leave to his heirs an estate in good condition. At first the term of service was set at twenty-five years; later it was reduced to twenty. Even more important than these limitations on the duration of service were more liberal policies in granting long leaves and earlier retirement. The most common method for overcoming the roadblocks in the path of retirement was to obtain frequent extended leaves of absence. One could obtain such leaves rather easily, especially in time of peace, if one were willing to pay overt or disguised bribes to superiors and officials.[73] Anyone who really did not want to serve any longer and who was not irreplaceable could obtain long-term leaves (virtual retirement) by petitioning the monarch. Yet complete retirement before the prescribed time was granted reluctantly and infrequently. Moreover, under ordinary circumstances retirement did not protect a nobleman from recall or various temporary government assignments.[74]

The unsuccessful attempt at restricting the autocracy at the accession of Anne in 1730 need not be described here.[75] But it is interesting to examine the ideas and attitudes pertaining to service that were expressed by groups of the nobility in the projects circulated at the time. The striking feature of these brief and not very searching expressions of opinion is the absence of any arguments against compulsory service as such. And why should it have been otherwise? Not only was service the traditional and accepted pattern of life for the nobility, but the class's privileges, status, and hopes of playing a leading role in the state depended on it. Nor had the nobility any serious grounds around 1730 for dissatisfaction with its position. Competition from the non-noble classes had not been serious; the government had relied mainly on the nobility for its service personnel, and the nobles had shared with the state the political, military, and cultural progress made by Russia since the accession of Peter the Great. The state's new glory and prestige reflected on them too, while the accompanying economic and political gains yielded direct material benefits for many individual noblemen. If the task was hard and the effort great, the rewards were great also.

There were only a few hints that special hardship cases be taken into consideration. However, there was a desire— by no means unanimous—to see the permanent nature of service obligations somehow alleviated.[76] Make it possible for us, some nobles argued, to return more frequently and for longer periods to our estates and our domestic concerns. In peacetime, while their services were needed only for routine garrison duty, it was felt that a sizeable proportion of the officers should be allowed to go home. This would not harm the interests of the state, and yet it would confer great benefits on the individuals concerned, their peasants, and—ultimately—on the country at large. This was the same argument that had been advanced by the high dignitaries in 1727.

More important, perhaps, than concern for their economic welfare was the concern of the noblemen for their status. A most important subjective reason for their intense dissatisfaction with the service rules was the requirement introduced by Peter the Great that the nobleman had to begin his service career at the bottom, even below the hierarchy established by the Table of Ranks. Noblemen had to enter the army as common soldiers or the navy as apprentice seamen; moreover, they were subjected to the same harsh discipline and brutal forms of punishment as their non-noble fellow soldiers and sailors, and they were compelled to carry out the same arduous and unpleasant tasks. Only after such an apprenticeship was a nobleman promoted to the lowest grade of the Table of Ranks. He then had to spend more time and effort climbing the ladder of ranks gradually—on the basis of merit and performance alone (if he lacked influential supporters and patrons)—before he could become a full officer. Many nobles—especially those with less intelligence, education, and ambition—remained noncommissioned sergeants, corporals, and even privates throughout their entire service career.[77]

Peter had justified the new rules of service by pointing out that no one could be a good officer and command men if

he had not first learned how to obey. In the absence of adequate schools or training programs, this knowledge could be
acquired only through experience, *i.e.* by coming up through
the ranks.[78] Yet Peter had provided that some posts be open
only to nobles and that noblemen be given preference in
certain kinds of training and experience. But until enough
nobles had been trained, anyone who was qualified could be
taken.

Still more galling to the nobleman was the situation in
which he found himself in the civilian administration. The
average nobleman felt ill at ease and thought it beneath his
dignity to deal only with papers and to rub elbows with
low-born clerks who were more efficient, experienced, and
aggressive than he. As a result, most of the paperwork was
left to commoners, and this in turn fed the nobility's dislike
for the administration and its officials.[79] Although Peter the
Great had tried to reserve the highest administrative posts
for members of the nobility, the lack of adequate candidates
often compelled him to appoint the low-born and the foreigner. Since the Table of Ranks provided for automatic
ennoblement upon reaching certain grades in the administration, clerks of common origin swelled the ranks of the
nobility and, once ennobled, rose fast to the highest posts.

Even before the death of Peter the Great, but more loudly
and insistently afterward, the nobility argued that all positions of responsibility in the administration, as well as in the
army and navy, should be the exclusive preserve of the nobility; the ordinary clerk of low birth—whose services could
not be dispensed with—should not be promoted beyond a
specified rank.[80] They also argued that noblemen should not
be given menial jobs or suffer the indignity of degrading
punishments. What did it mean to be a nobleman, they asked,
if it did not imply being treated in a different way and assigned other tasks than was a commoner? Was not the modern education of noble youngsters, as well as the sacrifices
of their parents in training their sons to be leaders and noble-

men, worthy of the state's gratitude? The nobility demanded that this spread of education be recognized by waiving the requirement that the nobility enter the civil service at the bottom of the ladder; if a nobleman were properly educated, they argued, he should be appointed directly to a supervisory position in the administration. The nobles also demanded special facilities for schooling and preference for children of the nobility in promotion to officer rank.

The arguments in support of these claims for special treatment in service promotions no doubt sound quite insincere and offensively spurious, but they illustrate the nobility's growing self-esteem and throw some light on the question of self-definition faced by the nobility in the eighteenth century. It was normal in the eighteenth century for noblemen to claim posts of importance on the grounds that in itself the fact of nobility automatically conferred the right to preferential treatment. Quite characteristic of the noble mentality, however, was the argument that a nobleman's status and self-respect suffered from having to serve alongside commoners, to have to take orders from them and even submit to their *brimades*. And since an administrative official often held in his hands the honor, property, freedom, and future career of the Emperor's subjects, how could a commoner without the refinements of heart and mind that come with European and literary education be entrusted with such responsibility? Never would he be able to perceive the human element of the situation: at best he would act on the basis of abstract notions and general rules interpreted literally; at worst he could be swayed by bribery. The nobleman's educational and cultural progress since Peter's reign, on the other hand, eminently qualified him to make decisions affecting the welfare of other human beings. Leaders in culture, leaders in the military, possessed of lofty concepts of honor and justice, they alone were qualified and entitled to the governance of men.[81]

But even while the government was prepared to give the

nobility preference in the administration, noblemen remained reluctant to join the administration. In spite of special advantages and the promise of favors, they preferred to serve in the army, especially if it was possible to join the regiments of the Guards, where promotions were more frequent and rapid. After he had received a Western education at some sacrifice and inconvenience to himself, the nobleman did not want to shuffle papers in a dingy office for a poor and irregularly paid salary and with few prospects for rapid promotion, recognition, or rewards. As a matter of fact, the government tended to undo with one hand what it tried to build up with the other. It did hold out rewards and attractions to the administrative branch, but as military requirements (fancied or real) came first, its policy was to give preferment and recognition to officers (and courtiers) and disregard the interests of those who did the routine work in the bureaus.

The dissatisfaction of the nobility with service patterns was expressed in its demand for recognition of its status during the crisis of 1730. All professional experts and leaders insisted that officer rank could not be granted every nobleman at the start of his service career if the hard-won qualities of the new modern army and administration were to be preserved. But the nobility requested that provision be made to give special training to its members so they could attain officer rank rapidly. Together with requests for automatic retirement after twenty to thirty years of service, it was the only concrete demand referring to the service pattern that was made at that time.[82]

Peter the Great had already thought along similar lines: he had established an in-training program in the Senate for young noblemen. It had been his hope that the School of Navigation and the Academy of Sciences would provide the required special training and general education for children of the nobility, so that the period of their active apprenticeship in the lowest ranks could be reduced. He had also given preference to nobles in making appointments to the regiments of the Guards, so that the Semenovskii and Preobrazhenskii regiments were largely manned by children of the nobility. Noncommissioned and junior officers from these regiments received correspondingly much higher ranks when they were transferred to regular army units or assigned to other institutions.[83] The establishment of the Corps of Cadets in 1731 was a response to the need for giving privileged service status to the nobility. Later, several other schools of a similar type were opened.[84] Admission to these privileged educational establishments was open only to children of the nobility, and graduation from them automatically carried appointment to the lowest full officer rank. Fulfilling a genuine need, these corps of cadets became very popular and very influential on the subsequent development of the Russian élite.

In fact, the very definition of the nobility was at stake. No protest was made in 1730 against the Table of Ranks, as the rank-and-file nobility was interested mostly in preventing the old and prominent families from consolidating and increasing their power. In opposition to the Supreme Privy Council's attempts at restricting the autocratic power of the new Empress, the nobility (*generalitet* and *szlachta*) raised the standard of autocracy. This defense not only illustrates the average nobleman's dislike of the oligarchy of the Supreme Privy Council, it also showed clearly that the Russian *szlachtic* acknowledged the fact that everything, including noble status and privileges, depended exclusively on the monarch's will. In other words, it meant that it should be possible for all nobles to attain the highest ranks and positions by virtue of their merit duly recognized by the sovereign. It was—to use an anachronistic terminology—a doctrine of "open opportunities to all" within the nobility,[85] stressing services rendered to the state and the monarch and the fulfillment of the nobleman's obligations of cultural leadership with regard to the country and people. The notion of cultural leadership

injected vagueness, if not outright confusion, into the definition of nobility. What was more important for noble status:
the grade attained in the Table of Ranks or the level of culture and education displayed in one's way of life? [86] Peter
had assumed that eventually a nobleman would have both
rank and a "cultured way of life." But could one be sure?
Peter's own experiences with the education of the young
noblemen of his time should have been a warning. This double standard was to bedevil the self-image of the Russian
nobility throughout the eighteenth century and leave an important legacy for the first generations of the intelligentsia.

Under the circumstances, any drastic change in the pattern
of the relation of the nobility to service and the state was
foreclosed, unless it was brought about by the state itself for
the sake of its own interests. The argument that during her
reign Anne gave satisfaction to the demands voiced in 1730
because she owed everything to the nobles does not seem
very convincing. As a matter of fact, liberalization of service
conditions, for example permission to retire after twenty-five
years of service and more liberal leaves of absence, came in
1736, *i.e.* some years after the accession of Anne, and hence
can hardly be considered to have been made under pressure
of the events of 1730. (Incidentally, these leaves were easily
canceled when it suited the government's interests, for example in 1740.) Essentially, the principle of service remained
untouched, and even its implementation did not change ap-
preciably until the 1760's. The nobleman was expected to
serve for the best part of his life, for at least twenty-five to
thirty years, and only under Elizabeth did retirement become easily possible after twenty years of service.

Of course, there were periods when the government was
quite lax in enforcing these rules. But the pattern as such
remained intact, and, more important, it was accepted as
natural by all the nobility. Memoir after memoir reveals
that a nobleman never even conceived of the possibility of
not serving, unless he were crippled or disabled. True, many

nobles wanted to put off the day of entrance into service as long as possible; after all, the normal start was at the age of fifteen! Naturally, everyone also endeavored to find the easiest kind of service, with the greatest promise for rewards and advancement. But this should not be construed as evidence that the practice of service itself was put in question. Those who tried to delay their entrance into service, those who tried to retire early, those who overstayed their leaves, as well as those who went into hiding to evade service altogether (this became relatively rare from the second third of the century) knew well not only that they were breaking the law, but also that they were doing wrong morally. It was a violation of the duty and obligation imposed on them as members of the privileged élite, and when they were caught, they accepted their punishment as deserved.

Under the impact of Peter's reforms, westernization had become the avowed goal of the Russian government and ruling class, and state service was unavoidably pressed into contributing to its realization. The nobility thus accepted service as its normal way of life because of the vital didactic function it had come to fulfill. The first emperor had modernized the military and administrative establishments to reflect Western techniques, models, and rational concepts. To participate in the work of these establishments, the noble servicemen had to acquire some technical skills—mathematics, engineering, ballistics, navigation, or architecture for the army and navy, or law, political economy, and languages for the administration.

The inadequacies of the Russian educational facilities (to be discussed in Chapter Four) meant that the regiment, the ship or the administrative office had to make up for the deficiencies of their staff by engaging in educational activities. This did not necessarily mean establishing regular schools in the regiment or administrative office.[87] More often it was a junior or noncommissioned officer or a clerk who taught the children of officers or the young servicemen languages, a smattering of mathematics, law, or fortification, as the need dictated. Much information and many skills were also acquired merely in the course of learning to perform service tasks.[88]

But not only in the restricted sense of book learning did service act as a form of schooling. It also introduced the young provincial noble serviceman to "civilization" in general and to Western notions of culture in particular. The most effective and comprehensive form of this kind of educational experience was found in the Corps of Cadets. But Western culture and civilization were also acquired within the ranks of the Guards regiments. In the Guards, the young provincial came into contact with officers (and soldiers and noncommissioned officers as well) who had received a good education and had been brought up in the big cities of the Empire. Serving in the Guards the youngster found himself close to the Court and, provided he had acquired the proper forms of dress and manner, he could participate in the social and cultural life of St. Petersburg (and, on occasion, Moscow). No wonder that many an uncouth provincial youth discovered himself and his hidden talents for art, literature, or philosophy while serving in the Guards.[89]

But the Guards regiments were not alone in fulfilling this cultural function. Service in ordinary army and navy units, or even local administrative offices, might offer similar opportunities and have a similar impact, albeit on a less sophisticated level. How many young nobles received their social polish and their "culture," or had their curiosity and thirst for learning awakened, through contacts and experiences in service? Until the very end of the eighteenth century, the Russian nobleman could lead but an isolated life in the countryside. The trips to the nearest important town were infrequent, and in most instances the town itself did not provide stimulating educative company or experiences. Service became the young nobleman's first genuine contact with the wider world, and his first opportunity to discover and share new knowledge and ideas.

For some, service also provided an opportunity for traveling in foreign lands. Before foreign travel had become a common practice—at least for the few rich or lucky young nobles—participation in military operations was the only way by which the average serviceman could get outside Russia. A strong educational impact was made through direct contact with Central and Western Europe in the course of military campaigns abroad, such as the Seven Years' War and the wars against France at the end of the eighteenth century. In addition, garrison service in the newly conquered Baltic provinces (and later in Poland and Finland) gave the Russian nobleman direct access to the way of life, customs, and language of the West. True, only a minority appear to have benefited from the experience of the Seven Years' War or from being stationed in the Baltic provinces. The average Russian nobleman was still too unsophisticated, coarse, and ignorant to appreciate what the new environment had to offer. Most were content with having a good time, drinking, and chasing after girls; and their coarseness hardly helped them gain admission into good German society.[90] But the few who were prepared by previous education, or were endowed with an inquisitive and open mind, did discover a new world.[91] When access was gained into a German bourgeois or even noble household, the benefits were immediate and great. The Russian learned the German language, and might take to reading relatively sophisticated books; on occasion he might become interested enough to pursue his studies further. Last but not least, he became acquainted with the amenities of life common in these provinces but still unknown or rare in Russia proper. On his return to Russia he might attempt to introduce these new things in his own house, and try to change his way of life to satisfy his newly acquired interests and tastes.

Service thus became a pathway to education and westernization for most noblemen, as well as a critical catalyst in
their very rapid cultural transformation. The Russian nobleman of Elizabeth's time, less than one generation after the
death of Peter the Great, bore no resemblance to his grand-
father, or even father. In view of Russia's previous isolation
and the small number of schools and teachers, such a rapid
transformation of the ruling class could not have been accomplished without the help of service in the army, navy, and
administration. Westernization affected even dress: by the
middle of the eighteenth century even the most backward,
uneducated, and tradition-bound petty nobleman in a faraway corner of provincial Russia (*medvezhii ugol*) was
wearing "foreign" (*nemetskii*) dress, usually an adaptation
of the uniform he had worn in service.[92] Whatever knowledge
and intellectual interests the provincial nobleman could display in retirement, he had acquired during his period of
service. Social contacts and friendships, an interest in what
was going on in the wide world, especially at St. Petersburg
and at Court, were stimulated and kept alive by service
experiences and memories.[93]

But although the didactic role of the service in developing
Russia's cultural élite should not be underestimated, certain
aspects of this process of westernization proved to have undesirable long-run effects. As ties to the home estate and
province were loose and fluctuating, and as family bonds
were essentially emotional and personal, devoid of the geographic roots and local solidarity that distinguished the
family patterns of the West, service alone provided a coherent
institutional framework for stability. This was particularly
true in schools and regiments. Pushkin intended more than a
poetic figure of speech when he said, "Tsarskoe Selo [*i.e.* its
boarding school] is the fatherland for us." [94] What he said
about himself and his friends in a spiritual and social sense
was also said by succeeding generations of graduates from
the Corps of Cadets and other special service schools. The

Guards regiments, too, fostered this sentiment, for service in them could be lifelong if one wished to make it so. Groups based on service and school connections acted as substitutes for weak family ties. In more than one sense, the Masonic lodges, the secret societies of the 1820's, and the circles (*kruzhki*) of the radical intelligentsia were an extension of these service-connected solidarities.[95]

Service made for a cultural rootlessness as well, involving more than merely the breaking of ties with the countryside that accompanies all modern urbanization. For service in the cities and capitals meant involving oneself in a new, emerging type of culture that had little in common with traditional Russian life. Not only was this culture primarily urban (after all, in the eighteenth century the discrepancy between town and country was not very great), but it aimed at resembling the culture of Western Europe as closely as possible. For the French nobleman, for instance, residence in the provincial or national capital merely implied a more intensive and satisfying experience of his normal cultural pattern;[96] for the Russian it meant adopting a new pattern altogether. Costume and speech, activities and rules of behavior were new, more or less successful copies of Western models. In becoming a part of this new environment, the nobleman acquired the habit of looking to Western Europe as the only source of norms to emulate. His contact with the traditional pattern of the countryside and his understanding of the people were destroyed; they remained only as a pleasant diversion in the summer.[97] Looking to the West for inspiration and models (though frequently also condemning it), he lost his ties with his own country's tradition and culture and began to feel foreign and superior to it.

Drawn into foreign culture, the service nobleman endeavored to bring up his children in foreign ways and, if he had the means, to travel abroad and become acquainted with the models directly.[98] Of course, in itself travel does not necessarily contribute to a feeling of rootlessness; if the traveler has firm ties and commitments at home, the experience abroad acts as a counterpoint to the familiar pattern, and only its valuable elements are assimilated. In such a case, direct foreign experience serves to reinforce the awareness of one's own identity and ties to one's homeland and its people. But while broadening the traveler's intellectual horizon and deepening his sophistication, these foreign experiences do not bring about social or psychological changes. If on the contrary the traveler aims at identity with the foreigners and rejects his home patterns (because they seem too primitive), then travel only reinforces his alienation from his own milieu. We can observe the phenomenon today in students and travelers from the developing nations who, after a long stay in the West, feel alienated and rootless at home. This is exactly what happened in Russia in the eighteenth century (and even in the nineteenth). Foreign travel and residence either "denationalized" the Russians or (as a protective reaction) drove them into parochial and sentimental chauvinism. In both cases they became foreign to their own country—either because they had become pseudo foreigners or because their chauvinism had no place in a country that was drawing away from the traditional patterns they had allegedly rediscovered while abroad.[99]

Notwithstanding the alienation and rootlessness it engendered among the nobility, however, the service pattern contributed to the westernization of other segments of Russian society by offering the nobility an unexpectedly wide opportunity to play the role of teacher. The serviceman was well placed through his official position in the civil administration and his social role in garrison towns to transmit his newly acquired Western culture, however superficial it may have been. And he did so eagerly. Filled with a sense of accomplishment, he felt that it would be beneath a gentleman's dignity not to live according to Western fashion and customs, to be devoid of literary and intellectual interests.[100] In his proselytising enthusiasm he was supported by the state, eager to have all the nobility, and as large a segment of the nation as possible, modernized and westernized. As part of their duties, members of the administration introduced Western patterns of social life, intellectual fashions, literary and dramatic interests to their subordinates and the population under their care.[101]

These noble servicemen gained prestige from the fact that they had a much higher level of culture and sophistication than the people around them, and that they had literary and intellectual interests (however mediocre compared to the true élites of St. Petersburg or Moscow) that they continued to pursue as much as possible. These servicemen became the élite of local society, and their example was followed. On duty in remote and forsaken corners of the Empire, the serviceman found solace in his role of promoter of good manners, taste, education, and culture.[102] The history of the cultural development of Siberia, for example, is testimony to the great role played by the officials in bringing the life of the spirit to that remote province.

In the same didactic vein servicemen-administrators were directly involved in trying to transform conditions in Russia.[103] As members of the central administration, they participated with the state in the modernization of institutions and their extension to all corners of the Empire, the "rationalization" of administrative and military practices and techniques, and the stimulation of economic development.[104] By putting "rationality" above "tradition," they thus followed in the footsteps of Peter the Great, who had initiated this approach by making the state the transformer of society.[105] Russia's administration was active, not passive; it looked to the future instead of following a direction defined by the past.[106]

Such was the general attitude and outlook on administration absorbed and largely practiced by the service nobility. The notion that the government could do anything led to the belief that, therefore, its servants should have free rein to act in accordance with the dictates of rationality and the requirements of their specific goals. Hence the ruthless attempts at imposing new ways, values, and patterns on a reluctant population. Servicemen reasoned that these new values were derived from the best principles available to the period; since other countries had done well by them, Russia must do the same. Opposition was to be swept aside by any means; the claims of historical tradition or regional and local peculiarity were not to be acknowledged. To the extent that they were conscious of what they were doing, the officials were not to be turned from their path, so that their actions and methods were much more tyrannical than they needed to be. They transferred to the realm of civil administration the attitudes and practices of blind obedience and complete subordination developed by the rigid bureaucratic order and hierarchy of the military establishment. If a peasant serf could be turned into an obedient automaton performing whatever his officers ordered him to do for the sake of a goal only the central authorities knew, if peasants and even noblemen could become mere cogs in a big, impersonal machine, why should the same not be possible with the rest of the population?

Since these attitudes were partly rooted in the relationship of the nobleman to the serfs and common people, we turn briefly from the nobleman's public life as a serviceman to his role as a land- and serf owner. Without a doubt serfdom—the economic mainstay of the nobility and the dominant feature of the country's social structure—played a paramount role in shaping human relationships and attitudes in Russia. The brutality, exploitation, and horror of serfdom not only left an indelible imprint on the mentality and behavior of the peasants, but also quite naturally affected the attitudes of the nobility, though perhaps less profoundly. Much has been written on the economic exploitation of the serfs; still more has been written about the cruel and capricious mistreatment they suffered. True, there still is room for a dispassionate description of the actual working of the estate system in Russia and for an exhaustive analysis of its economic aspects.

But these topics belong in the domain of the economic historian, and we shall not be concerned with them.[107] Here we wish only to sketch very briefly the psychological reactions and mental sets of the *nobility* that were directly shaped by serf relations and conditions. Admittedly, this is only part of Russian reality, but it is an aspect that has been insufficiently commented upon, in spite of its role in shaping ideological attitudes.

The state had given to the landowner a power over his peasants that was almost the full counterpart of the Tsar's power over all his subjects. The landowner was master of the activities of his serfs, completely and unchallengeably; he could do whatever he wished with them, except to kill them (and in practice even this limitation was not always enforced). Little wonder that the nobleman transferred the attitudes he had acquired as the Emperor's serviceman to his relations with his serfs.

The nobles as a class had watched a strong will transform a whole social group within a generation. If the autocrat—*i.e.* the state—could impose a new system of values and pattern of life on the nobility, and in so doing lay the foundation of Russia's glory and modernization, why could not the individual nobleman emulate his sovereign? Why could he not do with his peasants what Peter had done with the nobility? Such was the naïve reasoning of many noble servicemen, encouraging them to attempt to implement their newly acquired notions. But what was passing whim for some became an all-pervading passion in others. Noblemen became interested in their serfs merely as material for social and cultural change, sometimes even at the expense of their genuine economic self-interest (not to speak of the peasants' happiness). By an all-too-common paradox, the subordination of private economic interest to cultural modernization intensified the oppression and exploitation of the serfs.

The nobleman frequently tried to run his estate the way he had been accustomed to run a regiment or administrative office. He issued rules regulating the daily activities of his peasants and domestics that at times reached ridiculous extremes of pedantry and pettiness.[108] On occasion he would follow the military pattern of organization, at other times he imposed comprehensive codes (in imitation of natural-law legislation) regulating every facet of life on the estate. There is no doubt of the strong element of play that underlay this type of behavior. It was a carry-over—as we shall see—of the nobleman's childhood play experiences with serf companions.

But what was amusement to the landowner entailed a heavy burden for the peasantry.[109] The fact that the nobleman organized his own life along a similar pattern of play-acting and imitation of military procedures—wearing uniforms, devising entertainments with his guests in imitation of military festivities[110]—was of small consolation to the serf, who had never been in contact with this form of life and whose own traditional pattern and required activities were thereby thoughtlessly disrupted. The habits of ordering people about capriciously, of trying to reorganize the institutional patterns of life on a sweeping scale, that the nobleman had acquired in service were carried over to the running of his estates. We have countless examples of radical changes of mood that led to the complete rebuilding of areas of an estate, sudden changes in the work schedule, drastic alterations of gardens and parks and interiors of mansions, capricious and sweeping changes in the domestic regulations pertaining to the conduct and life of serfs.[111]

The result of all this was to hasten, or consolidate, the emergence of "two nations" (to use Disraeli's famous phrase coined in another context): the nobility and the peasants (or rather the educated class of servicemen and the commoners in general). All efforts of the landlords to impose changes and new patterns (whether these were beneficial or not) on their serfs only increased their alienation from the people. Not only was the serfs' economic and legal situation horrible, but even the language and the feeling of belonging to the same nation, which they once had shared with their masters, were rapidly lost. To many serfs their masters were like foreign conquerors, hardly better than the Tartars, against whom, of course, everything was permitted.[112] The peasant revolts, when they came, for example the Pugachevshchina, were terrible. Whenever they could the peasants destroyed the nobles and their property with passionate hatred, as if they wanted to eradicate everything connected with the nobles' values and way of life. Nothing but mutual suspicion and fear could come of the gap dividing serf from master.[113]

The experiences and relationships we have just described could only deepen the sense of alienation and rootlessness felt by reflective and enlightened noblemen. They were becoming ever more conscious of the fact that they had become strangers to their people. Their feeling of insecurity had several components: on the lowest level was an almost instinctive fear of those whom they had oppressed and exploited. On a higher level the noblemen felt that they lacked a milieu responsive to their newly acquired way of life and interests—they felt the pangs that come from being "modern" in a "primitive," "traditional," and jealous environment. Finally, on the highest level was insecurity mixed with strong feelings of guilt for the treatment meted out to the serfs and for not having drawn the peasantry into Russia's emerging European civilization.[114] But most important in the long run was the gradual realization during the last third of the eighteenth century that, in order to teach the peasants to behave like men, the nobility first had to give them the status of human beings.[115]

The westernization of noblemen through the service had its impact on their traditional quest for a clearer definition of noble status. Under Peter the Great, the nobility had pleaded for more indulgence for human weakness and greater leniency in dealing with the problems that arose from adapting to new

ways. But by the middle of the eighteenth century the nobility argued that their own energies and dedication beyond
the strict call of duty to the new state had transformed them
into civilized and sophisticated individuals. They had demonstrated their high sense of honor and responsibility by will-
ingly accepting the obligations of their status, including their
role as *Kulturträger* (culture-bearer) in Russian society. They
contended that the nobleman was now a different breed from
the commoner. This was not because the nobleman was
descended from a different racial or ethnic stock,[116] and not
merely because in the past his family had held high positions
and enjoyed privileged status in the state.[117] No, the nobleman was distinguished from both his Muscovite ancestors and
the common people by his achievements in Western culture
and education.[118] The nobility demanded, therefore, that the
state recognize their achievements by respecting the nobleman as a valuable, sensitive human being, rather than as a
mere cog in the machine of the state; they asked that their
spiritual qualities and cultural achievements be honored.[119]

The decades that followed the death of Peter the Great
witnessed efforts at setting clearer and more exclusive rules for
determining membership in the nobility and preferment in
service. But curiously enough, there was nothing even like a
serious effort on the part of the "old aristocratic" families
(such as there were) to bring back the old times. In fact, the
old nobility, the boyars, did not make any comeback, nor did
they ever seriously attempt it. The establishment of the Supreme Privy Council, which is often considered the expression
of such an effort, was in fact something else. While including
a few representatives of "old aristocratic" families (Golitsyn,
Dolgoruki), the Supreme Privy Council consisted mostly of
prominent dignitaries of Peter's time. This was certainly the
case not only of Menshikov—who, it is true, was eliminated
in 1727—but also of Osterman, Iaguzhinskii, Golovin. In fact
many members of the old families had become identified with
Peter's reign and reforms. We need only to recall the names

of Sheremetev, Romadonovskii, and Apraksin. The two famous Golitsyns (Dmitrii and Mikhail) and the more intelli-
gent Dolgoruki (Luke) were as much the "fledglings of
Peter's nest" as a Menshikov, Shafirov, or Golovin, the only
superficial difference being that they bore old names. Nor did
their policies in any way signify a return to pre-Petrine traditions. They were, rather, continuing Peter's work, though at
a somewhat slower pace and with greater concern for the
welfare of society as a necessary prerequisite for satisfying
the interests of the state and government. It is true that the
Dolgoruki clan tried to secure a dominant position through
marriage links with the monarch, and raise their family above
all others in the same way the Naryshkin and Miloslavskii
had tried to do in the seventeenth century. Theirs was merely
a search for court favor, similar to Menshikov's plan in 1727
or to the efforts of favorites under Anne, Elizabeth, and
Catherine the Great to use their "good fortune" in furthering
the family's material interests.[120] There never was any question of the Dolgorukis attempting or even intending to restore the boyar duma, the Muscovite pattern of court and
service life, or go back on the cultural, military, and political
transformations of Peter's reign.

What then was the significance of the crisis of 1730 for the
definition of the nobility? The major significance of the events
of January–March, 1730, consisted in the almost unanimous
opposition of the nobility to the formation of a true aristocracy
based on family, wealth, political influence, and power.
Dmitrii Golitsyn's plans revived the fear—subliminally ever
present in the Russian political consciousness—of a return to
the time of appanages, with its splintering of sovereignty,
weak authority, and divisive conflicts. Affected as he had been
by the concepts and experiences of Peter's reign, with its
emphasis on service, the average Russian nobleman was not
willing to believe that rights and privileges granted with his
help to a select group of nobles might then be easily extended

to the entire class. Nor did the actions of the Supreme Privy Council, it must be admitted, inspire the nobility with confidence in the likelihood of such a development. In the final analysis, by restoring full autocracy the crisis of 1730 reinforced the concept of the nobility as a body of equal servicemen whose individual and group status depended exclusively on the will, favor, and interests of the Autocrat.

One has the impression that the men taking part in the events of 1730 avoided dealing with the ticklish problem of the definition of nobility because they themselves, in their own lives and careers, illustrated the ambiguities and benefited from the contradictions inherent in the post-Petrine status of the Russian nobility. It was to the advantage of the majority that the question of definition of the nobility be left somewhat vague. The generation of the many who had obtained nobility and prominence thanks to the legislation of the first emperor obviously wished to prevent a return of the family principle as the deciding factor in public status. Clearly their present status, as well as their future prospects, were closely linked to the new opportunities opened up by Peter's transformation and modernization of Russia. Only service, pure and simple, could secure their gains and aspirations, and for this autocracy seemed to be the best safeguard; the absolute ruler alone could adequately reward and promote within the framework of the new social and administrative hierarchies. All those who were high-minded and ambitious, loyal and conscientious, were entitled to feel that service was open to them and that given an initial start anyone had the possibility of rising to the highest rank. No one should be deprived of this opportunity because the highest functions and most desirable rewards had been preempted by a group of individuals by virtue of their birth and the privileged status granted to their family by some kind of contract. Such special rights and privileges, the Russian noblemen were firmly convinced, could only lead to a splintering of sovereignty, to an end to the concentration of authority in the hands of one individual that alone had secured to Russia its present glory and power.

In this we may see a tacit recognition of the fact that the reign of Peter the Great had given the Russian nobility a new status, had endowed the individual nobleman with greater personal dignity. While this new situation entailed some hardships and dissatisfaction, there was compensation in the knowledge that one served the interests of a great state, an internationally recognized power. Peter's reforms had shown the way for Russia's cultural and political progress; the state had taken the lead in this task, associating the nobility with it, and its rewards were beginning to be shared equally by the sovereign and the nobility.[121] The victory of an oligarchy or aristocracy might undo these gains, more particularly since, intent on satisfying their own selfish interests, the oligarchs would neglect the state's function in modernizing and westernizing the country. The rank-and-file nobility, however (especially the more energetic and ambitious), wanted to go still further in the direction indicated by the Tsar Reformer; in their opinion this was possible only under the leadership of the state and with the active participation of the nobles; careers and high ranks open to all on the basis of service performance were the basic institutional tools. It is no accident that the most cogent, popular, and effective arguments against the Supreme Privy Council "conditions" in favor of the maintenance of autocracy came from the pens of men like Prokopovich, Tatishchev, and Kantemir. The selfish interests of the majority of nobles combined with the interests of the state as defined by Peter the Great to defeat any attempt to transform the pattern of service and merit in favor of set privileges and special status of hereditary family groupings.

In the reign of Anne, many newcomers (quite a number of whom were foreigners, mainly Germans from the Baltic provinces) rose to high positions in the state. It is interesting to note that, in spite of the influence wielded by the Baltic German noblemen who had entered Russian service, no serious attempt was made by them to introduce the Baltic pattern of estate privileges and local authority.[122] In part this may have been because they sensed that the Russian nobility would have been disinclined to imitate the "Germans," who looked down on them. In addition, the German favorites well knew that their own position depended on a strong autocracy assisted by a dependent and servile Russian nobility. All the efforts the Germans made in behalf of the status of the nobility were to enhance their own position in the Baltic provinces and preserve the special local rights and privileges that were theirs upon entering Russian service.

The law and practice of accession to noble status remained unchanged during the decades following 1730. The Petrine ambiguities remained, and although the number of ennoblements decreased somewhat (if we except Elizabeth's wholesale promotion of all the members of the Guards regiment that helped her gain the throne), service continued to be the main factor in establishing nobility. A subtle shift of a subjective-psychological nature did take place, however, and served to confuse the situation still more. This was the emergence of the notion that belonging to the nobility implied following a particular way of life and therefore having certain psychological attitudes and characteristics of mind. The concept of nobility became associated with a high level of education—more specifically with a foreign-style education, the wearing of foreign dress, and an acquaintance with foreign literature, ideas, languages, and habits. Imbued with his new role of bringing European civilization and cultural progress to Russia, the nobleman could not remain the lowly servant he had been in Muscovite times. He was no longer a servile, boorish, and ignorant individual inseparable from his family and class; he had acquired a sense of personal dignity and worth. In fact, as well as in name, he had become an honorable and educated individual whose personality had to be recognized and respected. In short, it was argued, to be a nobleman was to be someone who could be identified at first glance as a gentleman (*barin*).

Obviously, this was the ideal to which every nobleman aspired, but which not every nobleman could attain; nor were the exalted notions about personal dignity, education, and a cultured way of life necessarily translated into the treatment the noblemen gave their serfs, servants, family, or subordinates.[123] The fact was, though, that members of the nobility were developing a sense of being an élite by virtue of their way of life and their cultural and educational sophistication. The state and the common people both tended to accept the nobility's new self-image, in part because it was safer than any alternative images, in part because Peter's heritage precluded any other choice anyway.

That such an approach to a definition of nobility was not very serviceable for legal and administrative purposes is obvious. It is interesting that it was essentially a matter of self-definition and social acceptance. The individual himself had to be made to feel that by his way of life he possessed the qualities and qualifications requisite for belonging to this élite, and the other members of the group had to accept him. The basic criterion for membership in the élite group was the sharing of similar ideals and patterns of behavior and education (not unlike the practice of co-optation and the sharing of common aspirations that were to determine an individual's belonging to the intelligentsia). As far as the nobility in the eighteenth century was concerned, such an attitude led to two conflicting results. On the one hand it served as a very rigid principle of exclusion, for in the eighteenth century very few (if any) commoners could hope to obtain the education and cultural polish required to belong to the nobility. Yet it was not impossible for a few talented and energetic children of the clergy or of lower clerks to "pass" into the nobility, thanks to their better education and the Table of Ranks. Once they had accomplished this they merged fairly easily with the mass of the nobility.[124]

On the other hand, the very same attitude made for greater equality among the noblemen themselves, blurring somewhat the distinctions of rank. More important still, it blurred the difference in origin among the nobility: old families, low-class gentry, and foreign nobility, newly ennobled, were all made equal by their way of life, educational level, and intellectual accomplishment.[125] The belief grew that only two things were essential for the truly sophisticated nobleman: state service and cultural leadership. Hence his readiness to "accept" as his peers individuals only recently ennobled and (in the nineteenth century especially) even commoners who had attained a high level of cultural accomplishment, and who as genuine members of a cultural, and by implication ideological, élite, led a life that was "noble" even if their legal status was not. In this way the distinction between nobleman and commoner was well nigh obliterated for educated Russians active in the cultural and educational domains (academic world, high technical bureaucracy, and, at the end of the nineteenth century, even high-level, sophisticated economic activity).[126] And, indirectly, this attitude helped give the intelligentsia its special status and recognition in society.

Although the basic elements that went into a definition of nobility emphasized personal merit and cultural accomplishment, the notion of hereditary transmission could not be disregarded completely. Indeed, the very stress on a common way of life and on the sharing of cultural and moral values (particularly a sense of personal honor, responsibility, and dignity) were to justify the hereditary character of noble status. In the eighteenth century, of course, only noblemen could offer their children the family environment and education necessary for the development of these qualities and habits. Under Russian conditions, however, such an argument led to a rather curious paradox, which members of the lower nobility (and later the *raznochintsy*) were quick to perceive and stress. For the Russian nobility had in fact acquired these tastes, ideas, and culture only because the requirements of state service set up by Peter the Great had created the way of life and attitudes that were now considered the hallmark of nobility. Everybody agreed that had these criteria been applied to the nobility of Muscovy, all but a very few exceptional individuals would have had to be excluded. But if the state, by means of schooling and service, had forced the nobility to become what it was, there was no reason why a commoner subjected by the state to a similar process of education and "civilization" could not develop these same qualities.[127] The argument that the nobility alone had an inherent predisposition to benefit from the experiences of service and education could not be very convincing to contemporaries. Thus the arguments in favor of an hereditary oligarchy with special privileges and status advanced by members of old families crumbled by themselves, precluding the rise of a genuine Russian aristocracy in the West European sense.

By the same token, the nobleman who had not acquired these traits of mind and heart, whose way of life did not conform to the accepted ideals of culture and education, could not truly be a member of the nobility. Russians in the eighteenth century (and later) felt strongly that the ignorant, boorish, and bigoted nobleman devoid of any worthwhile interests and vegetating all his life in a far corner (*medvezhii ugol*) of provincial Russia, an individual who himself lacked a sense of his own dignity and worth and arrogantly denied the presence of these qualities in others, was not truly a nobleman, whatever his genealogical tables or letters patent might say. The "true nobleman," the "true son of the fatherland" (as he was frequently called in the eighteenth century), was ashamed that the provincial boor belonged to the same social class.[128] What was primarily objectionable in these provincial boors was this lack of a sense of social or national responsibility.

There was an easy way out of this condition, however: to enter service. Service would bring the uncouth provincial nobleman into contact with educated people, novel ways, and other provinces and countries. If some boorish provincials had seen service and had remained untouched, this was because they had served in very low ranks and for relatively short periods; they should have stayed in service longer and returned home only after acquiring more culture and polish. The very definition of nobility as a way of life, instead of undercutting the didactic role of service, strengthened it.[129]

Definition (and by implication rights) of the nobility was one of the major issues that came up for debate in the so-called Commission on Codification of Catherine the Great in 1767.[130] Essentially, the discussion centered on the question of whether the nobility was and should be an open class or not; whether new men should readily gain access to it through normal channels of promotion, or whether its ranks should be closed forever. The issue could not be stated in such simple terms because of the very make-up of the Russian nobility. After all, it was not long, at most only a generation, since the openness of the class had permitted the father of many a deputy (or of his electors) to join its ranks. Even the spokesmen for a closed nobility could do no more than advocate barring access in the future.[131]

Whether the Russian nobility was a closed or open class depended, in the final analysis, on how it was defined. Essentially this issue became a debate between those who recognized only nobility through birth and those who defended ennoblement through service. By and large, deputies representing the old established nobility of central Russia, especially around Moscow, advocated closing the ranks of the class to newcomers and insisted on the importance of heredity and birthright. Noble deputies from outlying regions and representatives of special groups—frontier regiments, Cossack hosts, non-Russian natives, towns—demanded the preservation of the principles and practice of ennoblement based on

Peter the Great's Table of Ranks. In short, those who had attained nobility long before and whose status was secure wanted to deny access to their privileges to newcomers. But those who had become nobles only recently, who wanted to rise higher still, and who hoped to see other members of their family or class follow in their footsteps, staunchly defended the principle that service continue to be the principal avenue of access to the nobility. In addition, a few meek voices defended the proposition that nobility should reward not so much service to the state as service to the community and nation; hence, accomplishments in economic or professional pursuits should also become grounds for ennoblement. A few deputies tried to connect economic success (*i.e.* amount of property) and nobility more directly by providing that specific noble status (a title, for example) should automatically give one the right to a specified amount of real estate.[132]

None of the deputies, even those dissatisfied with it, denied the heritage of Peter the Great. Peter's reign was viewed as a necessity—an emergency—and this justified some of its features. But now that the emergency had ended, argued those who wanted to close access to the nobility, there was no need to continue the practices produced by it.[133] Yet the very acknowledgment that Peter's policies had been necessary meant recognizing and accepting the state's leadership, its willful creative role, and the paramount importance of the nobility's service function. The discussions that went on in the Commission show quite clearly that the nobility was incapable of abandoning the notion of service as the foundation of its very *raison d'être*.[134] Even the defenders of the principle of heredity were really arguing that the service performances and high deeds of ancestors justified present-day noble status. And they conceded that even noblemen who inherited their status had to continue to serve their state and country or risk losing their moral—and in extreme cases legal—right to this status.[135]

But although the nobles did not wish to see the service

pattern itself abolished, they did argue that its compulsory character be removed. They contended that the nobleman's education and culture were the guarantees that he would perform his obligations conscientiously. It was therefore not only unnecessary but humiliating to drag a nobleman into school or the service in the same degrading manner in which the peasant recruit was sent to the army, by threats of dire punishment. A well-born nobleman would do his duty voluntarily. And if he failed to do so, the most telling punishment would not be the physical and psychological crippling of him, but rather the contempt of his fellow nobles, his shame and dishonor, and the recognition that he no longer deserved membership in the nobility. True, compulsion had been necessary under Peter the Great in order to deal with ignorant and stubbornly conservative Muscovites. But for the new nobility, an appeal to its sense of honor and pride would be more effective than threats. If the government would give adequate public recognition to service, all nobles would naturally continue to serve, and they would do it better as a matter of honor than of fear.

The interesting point, of course, is the extension of the meaning of "service." For defenders of the principle of heredity like Shcherbatov, it was no longer merely service to state and monarch that determined noble status, it also was service to society and to the country. This service could take the form of cultural and intellectual leadership, but it could also mean leadership in fostering the nation's economic and social progress. For instance, by virtue of his being a landowner the nobleman could help promote the national economy, introduce new techniques, and raise the level of productivity. By sharing the benefits, as well as the lessons, of modernization with his peasants, the nobleman served the country and justified his membership in the privileged élite.[136] There is little doubt that the argument was largely dictated by selfish "class interests" on the part of the well-entrenched nobility. But an equally important justification for the nobleman's monopoly of all important functions and benefits in state and society was his function as teacher and guide of the people.

The lack of a precise definition of nobility, coupled with the conflict of opinion brought out by the discussions at the Commission on Codification of 1767, stimulated a quest by the nobility for corporate status—that is, creation of an institional framework, in part administered by the nobility itself, for dealing with the nobility as a group. The quest for corporate status entailed two basic demands: (1) the working out of rules for identifying and registering members of the nobility, and (2) provision of a foundation for the nobleman's security of person, status, and property. As the latter meant specifically the noblemen's absolute control over his serfs, the quest for corporate status may be seen also as an instrument for social domination and economic exploitation. There is no doubt that economic exploitation was of vital concern to the nobility, but besides not being directly relevant in our context, it was not the most essential consideration, Soviet opinion to the contrary notwithstanding.

Only a satisfactory basis for definition of nobility could enable the "corporation" to serve as registrar for membership in the class. The debates of 1767 having left the matter of definition pretty much in the air, the very foundation of corporate organization was weak. Any definition provided for by the draft proposal of 1767 on the status of nobility was based on service—in other words, on something only the state could determine and certify.[137] It is true that the proposal left room for the notions of a noble way of life and orientation (*Gesinnung*) as factors in determining nobility, which to some extent were a matter of consensus among other members of the group. Here the nobility's corporate organization could provide institutional means for supervising and enforcing the relevant norms. In Russia, then, the notion of corporate organization rested on an ambiguity that became manifest in the lack of solidarity among the nobility's deputies at the Commission of 1767. The advocates of service as the principal source of noble status wanted a "corporate" framework only so that the promotion and registration of noblemen would be decentralized and therefore be more efficient; this meant the establishment of local offices of the Heraldry. On the other hand, those who insisted on the importance of birthright and the noble "way of life" wanted the very decision concerning membership in the nobility to rest in the hands of a local assembly of noblemen.

Actually, however, the noblemen's principal demand was for security of person and property. Any corporate organization of the nobility, it was felt, should therefore be mainly concerned with protecting this security, which the nobles felt they had lacked and which was vital for proper performance of their service obligations.[138] It would be anachronistic to see in this demand merely a spurious cover-up for selfish interests, although no doubt such a thing played no small role. Yet there was also an objective basis for the argument: the nobility had clamored for security of person and property constantly since Peter's time.[139]

It was proof of the autocracy's unchallenged power that security for the nobility was given legal guarantees only in 1767 (which were restricted to the deputies to the Commission). To most Russian noblemen and their deputies at the Commission of 1767, corporate rights meant that a nobleman could not be arrested and kept in prison arbitrarily, that his property could not be seized or confiscated without the observance of uniform rules of procedure, and that when accused of a crime he could not be subjected to degrading treatment until he had been deprived of his noble status by decree of the courts or the Emperor. It is interesting that the status of nobility was something the monarch or his appointed official could grant or withdraw; it was a matter of state policy, not an inherent quality or right.[140]

Corporate autonomy and privileged status of an estate are best secured when its members possess strong social and economic roots in a geographically limited area, and when they can perform clearly defined functions. This was the tacit assumption of those deputies who in 1767 asked that the local administrative functions of the nobility be extended. In essence what these deputies asked for was the right to take care of some administrative matters concerning their class and to help out in supervising the enforcement of law and order in the provinces; elected noblemen were to serve as assistants and adjuncts to the appointed state officials. These were requests, not demands, and their advocates put forth no historical, legal, or traditional justifications in support. If granted (as they were to be in 1775 and 1785) the privileges of limited local and corporate self-administration were to be a free gift of the state. But without local roots, functions, and strong bonds of personal solidarity, corporate autonomy was not very meaningful. This was pointed out by the deputies from the Baltic nobility, who were concerned with the preservation of their own traditional corporate rights and privileges.[141]

A solid local rooting of the Russian nobility had yet to be brought about. The act of February 19, 1762, could have been a first step in this direction. As a matter of fact, the act was not insignificant in encouraging a larger number of noblemen to return to the provinces and their estates and remain there. But it was not enough. Reorienting the nobility's interest toward economic enterprise would be another important step in the same direction, while the granting of full local administrative autonomy would serve as the culmination of corporate rights for the nobility. But a solid base for local economic enterprise required first a survey of resources and a better delimitation of estate boundaries, for their absence or vagueness resulted in acrimonious conflicts that prevented cohesion among nobles of the same district.[142] A solid and active estate structure implied local obligations and duties as well as privileges for its members. The Russian nobleman's obligations, however, were non-local. The nobility remained at the mercy of the state, with no other recognized function but that of state servant. So overpowering was the system of values based on state service that award of ranks and promotions by the government were expected for the performance of elective corporate functions on the local level. Failure to give promotions for such "service" by election resulted in the better and abler noblemen refusing to accept these functions.[143]

The government, however, picked up the question of the nobility's corporate status where the Commission of 1767 had left it.[144] Under the influence of contemporary Western ideas and models (perhaps also that of the Baltic provinces), Catherine the Great became convinced that a Russian estate structure should be established. This belief of hers was confirmed by the government's diminishing need for a nobility exclusively devoted to state service, since a sizeable "bureaucracy" (*i.e.* a group of people devoting their lives and energies to the military and administrative tasks of the government) had developed by then. Yet what was one going to do with the idle noblemen? They could, of course, sit on their estates and do nothing, as those who did not serve or had retired had commonly done since the seventeenth century. Under Russian inheritance customs, however, this would eventually lead to the decline of the family who lived on the estate, as the estate would be splintered further at every generation, and eventually the individual members of the family would sink to the level of their peasants.[145] To be a peasant meant, of course, to be unfree; how could the state allow the class of the unfree to grow at the expense of the country's leadership group? Moreover, with the disappearance of their economic foundation, the poor estate owners would no longer be able to perform the important function of policing their serfs; and the Pugachev revolt was too fresh in everybody's mind to view such a prospect with equanimity.[146] It was therefore essential to give the non-serving nobleman a positive function in society.

Of course the nobleman was usually the owner of serfs;

but although this privilege provided economic benefits, it did not entail specific political functions or rights. Moreover, this was not an exclusive privilege of the nobleman.[147] Under Peter the Great and his successors, the landowner, it is true, became responsible for his serfs' taxes and acquired wide powers of jurisdiction over them, but in both cases he acted as representative of the Tsar.[148] Nor did these rights give the nobleman specific privileges and functions in local adminis- tration and justice (except for meting out domestic punish- ments on the estate, which legislation of the eighteenth cen- tury was to make well nigh discretionary).[149] In his dealings with peasants and church the Russian nobleman was backed by the state in many ways, but unlike his counterpart in the West he did not possess autonomous *political* power merely by virtue of his being the owner of an estate.[150] There was no lord beside the Tsar; sovereignty was undivided and its exercise as centralized as technological conditions permitted. The Russian nobility had none of the local responsibilities and functions that distinguished the English gentry, nor did it possess any of the traditional political powers that lordship had conferred on the nobilities of feudal origin in France, Prussia, Austria, or Spain down to the eighteenth century.

It is well to remember that a gulf often separates economic advantage and privilege from political rights and power. The combination of the rights of private ownership with privileges derived from local political functions and power such as was enjoyed by the Junkers in Prussia was a far cry from the limited possibilities and circumscribed sphere of the Russian service nobleman.[151] Hence the latter's political weakness and ultimate dependence on the central government. In relation to the Tsar or Emperor, the nobleman was as much of a lowly serf as the peasant was vis à vis his estate owner. No wonder that it could be said with more than a grain of truth that Russia's two classes were both servile ones.

Participation in local administration and an important role in the economic and cultural life of the provinces, which would make the noblemen less dependent on the state and at the same time give them a new social role, was the solution that occurred to enlightened statesmen and officials in the late eighteenth century.[152] The acts of 1775 and 1785 were designed to give an institutional form to some of these considerations.[153] While the first dealt with local administration and the latter with the rights and privileges of the nobility, the two were intertwined and may be considered together. On paper the nobility received corporate status and autonomy with a fairly wide range of responsibilities in administrative, judiciary, and social matters on the local level. For the first time since Peter the Great (and in a sense for the first time in Russian history) the nobility, as a class, had become an objective legal entity, rather than a mere congeries of individuals.[154] The Charter of 1785 established something of a compromise between the advocates of service and the advocates of birthright as the source of noble status: the local assemblies of the nobility registered the nobles who owned estates in the province and kept lists of membership, but they could not decide who was a nobleman and who was not. This basic decision remained a prerogative of the state's Department of Heraldry and government offices concerned with service personnel.[155] In effect, the law recognized equality between nobility of birth and service, though the social reality was more questionable. But as the number of newly created nobles decreased and the procedures for ennoblement through service were more rigorously enforced, the distinction between heredity and acquired nobility ceased to have much meaning for educated members of the class. At the same time, greater stress was put on the "noble way of life" as justification for nobility.

To this end, noblemen obtained the right to have their own schools and to travel abroad freely. Moreover, according to the law of 1785, all noblemen were guaranteed security of person and property, and many civil law suits were to be taken care of by a court in equity whose members were elected by the local nobility. The responsibility for enforcing these acts was in large measure delegated to the nobility itself, through its local—district and province—assemblies and elected marshals. These elected officials had to keep accurate records of members of the nobility in their districts or provinces, register wills and deeds involving real estate, and act as guardians to orphaned noble children, seeing to it that the latter receive an education appropriate to their estate. Thus, the nobility of each province formed a legal corporation, a juridical person entrusted with safeguarding the members' interests and status. In addition, these rights and privileges were reinforced by the nobility's absolute and arbitrary power over the serfs and the election of "land captains" [156] who had numerous police duties on the district level. The captains not only sought out and prosecuted criminals, they also helped enforce laws and regulations, administered punishment to refractory peasants at the request of their owners, and collected various dues in kind and labor from the state peasants.

Actual practice, however, did not come up to the requirements of the law. An individual could lose freedom and property quite suddenly, without the protection of legal safeguards and orderly judicial procedures. Nor were members of the family and retainers immune from persecution. Even when illegal and arbitrary action of a governor or high official caused the loss of liberty or property, it was difficult, if not impossible, to obtain redress, particularly in the remote provinces east of the Volga and in Siberia.

In his thorough and highly interesting study S. A. Korf [157] has argued on the basis of government records that the nobility's corporate autonomy did not develop into a vigorous and fully grown institution, as had been the case with the Junkers in Prussia or the country squires in England. [158] Korf based his argument primarily on the behavior of the nobility's local assemblies and on the relationship that existed between elected officials and the government bureaucracy. But both these factors can be seen as part of a larger complex, all basically related to the service pattern and the centralized, autocratic character of the Russian state.

First, the nobility was inexperienced and not interested in corporate activities. Since before Peter the Great the Russian nobleman had lacked tradition and experience in acting as a member of a closed group. His sense of group solidarity was weak indeed, as we had occasion to observe when discussing the conflict between family and service orientations. The service obligation had taken the nobleman away from his home province and transformed him into an interchangeable part in an impersonal machine, preventing him from forming strong personal and group ties. The group solidarity of the Corps of Cadets and the Guards regiments, seemingly an exception to this rule, was oriented to service in the capitals; the individual cadet's or guard's participation in local corporate affairs was intermittent at best and had little impact on the provincial nobility.[159]

Furthermore, the service had inculcated in the nobility attitudes that were hardly conducive to genuine corporate life: lack of concern for local problems, a global, all-Russian point of view, the feeling that all problems were best taken care of by energetic military-bureaucratic leadership, and servile respect for those who held high office and rank. And on a practical level, since a nobleman could participate in corporate life in only one district or province, his standing and influence were limited if his attention and time had to be spent divided among the districts or provinces in which he had scattered estates.[160]

Since service continued to draw the more energetic, more ambitious, and better educated noblemen away from their estates, local assemblies were attended by the most ignorant, least capable noblemen. Many noblemen participated only passively in the assemblies, leaving the field to those who wanted to use elective office for personal advantage. Participation in local assemblies was frequently unruly and disorganized. Preference in elections was given to rank or government favor rather than to ability and independence, bribery in the form of gifts or illegal favors was common, and it was hard to enforce a consistent policy for any length of time.

As for the elected corporate officials, they never came to play the active and influential role that the terms of the legislation of 1775 and 1785 allowed.[161] Instead of developing into something like the English justice of the peace and county sheriff, elected Russian officials remained executors of the central administration's will and assistants of a centrally appointed governor. The lack of effectiveness of these officials was due to the same factors that resulted in the nobility's apathy about local affairs and that prevented the local appointed officials (as discussed earlier) from becoming dedicated to the interests of a specific region. Elected officials were rootless, lacking strong ties to the region in which they were elected, and which they helped to administer. Even they felt greater solidarity with state interests than with those of their provinces. The habits of obedience and respect for bureaucratic hierarchy fostered by the service prevented the development of a sense of dignity, self-reliance, or initiative. Elective positions carried with them no ranks or remuneration. Thus they remained inferior to the regular service hierarchy and actual state service.[162] The psychological impact was that since elected officials usually held only modest ranks, they tended to bow to the pressures of the governor and other appointed officials, who were usually higher in the Table of Ranks. Finally, the caliber of elected officials was reduced by the fact that the capable officials tended to be lost to service in the central administration. It was difficult for them to resist the lure of greater responsibility, a more sophisticated life, and the hope

of being more effective by going into service for the government and residing in the capitals.[163] Thus individuals were
frequently elected because of their high service rank or service connections (real or imaginary), but who were not capable and had little concern for genuine local needs.

Not surprisingly, given the prevalence of local apathy,
corruption, and disorganization, it was easy for the central
bureaucracy to intervene, partly to restore order and preserve
some legality in the proceedings, and partly out of a desire
to retain as much power for the central administration as
possible and make the elected marshals into the obedient instruments of appointed officials.[164] At first, Catherine the
Great sought to prevent flagrant interference by the administration. But she could not pursue the policy consistently,
for too many things going on in the assemblies had to be
stopped. She also soon became convinced that the very demands of efficiency required the administration's close supervision. Her successor, Paul I, disliked nobles who were not
in service and distrusted local initiative; he not only ap-
proved but required interference by the administration.
Alexander I and Nicholas I always favored the governors,
whom they viewed as their personal and direct representatives, and in so doing they helped to undercut the role,
power, and influence of the marshals of the nobility.[165]

Thus the pattern of service and the centralized and autocratic character of the government prevented the growth and
strengthening of corporate autonomy and initiative and a
significant transformation in the status of the Russian nobility. This is not to say that the Charter of 1785 had no part
in stimulating local life—political and cultural, as well as
social—and in laying the ground for the nobleman's greater
involvement in his estate and the affairs of his province. But
not until the emancipation of serfs had changed their role
in revolutionary fashion did the nobility seriously turn in
this direction; but even then the lead was taken by noble-

men who had service experience and were therefore able to transfer their notions of public duty and service to their new interest in local problems.

⁂

The disappointing experience with the legislation of 1775 and 1785 led to another attempt at redefining the role of the nobility in terms of estate rights and corporate autonomy. This time the initiative came from a small group of noblemen who tried to connect the nobility's economic and social leadership with basic rights for the individual nobleman. The Charter of 1785 had formally exempted the nobleman from direct taxes and corporal punishment, but nothing beyond that.[166] In almost all respects the nobleman was as much subject to the arbitrariness of the sovereign and his agents as the lowliest serf was to that of his master.[167] Paul I's reign was a telling reminder of the nobleman's precarious situation vis à vis the state, and it paved the way for an attempt at introducing an "aristocratic" constitution in the first years of the reign of Alexander I.[168] As a matter of fact, it was not the first attempt, for the discussions concerning the status of the nobility in 1762 and in the early years of the reign of Catherine the Great had contained similar implications. The lead had been taken by the Vorontsovs and Nikita I. Panin; they failed because of Peter III's overthrow and Catherine's refusal to accept Panin's project for an advisory privy council. In her refusal Catherine was supported by high-ranking service nobles who, like their predecessors of 1730, preferred to rely on the autocracy and its rewards for service.[169]

While elements of the Panin-Vorontsov program could be traced to the conditions and projects of 1730, the immediate source of inspiration was conditions in contemporary Sweden and England. This is not too surprising, since the Panins and Vorontsovs and their friends were among the most sophisticated members of the nobility, men with wide intellectual interests and direct experience of Western European political life. They were "aristocrats" in the special sense that they combined noble birth (although they did not belong to prominent pre-Petrine families), education, and wealth with high service rank and experience. Ironically, their "ideology" was a product of the nobility's service pattern, for it was based on success within the service hierarchy and on those benefits that accrued from an individual's acquiring cultural and social sophistication in state service.

What could their plans and proposals mean in terms of the Russian nobility's status and future development?[170] For one thing, they laid the foundation for the transformation of the Russian autocracy into a *Rechtsstaat*. This *Rechtsstaat*, for the time being at least, would benefit only the upper rungs of the nobility, but might later include all noblemen. It was a *Rechtsstaat*, moreover, that implied some degree of participation by the top élite in the political and administrative processes of government. One might say too that the proposals of the Panin-Vorontsov group aimed at transforming the upper stratum of the Russian nobility into a genuine estate (*Stand*) in the Western sense, with intangible rights and privileges, access to membership almost exclusively by birthright, and implying (without requiring it) that its members accept public responsibilities, deriving from their cultural and economic leadership.[171]

It is important to note two points: First, as set forth by Panin and Vorontsov, the upper nobility's new role and status were to be the free gifts of the autocratic emperor. The aristocratic party expected the Autocrat to graciously grant their demands as a reward for the nobility's cultured accomplishments and services during the last three quarters of a century. Was it not a fitting and natural culmination of Peter the Great's reforms, which had aimed at reshaping the leadership of the Russian nation in the image of European élites? Yet, counting only on the good will of the Autocrat, the leaders of the aristocratic party could not (and did not) enlist the support of the rank-and-file nobility. The average nobleman, therefore, remained largely ignorant and unaffected by the efforts made on behalf of his class.

Second, the new status of the élite was to ensure the individual nobleman security of person and property and safeguard him against the arbitrariness and tyranny of government officials. Curiously enough, in justification it was pointed out that the level of cultural maturity and sophistication attained by the nobility had made of personal security a *conditio sine qua non* of the individual nobleman's dignity and self-esteem. Dignity and self-esteem were in turn the essence of true nobility, and, in Montesquieu's famous formulation, a monarchic government required a nobility. The proposals clearly did not extend the benefits of the estate privileges to the poor, ignorant, non-serving provincial nobleman, whose level of education, culture, and economic prosperity hardly distinguished him from the wealthier peasant. Even the lowliest nobleman, however, would be protected against arbitrary personal abuse by local officials.

The aristocratic party also stressed the nobility's participation and leadership in economic life. The enlightened aristocrats clearly understood that the haphazard and slothful management of estates by the average nobleman was personally ruinous, and a handicap for the development of the nation's wealth.[172] It was the duty of the nobility as a genuine élite and a privileged estate, to improve its economic basis. Related to their economic concern was this group's feeling that there was an urgent need for some decentralization (*déconcentration*, the French would put it more precisely) of the administration and judiciary. To this end they advocated the establishment of "branch Senates" in the provincial centers and to let the local courts decide in the last resort the majority of smaller civil and criminal cases, thereby giving greater scope to local and individual enterprise.

These proposals aimed in effect at transforming the Russian service nobility into a class of landowning, locally rooted, and privileged individuals, possessing a high level of education and culture, entrusted with local public affairs, and contributing actively to the economic and social progress of the nation.[173] Such a transformation would justify the special privileges of individual dignity and economic security that the state would grant to members of the nobility.

In its efforts at redefining and transforming the nobility, the aristocratic party was opposed by high-ranking members of the central administration and by personal advisers of the Emperor—not all of noble origin—who might be called the "bureaucratic élite." The aristocratic party thought in terms of a gradual evolution through the creation of an estate that —over a period of several generations—would include all those who had demonstrated their active leadership in the economic, cultural, and public life of the nation. The bureaucratic élite, on the other hand, was guided by two notions: First, any rights and privileges consistent with a *Rechtsstaat* that the Emperor might grant should apply to the *pays légal* as a whole; secondly, these rights and privileges should be derived from general principles, amenable to philosophic validation, and implemented by the Autocrat assisted by the regular bureaucracy. In short, the aristocratic party thought of a Russian *Rechtsstaat* as the culmination of an historical evolution that would first favor the top layers of the nobility and then gradually encompass the remainder of the population; the final form the *Rechtsstaat* would take could, therefore, not be foreseen, as it would result from the nation's actions and responses to the new pattern of development. The bureaucratic élite, on the other hand, aimed at establishing a *Rechtsstaat* by fiat of the state; it was to be clearly defined and fully implemented at once through the existing —albeit reformed—machinery of the state.

Neither group trusted or respected the average nobility.

But the aristocratic party hoped to raise most nobles to its own level of cultural and economic significance. If only the lower nobility (the argument went) had intangible individual security and property rights, they would develop their participation in many aspects of national life, not merely government service. The bureaucratic élite, on the other hand, distrusted the lower nobility, who—lacking a good Western education and ignorant of the principles of the Enlightenment—were reluctant to abandon the traditional routine of their way of life as well as their suspicion and dislike of Western values as a threat to their status and peace of mind.[174] In addition, the bureaucratically oriented group believed in speed, centralization, and uniformity, and in this they were in accord with the monarch.

The ambiguous nature of the Russian nobility, its service orientation and acceptance of the state's leadership, precluded a determined effort to loosen the reins of autocracy. Under the circumstance, the Autocrat had no difficulty in retaining his absolute power in full, not granting even the most limited political freedoms and individual rights. Nicholas I drew the logical conclusion from this state of affairs, and like Peter the Great he viewed the nobility primarily as a state service class. The nobleman who had not served was either suspect or despicable.

Again, the bureaucratic principle won out over the attempts at transforming the service nobility into a genuine estate with an autonomous corporate life, whose members' rights and privileges would be based on their creative and socially valuable roles in the economy, the local government, and the expression of ideas and opinions. Failure to create a genuine estate of the nobility perpetuated the average nobleman's rootlessness and dependence on the state; he continued to look to the state for guidance and leadership in all that concerned the country's development and transformation. There is no doubt that this heritage set the framework for the education and thinking of Russia's élite, which in the nineteenth century became the seedbed of the intelligentsia.

———•◦•———

In the course of the eighteenth century, a division began to take place between the nobility—who served only for a short while or not at all and who were shifting their attention to their potential cultural and social role in the country—and the bureaucracy—a new class of career officials (many of whom were non-noble by birth) who served in state offices.[175] The bureaucracy was taking over the positions of prominence and securing rewards, recognition, and high status, while the nobility was withdrawing from direct participation in the business of the state. This parting of the ways among Russia's educated élite, however, was not to be completed or attain paramount significance until the second quarter of the nineteenth century.

It is perhaps inaccurate to speak of the group of Russian career officials as a bureaucracy in Max Weber's sense, since it lacked several important characteristics of a modern bureaucracy.[176] For brevity's sake, however, we may speak of it as a subaltern bureaucracy: a well-defined, relatively closed group, operating according to set rules and developing its own pattern of thought and action in response to state requirements. This class also had a fair chance to perpetuate itself by giving its children a minimum of education so they could secure low positions and apprenticeships. In any event, this was a group on which the state could rely for the performance of routine office work (and at times even more), and in a highly centralized and paper-dominated administration this was an essential contribution to government. This group could also be counted upon to provide the government with a small number of higher functionaries with long experience in the practical side of administration. Such high officials of low birth who had risen through the ranks were just numerous enough in the latter half of the eighteenth century to act as a bracing element for the majority of noble dignitaries, mainly from the military, for whom assignment to the administration was only a temporary interlude.

This small nucleus of regular officials gave the administration some modicum of efficiency and continuity; by the same token, however, it also served to discourage innovation and creativity, for the low-born officials shied away from daring reforms and improvements. Even after they had been ennobled, these officials remained the creations and creatures of the bureaucratic state; they shared in *its* interests and not in those of the noblemen, who were trying to become a privileged, aristocratic estate. The low-born officials did not even share in the limited attachment to a landed estate, or in the kind of paternalistic concern for peasants that a nobleman displayed at times.[177] Thus they were most loyal and dependable instruments of the autocracy and made it impossible for the service nobility to form a solid united front against state and autocracy. In fact, they enabled the government and administration to feel less dependent on the services of the nobility.

In a loose sense, there was shaping up the rudiments of a bureaucracy whose members did not come from the bourgeoisie, as in the West, but rather from among the children of the clergy, low-ranking clerks and soldiers.[178] The state could now afford to rely on the services of only those nobles who wanted to give them readily, particularly since, for reasons summarized earlier, there was great likelihood that most nobles would serve anyway.[179] In effect, by the beginning of the last quarter of the eighteenth century the Russian state modernized by Peter the Great had met its institutional needs in two ways: state service had become the accepted pattern of the nobleman's life, and the nucleus of a small professional officialdom (not necessarily of noble origin) had been formed.

The state's confidence that its needs for officials would

always be met found its expression in the famous decree of February 19, 1762,[180] which made service optional for the nobility. Far from marking the nobility's "victory" over the state, as frequently stated, the decree of 1762 marked rather the state's declaration of "independence" from the service of the nobility. That is why even though it secured permission to remain idle, the status and rights of the nobility witnessed no change or expansion.[181] Whatever rights the nobility would obtain subsequently were to give further expression to the state's independence from its services. Thus the government attempted to direct the noblemen's energies into new channels outside of state service and make them more useful to both country and people by having them involve themselves more in their private affairs as landowners. No longer did the state need the nobleman for service, but it still wanted him to help westernize and modernize the country, to be a social and cultural leader of the people.[182]

The problems arising out of this attempt to give a new social role to the nobility were to give birth to the intelligentsia. For as the importance of their traditional role in the service diminished, the nobility began to become alienated from the state. The nobility had been the creation of the state, and in reward for its services to the state it had been allowed to gain high status and a number of important privileges with respect to the peasantry. Unlike its counterpart in some Western European countries, the Russian nobility had never controlled the state; it merely developed a sense of participation and partnership in the state's purpose. Of Russia's social classes, the nobility alone could feel a common bond and common interest with the state, especially when both were actively defending the independence of the national patrimony (sixteenth and seventeenth centuries) or working for the modernization and westernization of the country (eighteenth century). During the first half of the eighteenth century, the nobility felt that it was the state's partner and took great pride in Russia's new status of power and culture. In retrospect, at least, it seemed to the nobility that they and Peter the Great had worked in harmony to bring forth a new Russia and promote the true interests and glory of the fatherland. And now that the job was well under way, the state was telling the nobility, "The Moor has done his job, he may go now." [183]

The nobility's feeling of being let down, of not having been fully rewarded for its efforts, was expressed by the saying that the nobility had been transferred from the authority of the Armed Forces to that of the Interior. This sentiment became particularly strong after the organization of the provincial administration in 1775. From active participation and collaboration—however reluctant it may have been at first—in the life of the state, the nobility was "demoted" to the function of guardian of peace and social leader of the remote countryside, of caretaker of narrow local concerns. The state had become separate, in fact and purpose, from the nobility.

This feeling was accentuated by the bureaucratization of the new state institutions. Through Peter's reforms, the nobility had lost the Tsar as their personal lord; now they felt cut off from the very institution they had helped to establish. The ruler and his counselors had been displaced by an impersonal "office," in which a clerk mechanically applied universal rules, expressed in rigid written form, which took no account of special circumstances and needs of individuals. The service nobility developed the feeling that justice itself, the very possibility of finding redress, had been destroyed by the interposition of institutions and officials between the monarch and his subjects. Quite naturally much of the resentment was directed at the officials, who were blamed as the source of all the iniquities, injustices, and disasters in the nobleman's personal life and service career. Such resentment (and resulting hatred) was of course intensified when it was realized that many of the officials who apparently held (and in fact frequently did hold) one's fate in their hands

were lowly commoners. The unlucky noble serviceman readily believed that his fate was the result of a commoner's contempt for and dislike of the nobility, a belief that was not
diminished by the knowledge that so many of these officials
were not above the temptations of bribery.[184]

The nobility lost interest in the civilian administration
when it discovered that it could not attain the position of
monopoly it craved. Many noblemen now discovered the
need for another focus of attention, another object for their
loyalty and dedication.

———— ·•·• ————

Freed of its service obligation to the state, what could the
nobility do? It did not have any important and publicly
recognized social role to play except serving the state. This
was difficult to change overnight. The new interests and
roles that could arise from the noblemen's leadership in the
process of westernization and modernization, independently
of their function in the state, had not yet become of paramount concern or received public recognition.[185] In fact,
since Peter's reforms had substituted rank for every other
criterion in the dispensation of social and political status and
privilege, the nobility had demanded special preferment in
obtaining ranks and more rapid advancement through the
lower ranks of service on the basis of education and birth.
This same quest had assured the success and popularity of
the Corps of Cadets and the special military and naval
schools for noble children, as well as service in the Guards
regiments (whose ranks had a higher equivalent in the regular army) and at court (whose ranks could be advantageously
transferred to the civil service hierarchy). The worship of
rank as the basis of one's place in society continued after
1762. There might have been some question as to the necessity of serving for very long periods, but it was agreed upon
by all (including peasants) that a nobleman was nothing
without at least the lowest commissioned rank (or its civil

equivalent). This explains the great efforts made by well-to-do nobles to enroll their children into service, preferably the Guards regiments, at a very early age. Early enrollment was advantageous not only to give children a head start in their future careers, but also because without even a formal rank they were not really members of the privileged élite.[186]

So important was rank that there was little hope of inducing noblemen to take up an activity that held little or no promise of promotion within the Table of Ranks. To enroll and keep both students and faculty, the Academy of Sciences and the University of Moscow tried to obtain ranks or preferment in promotion for their staff and graduates.[187] The minutes of the Commission of 1767 show quite clearly that corporate self-government and self-administration were not separated from ranks in the minds of the nobility. Even the local elected offices, for whose preservation the Western nobility had fought so fiercely for generations, were meaningless and undesirable if not accompanied by promotion in the Table of Ranks.[188] Contemporary memoirs and belles-lettres are filled with instances of rank worship (*chinopochitanie*), and even in the latter all personages representing the uneducated, poor, and ludicrous noblemen—the comical stick-in-the-mud provincial *obyvatel'*—have either no service record at all or possess only the lowest ranks.[189]

The common people, too, paid great attention to rank: serfs took pride in their master's rank and even snubbed those whose masters held lower ranks. But even the more emancipated and progressive noblemen valued rank highly. In principle at least, rank was a function of service and therefore a function of one's usefulness to society and the state. It was therefore natural for service, even if temporary, to be considered the principal activity for a nobleman. The high premium put on rank by opinion and custom enabled the state to give the nobles their freedom without having to fear that they would completely desert government service.[190] The non-serving nobleman remained the exception, until the end of the eighteenth century and even until the 1840's. True, most nobles did not serve all their life, unless they had become exclusively professional officers or officials. After 1762 a nobleman served on the average for about ten to fifteen years, starting early, when about fifteen to seventeen years old, and he retired in his late thirties upon reaching a respectable rank (depending on ambition and luck, of course). In the literature of the time we meet mainly captains and majors in retirement, more rarely lieutenants and colonels—the former because they wanted to go on, the latter because they had become professional military men and had good prospects of becoming generals. If he had some bad luck in his career or if his family had grown too large, the nobleman might prefer to retire earlier and devote his time to the management of his estate. Historians have given too much attention to the cases of early retirement or resignation, the denunciation of certain phases or aspects of service. These cases have been prominently noted in documents and literature precisely because they were exceptions. After 1762, as before, service remained the normal path to status, greater prosperity, and full participation in the cultural life of Russia.

But was there nothing outside of service the nobleman could do to maintain his position in society and justify his cultural leadership? Our discussion so far has implied that, at least since Peter the Great, service was the only thing the nobleman could do legally and publicly, even at the expense of neglecting his own personal interests. True, Peter the Great had encouraged the nobility to engage in commerce and industry. But the nobleman who heeded this prodding still perceived it as part of his service obligation and expected recognition from the monarch in the form of service rank, or similar distinction, as well as an improvement in his own economic status. Even such a thing as building and keeping in repair a house in St. Petersburg was part of his service obligation.[191] When residence in a particular city to further the modernization and urbanization of Russia was considered a compulsory part of state service, was there much chance that any other activity encouraged or permitted by the state would be viewed differently?

By the middle of the eighteenth century, however, the nobleman's economic responsibilities and interests had won the recognition of the government. It became possible to obtain leaves or even permission to retire to take care of one's estates and business affairs. After he had been granted "freedom from service" in 1762 the nobleman could, in principle at least, pursue whatever occupation or calling he wished, for in Russia there was no genuine feeling for *dérogeance* (*i.e.* the notion that certain activities were demeaning to the nobility).[192] Wholesale trade, manufacturing, and the farming of excise revenues became acceptable occupations for the nobleman in the second half of the eighteenth century.

The ambivalence of the nobility toward non-service activities was reflected in the debates in the Commission on Codification in 1767. Some noblemen argued that trade, industry, and agriculture, oriented toward private gain, fulfilled a useful role, but since they were not a public matter the nobility should have as little to do with them as possible. Others argued that the state created by Peter the Great required a new economic foundation, and that private economic activity could play an important public role. It was felt that since economic activity fell within the domain of state concerns and could become an object of service, it should be a monopoly of the nobility. These nobles hoped that economic concerns would diversify the exclusive service orientation of the nobility. They argued that the nobility ought to take the lead in the country's economic modernization and development—a task for which its wealth, education, and administrative experience should have prepared it. It is interesting to note that, for both sides, narrow class interests were justified in terms of the nobility's function of service to the state.[193]

That eloquent spokesman for the exclusive rights and privileges of the nobility, Prince M. M. Shcherbatov, argued with fervor in the commission that noblemen should be given a solid and exclusive role in agriculture. This fitted well with their responsibility as serf owners. Agriculture, he pleaded, should provide the means for a modest living that would allow the nobleman to give some education to his children in preparation for their service careers. To protect the welfare and status of the nobility, Shcherbatov asked that the landowner be shielded from what he felt were the greedy, harmful, and unethical operations of merchants and financiers. Like the spokesmen for the aristocratic and feudal outlook of another age in Western Europe, Shcherbatov was suspicious of everything usually associated with the notion of "bourgeois spirit." In addition, he demanded that the merchandising of farm products (especially grain), the exploitation of subsoil wealth, the manufacturing of articles for sale and domestic use from raw materials obtained on the estate, and the right to engage freely in international trade become the exclusive monopoly of the nobility.[194]

While Shcherbatov himself remained a firm advocate of the nobility's obligation to serve the state, he hoped to mitigate the exclusiveness of service with economic activity. In a sense, he wanted to transform the Russian service nobility on the model of the English gentry as he saw it: landowners with serious economic interests and concerns performing an essential function of leadership by serving the state during their most active years and by rationally managing their estates and introducing improvements and innovations into the countryside after retirement.[195] Interestingly enough, Shcherbatov's position was not readily adopted by his fellow nobles. Many agreed with his denunciation of merchants and financiers; many supported his efforts at keeping the trader and the capitalist away from villages and estates; but few switched their major career activity to agriculture and economic enterprise.

A similar effort at breaking the exclusivity of the service orientation can be perceived in the Charter to the Nobility of 1785, to some extent in the Act of 1775 on the provinces, and in Catherine the Great's social and economic policies. She was eager to see Russia's agriculture modernized and the country's economic potential developed. In this the nobility had to play a leading role, and Catherine hoped to stimulate their interest along these lines.[196] In 1782 her government granted noble landowners exclusive rights to the raw materials found on their estates, in the hope that at least part of the nobility would turn seriously to economic pursuits.[197] Catherine had some measure of success: many a nobleman took to managing his estate more conscientiously and effectively, many introduced new techniques and crops. But much of it was merely a pastime.[198] The rational management of estates and "scientific farming," the maximization of income through modernization, did not come into their own in or before the second quarter of the nineteenth century, and even then only slowly and in a few particularly promising regions (*e.g.* the Ukraine).[199] Interested though he might have been in enhancing his own economic status and his wealth, the nobleman did not let himself be transformed into a gentleman farmer or an entrepreneur, as his English or Prussian counterpart had done.[200]

First, noblemen wanted to participate in the more sophisticated cultural atmosphere of the cities, something most of them could attain only through service. Second, the Russian nobleman, lacking local roots, did not know how to take advantage of the few opportunities to participate in local affairs that he was offered. He therefore remained at the mercy of officials sent from the capital, who even after 1785 were the true masters in the countryside, and deprived the nobleman of any serious desire to make local affairs his main concern. Finally, the effort and difficulties involved in making economic entrepreneurship rewarding under Russian conditions were easily overshadowed by the strength of the service tradition and the advantages offered by a successful career in service.

Nor was it easy for a Russian nobleman in the eighteenth century to make a career in the so-called free professions. Obviously, the obligation of service acted as a barrier until 1762, although decreasingly so. More important, however, was the fact that specialized training was needed for most professions, and there were few schools—and not even for all callings at that. Moreover, the young nobleman was frequently forced to withdraw from school to enter service, leaving the sons of the clergy and other *raznochintsy* to pursue the full course of professional training. But once he had been trained in law, medicine, or technology, what could the nobleman do? Law had obviously to lead to a career in the administration, for under the judicial system existing at the time the private exercise of law was out of the question. All evidence introduced in court was in writing, and the necessary papers were best drafted by a notary or clerk; lawyers did not appear in court, and whatever soliciting had to be done before the courts, the Senate, or the monarch was best done by an official or dignitary enjoying favor. The medical field was not easily accessible, for Russia had no decent school of medicine, and until late in the eighteenth century the profession was practically monopolized by foreigners, primarily Germans. In medicine, too, the only enticing opportunities were with the government, as public health inspectors, or in the army.[201] Last, the technical professions—mining, engineering, etc.—also almost exclusively led to state service, for most major enterprises using technically trained personnel were operated by the state, at least until the very end of the eighteenth century.[202] The few nobles who had obtained technical training (Tatishchev, for example) used their talents in the management of state enterprises or in the administration, and in this capacity they were assimilated into the military or administrative hierarchy of the Table of Ranks.

As for the academic field, it did not have much appeal for the nobility in the eighteenth century. It required arduous, long, and unrewarding training, and the competition with foreign scholars or *raznochintsy* with better preparation in the ecclesiastic schools was too great. But most important was the fact that the teacher (and even the professor, who frequently doubled as tutor) was considered merely a high-class servant. The scholar and academician was still such a rarity, since there were so few positions where he could be used, that an academic career had little allure and offered no visible rewards. The first Russian academic figures came from the clergy and it was not until the nineteenth century, with the foundation of new universities, that children of the nobility entered the academic field professionally. But in the eighteenth and early nineteenth centuries even a university career was a form of state service; it was not a "free" profession in our sense.[203]

In any event, so long as social status was determined by service rank, no profession could attract the nobility unless it also led to a place in the Table of Ranks. An officer could become an engineering or mining specialist, an administrator might become a competent jurist or pedagogue, but these were the unforeseen by-products of service careers that had started without such professional specialization in mind;[204] what really mattered were an individual's position and rank, not his professional or technical competence.

Not until the 1840's did the nobleman find new, promising fields in economic enterprise and the professions. Until almost the end of the imperial regime, public recognition and official reward in these new fields of endeavor came in the shape of ranks and titles from the Table of Ranks. The professional man of non-noble origin took advantage of this situation to further his career as well as the status of his family; through the Table of Ranks he could first become associated with the élite and eventually join the nobility. Not until the last quarter of the nineteenth century did the hierarchy of the Table of Ranks cease to be the principal gauge of success for the professional man, as well as for the state servant.

As we have seen in this chapter, service was the nobleman's principal activity; service provided the basic normative framework for individual and social relationships, and, with the reforms of Peter the Great, service rank became the only recognized form of noble status. Sensitive to the élite's scale of values, the common people spoke reverently of the "general," viewing this rank as the *summum bonum* in social status. Never did they think of "nobleman" with the same feelings of reverence and awe.[205] This concept of status made the nobleman primarily dependent on the state. He owed little to his family's history or local power. Everything he had —his person, property, and family status, as well as the future of his children, were at the mercy of the sovereign power. Nobility was therefore a status that could be easily lost. This basic feature explains the nobility's underlying feeling of insecurity,[206] a feeling heightened by the geographic and cultural rootlessness of the nobility that was caused by the service pattern and the rapid process of westernization.

Service became the expression of a social and moral ideal, used to justify an individual's privileges and special rights. If a nobleman became exclusively concerned with pursuing his private interests and satisfying his selfish ambitions outside of service, it was felt that he had betrayed his duty, forsaken his *raison d'être*. To be sure, it was an ideal norm, and not everybody, by any means, lived up to it. But the pursuit of selfish interests outside of service was not sanctioned by moral approval or genuine recognition, as was the achievement of private economic advantage by the "puritan code."[207]

Unlike the West European feudal lord, whose concept of "service" was embedded in a framework of mutual rights and obligations, the Russian nobleman of the eighteenth century quite clearly was exclusively a servant of the state; in fact he was the agent of the latter on his own estate.[208] The stress was on the nobleman's usefulness to the state and to society at large, not his worth as a private individual or his role as a member of a special group.

Outside service a Russian nobleman in the eighteenth century had no socially meaningful and acceptable outlet for his talents, energy, and activities. Unless he served, the nobleman had to live in idleness; for even the management of his estates, under conditions of serfdom and Russia's economic backwardness, could not readily become a satisfying full-time occupation.[209] The following dichotomy was, therefore, established: usefulness and cultural progress in service or brutish backwardness and pursuit of private pleasures.[210]

Therefore, when the state's need for the services of the nobility was reduced by the rise of a professional bureaucracy, the rootlessness of the nobility was intensified by loss of its traditional function, and it began to become alienated from the state. The existence of serfdom isolated the nobility still further: a minority living cheek to jowl with a majority that it oppresses, and from which it differs culturally and spiritually, must experience great anxiety and virtual alienation.

Thus the situation of the nobility in the eighteenth century was fraught with ambiguity and paradox. Dependency on the state helped to foster worship of the monarch, but sometimes became transmuted into complete rejection and hatred. The people were disregarded by the nobility, yet feared; they were an object of protection and concern, and yet at the same time were subjected to the most tyrannical and brutal treatment. Culture was deeply respected as an essential component of individual and national progress; yet it was valued not for its own sake but merely as an instrument of state power to bring about modernization. These conflicts not only created a mobile—even potentially explosive—situation, they also produced rootlessness, alienation, and, paradoxically, a will to power for the sake of transformation. This will for creative action in social policy implied an orientation toward the future and a lack of desire to build on tradition. For Peter the Great had made such a sharp break in the consciousness of the eighteenth-century noblemen that to return to the pre-Petrine tradition would have destroyed everything the nobility had accomplished, everything it was proud of.

FOUR

Home and School

THE PATTERN of service resulting from Peter's reforms made its impact felt from the very beginning of a nobleman's life. If he was born on his father's estate, more often than not the father was away or had to leave soon to return to service. Not infrequently service obligations kept him away from family and estates for a very long time.[1] It was not unusual, at least during the first years of his life, for the noble youngster to grow up without direct paternal supervision. By and large, mothers did not discipline or supervise their sons much while the father was alive, even when he was away. Of course, there were exceptions—some mothers not only took care of the estate most efficiently and energetically but also played a major personal role in their sons' education.[2] Naturally, in many cases the mother provided emotional support, but usually her overall influence was limited, for throughout the eighteenth century (and even after) most noblewomen were, as a rule, quite ignorant, even illiterate.[3] Their interests were very limited and simple, their minds and manners uncouth, and they continued to live by the traditional precepts of the *Domostroi*.[4]

The small child was left to the care of nurses, maids, and *diad'kas*[5]—all of them serfs. His playmates were the children of household or village serfs, and only occasionally, when neighbors and relatives came to visit, did he enjoy the company of children of his own class and background. In most instances, serfs displayed warmth, even love, for their young master, which often contrasted with the parents' restraint in displaying such feelings, either for pedagogical reasons (the *Domostroi* had not yet been relegated to oblivion) or because they were taken up with their occupations. The physical wants of the child were satisfied promptly, at the slightest expression of desire.[6]

But supervision by serfs and the companionship of their children may well have had harmful consequences for the little master (*barchuk*): the child could hardly be taught self-restraint, and it was almost impossible to impose discipline on him. The serfs may have provided the child with a good deal of emotional stability (if one accepts the findings of some modern psychologists), but only at the expense of his ego and superego.[7] Only rarely did the parent take the side of the serf nurse or *diad'ka* against the child, and the traditional, rigid rules of the *Domostroi* came into play only for family reunions and similar festive occasions. For the most part, the child was free to do as he pleased with impunity. His life was anarchic and idle. He spent his time on the estate enjoying coarse animal pleasures;[8] only rarely could a mother or *diad'ka* effectively compel the child to work and learn. The loss of this freedom, when it later came, was naturally to be resented. But how could such children grow up respecting work and discipline?

Moreover, far from making for closer relationships with the serfs or obtaining a better knowledge of the peasants' way

of life and thought,[9] association with serf children only encouraged the noble youngster to order about, and "use" other
human beings for his own ends—a predisposition inherent
in all children but normally checked by the authority of their
elders. He saw how his parents tyrannized and abused his
nurse and *diad'ka*, their domestics and peasants, and he followed suit. The serf playmates also knew quite well, of
course, that they had to bow to their young master's whims
and endure his caprices and abuses, for protection or recourse against him could hardly be expected from his parents,
nursemaid, or *diad'ka*. If the young nobleman was sent to
the parish "school" run by the local priest or deacon to learn
his first letters and figures, he was given privileged treatment,
and his failures and pranks were punished by the beating of
his serf classmates.[10] This whipping-boy system, far from in-
stilling moral sentiments or fear in the young nobleman,
hardened him to the suffering of others and reinforced his
natural propensity to shift the blame onto his hapless playmates. The sight of a serf child whipped for his noble play-
mate's faults could hardly develop the latter's sense of justice,
responsibility, and self-restraint. Little wonder that when
Karamzin pointed out the moral evil of the situation, it was
a shocking revelation to the sentimental generation of the last
decade of the eighteenth century.[11]

While the pattern of the young nobleman's daily life at
home was one of freedom and indulgence, his social values
and public ideals were those of state service, of obedient
acceptance of its discipline and hierarchy. The nobleman's
service orientation, thinking, and education were thus in
sharp contrast to the freedom and anarchy of his early upbringing on the estate. This resulted in a tension, a polarity,
which contributed to the Russian nobleman's sense of being
merely an object of haphazard decisions by parents and
superiors, which may account for so much of his insecurity
and behavior. The normative pattern of eighteenth-century
Russia stressed the nobleman's duty to serve and be useful

to the state, the monarch, the country, and to engage in a purposeful public activity. A nobleman might be enrolled in a Guards regiment at birth, be promoted to corporal when he started his letters at home, and receive his sergeant's stripes when he enrolled in a regular school. The notion of rank as the most critical aspect of life thus came early and easily to the children of the nobility and provided a counterpoint to the anarchy and laziness of life on the family estate. To the noble youngster, rank was often a matter of play; but it was also a symbol of his future authority and obligations, as reflected in his acting out his rank at the expense of his serf playmates. Noble children often tried to realize in life the fantasies they had drawn largely from their readings and studies. We have of course all tried to act out our fantasies, imitating, for example, Robinson Crusoe on some island in a lake, or reliving Huck Finn's and Tom Sawyer's adventures. The point, however, is that we played the game with playmates who were our equals. In Russia, on the other hand, the game enabled the young nobleman to shape—or try to—the lives and behavior of playmates who had neither wills nor rights of their own.

Later in life this childhood situation would be given wider scope as the nobleman applied his service experiences and learning to the management of his estate and the government of his serfs. The resulting situations are often described to illustrate the personal quirks, the childishness, or lack of practical sense of the nobleman. But they also had serious consequences for the attitudes of the nobility. As a child the nobleman was fascinated by heroic or romantic tales; as an adult he would be captivated by the orderliness, clarity, and rationality he encountered in the service, particularly the military. As he had acted out his fantasies with serf playmates, so it would easily occur to the adult nobleman to enact the newly discovered service forms and rules on his estates either for the benefit of his adult serfs or for his own aesthetic enjoyment.[12] Had not Peter the Great shown the way by transforming his subjects in imitation of the West, mainly through military service? Naïvely, to be sure, but not unexpectedly in the light of his upbringing, the serviceman would later believe that he could run his household and estate like a regiment, dressing up his serfs in uniforms, with codes and rules to order their lives efficiently.[13] In addition, he was later to think that he was introducing to the countryside an "aesthetic" element of orderliness that provided a welcome contrast to the sloppiness (*khalatnost'*) of Russian provincial life.

Given the lack of supervision and discipline in the home life of a noble child, it is not surprising that his education frequently took place on a makeshift basis during the early years of his life. The rudiments of learning—reading, writing, some counting, as well as the catechism—were acquired at home, from a parent, a relative, or the village priest or sexton. In the latter part of the eighteenth century domestic serfs occasionally performed this service for their master's children. The results, as a rule, were far from brilliant, for the teacher himself was not overly skilled, and controlling the unwilling child was not an easy matter. Many a young nobleman was to come to service examinations and inspections (*smotry*) utterly ignorant of even the basic rudiments, and even almost illiterate.[14]

As the child grew older, two paths were open to his parents. If they were prosperous, a private tutor (or maybe several), a seminary student or some foreigner, was hired to continue the child's education. If suitable tutors could not be afforded or were not available, the child had to be sent away to a boarding school, to the Corps of Cadets in St. Petersburg, or to some regimental or technical military school in a provincial center.[15]

When a tutor was invited his success naturally depended on his personality, ability, and the conditions in which he was allowed to work with his charges. Russian eighteenth- and nineteenth-century literature is full of descriptions of the ignorant, fraudulent, coarse tutor of foreign origin. Contemporary memoirs give graphic illustration of the pupil's and parents' spite, lack of respect, and suspicion of the tutor from the seminary. The tutors—both native and foreign—had difficulty in overcoming their pupils' habits of freedom, indiscipline, laziness, and willfulness. The tutor's task was made still more difficult because his pupils always had the support and protection of their parents and particularly of their nurses and *diad'kas,* who resented being displaced by a newcomer, frequently a foreigner at that. Respect for academic learning did not come easily to the Russian countryside, and the conscientious and capable tutor had to wage a difficult uphill battle. Many tutors, even those with the necessary knowledge and ability, gave up the fight and contented themselves with coasting along, in the manner of Eugene Onegin's well-known *abbé.* Others became tyrannical taskmasters (often importing false learning) who, under threat of punishment, exacted from their pupils a mere parroting of their lessons.

Whatever the pedagogy, whoever the tutor, one thing remained constant throughout the century: a utilitarian approach to education. Education and schooling were considered necessary for promotion in service and for life in the proper circles of the capitals. As soon as the child had acquired the necessary minimum he was sent off to a regiment or government office.[16] There still was little feeling that education and learning were valuable for their own sake, as part of the development of the individual.[17] Only what was considered useful for a service career needed to be taught. As it happened, foreign languages and good manners were part of this narrowly pragmatic approach, which provided an opening wedge for a more sophisticated orientation. But education as an element of civilization and culture did not become accepted among the provincial nobility before the last two decades of the eighteenth century.

For a good number of noble children, especially during the first three quarters of the eighteenth century, schooling entailed being sent to some institution in the city. As a rule it was a boarding school, for few were lucky enough to have relatives or friends with whom they could live.[18] For many youngsters the experience of living away from home, and being more or less on their own, started very early indeed, sometimes at the age of six or eight. Even if the youngster returned home for the two months of summer vacation, his separation from the family was well-nigh complete.[19] He learned to get along with his peers and teachers, and developed interests and friendships that became more meaningful than his family. Frequently, he preferred to spend his vacations at some schoolmate's house, rather than go home.

But although the noble child learned to adjust to school life, numerous memoirs convey the impression that the break from the family and the estate was sudden, brutal, and frequently traumatic.[20] There were practical reasons for this: boarding schools were drab and gloomy—more like prisons or monasteries than places for learning and the joyous maturing of adolescents. Many schools in fact prepared for military careers in branches of the army or navy; sometimes they were directly connected with the local garrison. As antechambers to military service, these schools were subjected to the same discipline and formalism.

But psychological factors probably intensified the impact of boarding school. A modern psychologist might speak of the child as feeling rejected by his family and former environment—and at a rather crucial period of his physical and emotional development. Such an experience might well give rise to long-lasting resentment (in Scheler's sense). Of course, a child might adjust rapidly (although superficially) to his new circumstances by freezing in his feelings and rejecting everything that his childhood had stood for. Or, on the contrary, a child might cling to the past, surrounding it with a wistful aura, and yearning to return to the old freedom and protective environment.[21] These young noblemen closed their eyes to the new values and experiences and, like cattle, went through service blind to the new horizons opening up to them. This kind of service noble provided the main complement of the semiliterate noncommissioned officers and low officials peopling the remote corners of the Russian empire. We noted in Chapter Three their baneful role in the failure of local corporate life.

Being sent to boarding schools at an early age also induced a keen feeling of rootlessness in young noblemen, and the impact sometimes lasted for life. These youngsters felt the absence of strong ties to a specific locality, the feeling that their human environment was unstable and shifting. The great contrast between school and home life was bound to impress the youngsters with the idea that state service and separation from home life were fatefully connected. The psychological allegiance of many youngsters shifted dramatically from home and birthplace to school and impersonal service organization.[22]

This is not to deny that strong family bonds continued to permeate Russian life, among the nobility as much as among the peasantry.[23] But it may be worth remembering that strong family attachments are often by-products of social and geographic rootlessness when the family, especially the immediate family, becomes the only group capable of providing some sense of belonging and stability. It is no accident that the most rootless groups—persecuted minorities and exiles, for instance—frequently develop the strongest emotional loyalties to the narrower family.[24]

———— • • • ————

Let us turn now to a consideration of the type of education that was available to the Russian serviceman in the eighteenth century. Keep in mind that we are now dealing with a system that benefited only a segment of the nobility. It would be safe to say that while the rudiments of education were acquired by all nobles from the middle of the eighteenth century on, only a minority pushed their studies beyond this minimum.

The paramount factor in Russian formal education was the critical role of the state. Paradoxical as it may seem, the state played a much larger role in education and cultural life than, say, in the sphere of economic activity. In one form or another, the state provided the largest number of adequate schools for the nobility, a situation that stemmed from the determining role of the service pattern on Russian life. The early secular institutions of learning were dominated entirely by the service requirements of the state.

Russian modern secular and technical education had its origins in the reforms of Peter the Great. Of course, Peter did not start *ab ovo;* throughout the seventeenth century, efforts had been made to implant a modern secular type of education, at least for the upper rungs of Muscovite society. Although some successes were registered, notably the foundation of the Latin-Greek-Slavonic Academy in Moscow, the final results were meager: at the time of Peter's accession Russia still had no effective modern institutions of education. The story of Peter's establishment of the first Russian secular and technical schools—the school for mathematics in the Sukharev Tower in Moscow and the Nautical Academy (academy of navigation) in newly founded St. Petersburg—has often been told, and we need not repeat it.[25] To give these two professional institutions a permanent foundation, the first Emperor also established a network of elementary schools, the so-called "cipher schools." The latter, however, proved less than successful, and eventually they were merged with the newly created diocesan ecclesiastical schools.

It should be noted that in contrast to Western Europe, the Russian state had no competition from religious teaching orders or public corporations connected with the Church. Its nearest competitor, the ecclesiastical schools, were also indirectly under the supervision and control of the state through the Holy Synod, and after the final secularization of clerical domains in 1764, their finances were dependent exclusively on state allowances.[26] The clergy in fact tried hard to disassociate themselves from the secular and technical schools being introduced by Peter, and they avoided accepting responsibility for the cipher schools. But under pressure from the first Emperor and his successors, they had to give in, and eventually the ecclesiastical schools played a sizable role in Russian primary and secondary education. In fact, the ecclesiastical schools, particularly on the secondary level, came to provide merely another way to prepare for service. This was especially the case in the Ukraine, where many children of the poorer nobility attended these schools.[27]

As for private schools, they played a definitely subordinate role, for throughout the eighteenth century there were only a few private schools (almost exclusively in the capitals) with a very small enrollment.[28] The private tutors began coming into their own only at the end of the eighteenth century, and while they played a considerable role in starting a child's education, in only a few cases did they offer much more than the rudiments.[29] The state even exercised some control over private schools and tutors, though with only indifferent success, especially with the latter. Private boarding schools had to be certified by the state, and their programs were subject to state approval and guidance.[30] Further state supervision stemmed from the fact that, to secure admission to a public institution of learning from a private school, a state examination had to be passed.

Education in Russia was therefore an intrinsic part of service, and for the average nobleman school was the first form of service. In the eighteenth century the obligation to serve also implied the obligation to be educated.[31] The school vocabulary reflected this service orientation: to attend school was to be in the service, *na sluzhbe;* promotions to a higher grade and graduation were referred to in terms of receiving a rank. The staff of instruction and administration in educational establishments were referred to by such service terms as *komandiry* and *nachal'niki*. While this carry-over was strongest in the military schools, more particularly the Corps of Cadets, it affected nonmilitary schools as well. The organization patterns of service also served as a model for the daily routine of school life; rewards and punishments bore a strong resemblance to those of government institutions. In military schools military subjects foreshadowed the reality of service, and even in schools of "general education" many subjects and exercises could be made to serve as preparation for subsequent service careers.

Not surprisingly, schooling became compulsory, and, like all of Peter's measures, it was enforced with his customary zeal and harshness. To make sure that his injunctions on education were really obeyed, Peter supervised personally the progress of young noblemen. A passport system enabled the government to keep track of its potential servants. When he was first presented to the authorities at about the age of six to eight, each young nobleman was issued a passport valid until the next inspection, at which time he had to pass an examination.[32] In case of failure the passport could not be renewed, and the young man had to enter active service in a very low rank. A nobleman who could not satisfactorily pass an examination in the basic subjects could not become an officer, was not permitted to marry, and was considered legally a minor, regardless of his biological age.[33]

Under Peter's successors, the highest organs of the state, the Supreme Privy Council or the Senate, did the examining. Peter's requirement that a nobleman successfully pass a general examination to be considered legally of age and to be permitted to become an officer lost its rigidity in course of time, but the principle remained. As long as service remained compulsory, every nobleman had first to register for service and then obtain leave of absence to complete his education. Unless he entered one of the special service schools, such as the Corps of Cadets or the University Gymnasium, a young nobleman had to secure permission to study at home.

Youngsters were impressed and forced into schools; those who escaped and tried to take refuge in their families were sought out and brought back *manu militari*. As usual, neither Peter nor his assistants displayed common sense in enforcing the requirements of education and training: every available person was sent to school, regardless of individual inclination and ability. Peter assumed that anyone could do what he was told to—hence his discouraging lack of success in so many instances. Middle-aged servicemen were compelled to attend schools alongside youngsters; despite their manifest inability, both groups were kept at school, and no effort was spared—including the harshest punishments—to inculcate them with the rudiments of Western technology and culture.[34] After the Great Reformer's death, the Supreme Privy Council was left to deal with the most pathetic cases.[35]

Nevertheless, education did take hold in Russia, particularly among the nobility. This was due primarily to the rewards that education offered in the context of the service system:[36] since the Table of Ranks was the main avenue to membership in the nobility and the only means for securing or enhancing one's status, a successful service career was desirable; and for this, education was essential. The resistance to education has held the limelight in Russian historical literature, while the successes and enthusiastic reception given the new opportunity for education have gone unnoted. Peter was not alone in stressing Russia's need for modern, secular education; he had active support among both his own and succeeding generations.[37] In short, no more than a generation after Peter's death, education was accepted as a matter of course by the majority of nobles and in many instances even eagerly sought after. The early difficulties, the awareness of the great lag that Russia had to make up, the exhilaration of the first successes—all these perhaps help to explain the extraordinarily high value that successive generations of enlightened and forward-looking Russians put on education. Of course, Western Europeans also considered education a positive good, but they did not view it as the *sine qua non* of social progress and national power.

Since without schooling one could not rise above the lower grades of noncommissioned rank and their civil equivalents, the poorer members of the nobility began to agitate for better educational facilities, so that their children could be launched on a successful service career. As is well known, first there were efforts to make educational accomplishments a ground for exemption from service in the lowest ranks on a par with non-nobles.[38] This was the avowed purpose of the creation in 1731 of the Corps of Cadets (*Shliakhetnyi kadetskii korpus*). The establishment and great and immediate success of the Corps clearly illustrate the fact that without schooling the normal service obligations could not be properly discharged.

At a later date, and for a wider circle of students, the University of Moscow and the boarding schools attached to it played a similar role. Deputies of the nobility vociferously proclaimed to the Commission of 1767 that without schooling a nobleman could not secure an adequate service career.[39] To satisfy the growing demand for adequate schooling on the part of the less affluent nobility, it was proposed that schools be established in every provincial capital, if necessary at the expense of the local nobility themselves. It is significant that although service had ceased to be compulsory in 1762, the deputies continued to argue for schools in terms of service needs, thus nicely illustrating the prime importance the nobility continued to attach to service. Parents made sacrifices to engage tutors or send their sons to school only because it was deemed necessary and desirable for service.

This consideration affected even the outlook on the education of women. F. Saltykov, who had been among the first to advocate a modern education for girls, argued that only an educated woman was capable of raising useful servants of the state and of providing support and companionship to her husband in service.[40] This approach eventually culminated in the creation of the Smol'nyi Institute for Noble Girls, the function of which was to educate young women for their future role as wives and mothers of servicemen.[41]

Quite likely, of course, a genuine desire for education would have developed anyway, but in the thinking and writing of eighteenth-century Russians, considerations not based on service needs definitely played a subordinate role. In fact, because schooling was viewed exclusively in service terms, parents frequently did not permit their sons to finish their chosen course of studies, especially the more advanced academic ones. The most important thing a boy could do, after all, was to enter active service in order to make a good career early.[42] That is why Lomonosov and others strove, albeit with limited success, to secure a recognized place in the regular Table of Ranks for the faculty and students of the university. In a country where service rank was everything, advanced studies could have no appeal, they argued, unless rewarded by a proportionately high service rank. Lomonosov's specific proposals failed to be accepted, but with the spread of advanced learning, recognition was given to the importance of rank. A student graduating from the university was entitled to the lowest (fourteenth) rank; a "master's degree" conferred on the holder the equivalent of company officer rank; and the doctorate automatically gave an honorable position in the Table of Ranks.[43] On admission to the University of Moscow (the only university throughout the eighteenth century), students received permission to wear a sword and uniforms. The joy and excitement at the prospect of wearing a duly respected uniform was often similar to that experienced by a youngster about to be commissioned an officer.[44]

These were the basic attitudes and practices that survived in full force into the first decades of the nineteenth century.[45] Army service was not considered to constitute a break from the pattern set by the educational experience, but was rather a change of form, as can be readily inferred from the careers of the future Decembrists.[46]

The notion of a service-oriented education had a double aspect—each with its own dynamic. First was the narrowly professional side, dominant in the reign of Peter the Great and his immediate successors. In his educational measures Peter was motivated by purely practical considerations. He needed soldiers, sailors, and administrators acquainted with all recent technical aspects of their profession. Everyone in Russia had a specific public role for which he had to be properly prepared. Modern warfare, administration, trade, industry, and culture could not be carried on adequately without technical knowhow that could be acquired only in schools. This aspect continued to play a major role, of course, in all military schools, more particularly those of the technical branches, such as the navy, artillery, and engineering.

But even the narrowest professional training rested on the general culture that had become generally accepted in Western Europe, and the new professional schools could not avoid becoming schools of "general education." Peter realized that Russia needed men who would be able to participate in the progress of Europe—the Russian serviceman should be not merely a technician acquainted with Western know-how, but a genuinely cultured European *honnête homme*.

Thus Peter the Great introduced a dichotomy that the remainder of the eighteenth century was left to resolve. But for Peter and his generation, at any rate, *both* general and professional education had a distinctly instrumental orientation. This emphasis could be easily implemented, since Russian education was much less bound by tradition than that of Western Europe, and was therefore much more amenable to pedagogic innovations.[47] Such flexibility allowed for innovation which permitted the Russians to follow and even outdo the West very rapidly and effectively.

There was, of course, a corresponding negative side. Innovations were likely to be accepted too readily and uncritically, which resulted in a lack of stability and continuity for educational programs. Methods and content of education were quickly adapted to prevailing needs and fashions, to the detriment of the solid foundations that should have been secured first. Many educational institutions appear to have been built on sand, and the Western culture they imparted was a thin and fragile veneer. But most contemporary educators expected that the process initiated in the schools would continue in the service. Whenever this happened the results were beneficial and long lasting.[48] But if service did not carry further the westernization and cultural polish begun in school, the limited educational experience remained an artificial gloss that barely hid the uncouthness and ignorance beneath.[49] The vague Western notions that a nobleman had heard from tutors or teachers might even become a pretext for oppressing the serfs in a more "rational," hence harsher and more alien, fashion.[50]

The actual curriculum of the Russian school reflected the dualism between professionalism and general culture that had been introduced by Peter the Great. Secular education, in line with the needs of the state, began by being primarily technical. Among the subjects were those needed in the military and naval establishments—mathematics, ballistics, fortification, military engineering, etc. In addition, there were also drill and such physical exercises as were considered useful at the time. Under the army-minded emperors Peter III and Paul I in the eighteenth century (and under Alexander I and Nicholas I in the nineteenth), excessive attention was given to drill and parades,[51] even at the expense of other military subjects, not to mention academic disciplines.

However, in his own brusque and crude way, Peter the Great himself gave the initial impetus to the cultural side of education by requiring that servicemen be taught the elements of "gracious living" (demeanor, etiquette, dancing, fencing, etc.) as well as foreign languages. The Corps of Cadets went much further in this direction—its curriculum consisted of a survey of the major fields of knowledge and the cultural accomplishments of the time—and it set a standard to which other institutions aspired as well as they could.[52] We need not survey the curricula of the major institutions of education in detail, for they were patterned on that of the Corps of Cadets. And that the basic character of the school programs had not changed by the beginning of the nineteenth century is shown by the prospectus of the Boarding School for Nobles in Moscow during the reign of Alexander I and the establishment of the *lycée* at Tsarskoe Selo.[53]

As in Western Europe at the time of the Renaissance, this general education was at first rather encyclopedic, since education was equated with factual knowledge.[54] It was believed that unless the Russian acquired a smattering of everything that the West had to offer, he could not be considered educated or even civilized. Foreign languages—especially modern ones—held the first place in the curriculum because they gave direct access to Western knowledge and culture.[55] Prior to the last quarter of the eighteenth century not enough had yet been translated to satisfy the curiosity and needs of the Russians; although the basic classical literature was available in Russian translations, they were rarely of a high order. Before the establishment of the "Society laboring for the translation of foreign books," [56] the Russian Academy (*Rossiiskaia Akademiia*), and the publishing activities of Novikov, the largest portion of Western civilization was accessible only through a knowledge of foreign languages.[57]

Second place in disseminating Western culture was held by literature and drama. The romance, and later the novel and moral tale, played a most significant part in acquainting Russian readers with Western customs, fashions, and ideas. The schools were of primary importance in making this literature available to a wider public in Russia: first, of course, foreign languages were studied in the schools; second, and no less important, the schools acted as the first "translation bureaus" in Russia. Thus, regular translation work was first undertaken and published in the Corps of Cadets. Translations consisted mainly of belles-lettres, periodicals, and similar entertaining reading matter, in addition to technical books. The Corps of Cadets in the first half of the eighteenth century, the academic gymnasia and boarding schools for noble pupils in Moscow and St. Petersburg in the second half, and the provincial centers at the end of the century became the chief propagators of Western spiritual culture.

As the eighteenth century wore on, two trends developed: first, cultural subjects began to take precedence over technical subjects, which became associated with "common" occupations and physical hardships.[58] Second, it was realized that it was not enough to have *"une tête bien pleine"*; it also had to be *"bien faite."* More important, there also had to be the ability and will to create culture anew and impart its benefits to others. A "culture of the heart" was therefore needed even more in Russia than in the West because of the obligation the educated class had incurred toward the people. The pedagogical ideas of Locke and Rousseau, which became dominant in Russia in the second half of the eighteenth century, strengthened this attitude and provided some concrete suggestions on how to develop the culture.

It should be noted that the notion of moral responsibility as an ingredient in Russian education had developed early—a result of the goal of utility for the state and service.[59] The moral aspect was to remain strong, even after education had become primarily an adornment of the noble way of life, as it had been in Western Europe since the sixteenth century. In principle, at least, education imposed on the nobleman who had enjoyed its fruits the obligation of helping to "civilize" his fellow men, particularly those directly under his power, whether in service or at home. In Russia (as in America in the late eighteenth century and throughout the nineteenth) the notion developed that enlightenment acquired through education, being the most important avenue to material and spiritual benefits, imposed the moral obligation to spread the latter as much as possible. Hence the strong resentment by the educated of the bureaucratic high-handedness that threatened their newly acquired dignity and sense of responsibility, while preventing them from fulfilling their social purpose, as they had come to define it. The moral component imparted to Russian education an "evangelical" tone: educational institutions were conscious of doing a job of spiritual as well as intellectual redemption by preparing the student for his proper cultural role and moral calling. These were—in Max Weber's definition—"bourgeois" values, but they were accepted by educated Russian noblemen because they were the natural result of an education geared to the requirements of state service.

For similar reasons, perhaps, eighteenth-century Russia looked to Germany for its main source of inspiration in educational matters, in terms of both practice and personnel. Russian schools were staffed primarily by teachers of German origin (although occasionally they were English), protestant and bourgeois.[60] Their personal influence was reinforced by the natural-law philosophy in which they were grounded and which they taught. Only in the last quarter of the century, primarily among private tutors and exclusive boarding schools, did French aristocratic pedagogical influences on the seventeenth-century Jesuit model become apparent, paving the way for the formation of an idle aristocracy.[61] For most of the rank-and-file nobility, the service-oriented, utilitarian, vaguely "evangelical," "bourgeois" pedagogy remained the dominant educational influence. Alongside the relatively open character of the Russian nobility (due to the Table of Ranks), this pedagogical orientation formed in the nobility a self-image and social ethic much more like those of the Western bourgeoisie than of the feudal aristocracy. It was, therefore, easy for a portion of the educated Russian nobility to become transformed into a socially conscious, progressive intelligentsia in the modern sense.

By the end of the eighteenth century, under the influence

of I. I. Betskoi and others, the schools of the nobility consciously proposed to shape a new humanity in Russia on the model of Western Europe and, if possible, to improve on it.[62] The major concern was to mold the "entire man"—particularly his heart and spirit—thereby endowing each nobleman with a new dignity and worth. In accepting the task of creating new men, the schools tried to isolate the students from the outside world as much as possible. In particular, their pupils were to be shielded from the family milieu that had not yet acquired a Western polish and outlook. The desirability of isolating the pupil from his normal milieu found general acceptance, even if it was not always practiced. The schools aimed at substituting for the family, and in many instances they succeeded.[63]

Thus for perhaps the first time in their lives, the children of the nobility—whose rootlessness we have described—developed close attachments and strong feelings of solidarity;[64] this feeling of belonging sometimes extended even to students who lived at home. But it is important to stress that this bond was based on sharing in a common process of intellectual and psychological maturation—the discovery of a new world of the spirit. To the extent, therefore, that the school succeeded in shaping a new type of man, it helped to reinforce a special feeling of "cliquish" solidarity that set the students off from their home environment, their elders, and —most significantly—from the state, which acted as if the new type of man did not yet exist.

The students in these schools also experienced acutely their isolation from the rest of Russian society. The "new type of man," whose mental makeup and spiritual requirements were the products of the Russian educational system, failed to find a responsive environment. All too often, this led to the new man's early death (figuratively speaking). How many followed the easier path and became part of the very milieu they had learned to scorn in school? How many educated noblemen, graduates of these boarding schools, when they found themselves in the harsh, uncomprehending and almost alien environment of service became disenchanted and embittered? They were bound to feel their isolation and exclusiveness ever more strongly, and they reacted by violently rejecting the Russia for which in truth they had not been prepared and with which they could not cope. Their bitterness nourished the "intelligentsia," whose members revitalized the strong bonds formed at school. The pattern of circles (starting with the ones organized by the Turgenev brothers around 1801), was a direct result of this blend of isolation and solidarity.

The sense of being isolated from Russian reality experienced by so many of these young people was heightened by the ideological orientation of their studies. The "new Russian man" was in fact similar to the enlightened nobleman of eighteenth-century Western Europe. As we well know, the eighteenth-century "intellectual" had a tendency to be abstract, system loving, and even a bit Utopian.[65] How much more was this the case of the educated Russians, for the implications of their new Western learning were not toned down by the force of past traditions. Their acquired knowledge was almost exclusively foreign: foreign languages and literatures, history of the world, classical, Western philosophy and law, etc. It is, of course, an exaggeration to say that the young nobleman out of school did not even know Russian, but it is true that he did not have a "common language" (in the more basic sense) with the people. At home in the literature and history of Western Europe, the young Russian nobleman was quite ignorant of Russian letters and the past of his own homeland.[66]

Of course, Russian subjects were not completely neglected. To begin with, the Russian language was practiced and its grammar taught. There was also the Russian Orthodox religion, though the exact nature of its role still awaits its historian. Beginning with the second half of the eighteenth century, after a brief flurry of effort under Peter the Great,

Russian history, literature, and law were taught more and more, and they became more widely known. But they did not hold the center of the élite's attention, and very often they served only as an external mask or costume for basically Western notions, patterns, and feelings. As a matter of fact, the introduction of national elements and the development of a "national consciousness" were to a significant extent themselves the by-products of the Western influence.[67] It is not easy to find out how these national elements affected the self-image of the nobility. But it is fair to say that the emotionally potent aspects of Russian reality did not come through school. They were rather due to an early exposure to village life, to the tales of nurses and peasant tutors, more rarely to the influence of grandparents. The school gave only a somewhat dry and uninspiring catalogue of facts concerning Russia's past—frequently clothed in "Western" costume—or sang paeans in praise of Russian rulers and feats in the mistaken belief that these could lead to a genuine understanding of national traditions.[68]

The inability to fit Western learning and culture into a Russian context also reduced the effectiveness of sojourns in Western Europe—which sometimes climaxed the young Russian nobleman's education—and further alienated him from the state. Throughout most of the eighteenth century, with a few very rare exceptions, the Russians did not know the equivalent of the English grand tour.[69] But quite a few young nobles did see and study Europe before embarking on their regular service careers. As is well known, the practice had its origin in Peter's sending young men to learn navigation and similar crafts in Venice, England, and Holland.[70] Later in the century, such trips abroad no longer focused on the acquisition of technical knowhow, but on the study of traditional humanistic disciplines. In many cases, young Russians were sent abroad by the government, which supported them—albeit in quite a niggardly fashion, as Radishchev and his fellow students experienced at Leipzig. Upon their return they were expected to fill responsible posts in the state service. The training received during these stays abroad was largely determined by the needs of the state: it might be technical in a broad sense, as in the case of Lomonosov; but in the majority of cases, it was legal and philosophic, to prepare candidates for the judiciary and civil administration.[71] The purpose of these journeys abroad being strictly didactic (and the travelers' activities and purse being strictly supervised by the government), the young Russians acquired a great deal of valuable knowledge, but they seem not to have had the opportunity (or desire) to penetrate Western life and fully absorb the new environment. By and large, their experience was restricted to university life (and in a limited fashion, at that) and the professional-academic class of Western Europe. Toward the end of the century the situation changed, and something like a grand tour became fashionable in some circles. The Russians toured Europe by going from one famous public or private institution, gallery, celebrity, or professor to another, and they brought to this task the earnestness and eager desire for enlightenment that in our own century are displayed by students and visitors from underdeveloped countries.[72]

The students returned burning with the desire to be useful, to apply for the benefit of their country and government what they had learned abroad. They did not fully appreciate (and it is evidence of their failure genuinely to understand the dynamics of Western life) that their newly acquired knowledge was directly related to conditions in Western Europe and that it could not be transferred mechanically to Russian circumstances. Nor did they understand the vastly different social and cultural role played by the intellectual élite of Western Europe in developing the notions of law and principles of government they had learned about and wished to introduce into autocratic Russia.[73] Little wonder that they had to make the bitter discovery that they could not apply their knowledge in the way they had hoped. They found themselves frustrated at every step by the sociocultural reality of Russia and the practices of the autocracy. Disaffection, even alienation and revolt, were their natural reaction.

For its part, the government no doubt was disappointed too. The money and effort expended to have these young men well trained in the West did not bring the expected results. Instead of being useful, enthusiastically loyal, and grateful public servants, many who returned from foreign schools proved critical of Russian conditions, ill adapted to the *modus operandi* of the imperial administration, and all too often filled with knowledge that had little application in their homeland. The government did not view favorably the returning students' claim to higher knowledge and wisdom. In some instances the misunderstanding was particularly great because, in the minds of the high court dignitary, Western Europe meant primarily the social graces and glittering civilization, while for their earnest young subordinates it connoted a deeper spiritual life and a disciplined dedication to learning.[74]

All this resulted in a curious paradox. In the process of using Western education in order to satisfy its immediate practical and technical needs, the government helped to create a leadership group with a Western outlook and way of life. But the Western education received by the Russian élite provided the basis for a new self-image both for the nobility as a class and for noblemen as individuals. The nobility's newly acquired way of life—combining education and service —was its own accomplishment, its major *raison d'être*, and its basis for claims to special treatment and rights.[75] A cultured and educated way of life became in itself the mark of the nobility. No one who lacked a Western-type general education could in truth be considered a member of good society or (in fact if not in law) claim all the privileges of noble status. Those who lacked the proper education and did not lead "civilized" lives, even if they were in service and possessed wealth, could not be considered full-fledged members of the nobility.[76]

The nobility's new self-image supported two distinct but equally important claims: First, respect for the cultured, educated individual, and protection against the indignities of arbitrary or tyrannical acts by government officials. This demand reflects the impact of Western ideas and values, for the individual personality had not been an important independent element in the social and cultural life of Muscovite Russia,[77] and for political and legal purposes even in the eighteenth century an individual was granted certain public characteristics only by virtue of his belonging to a specific group. Moreover, as the reign of Paul I was to remind the élite, the individual Russian—whatever his position—was at the mercy of the ruler and his agents. The well-known remark of Emperor Paul that a man was a distinguished individual only so long as he, the Emperor, spoke to him may have been apocryphal, but it well described the situation.

But at the same time the government had helped to create individuals capable of thinking independently of their family, class, or nation. Education stimulated in many noblemen the desire to live in a cultured manner, to make individual use of their newly acquired or discovered potential. Freedom from compulsory service was to provide the means for satisfying this desire for many; but even within the framework of service the educated individual endeavored to create conditions suited for such an existence (and frequently succeeded).

This new sense of individualism helped to create a sense of separateness from the state among the educated—a feeling that the state ought to remain outside the everyday life of a civilized human being.[78] Quite naturally, whenever the state took tyrannical and arbitrary actions, it aroused the passionate anger of those who had but recently freed their souls and minds to discover their own personal worth. The result was antagonism to and "alienation" from the state. Although it is anachronistic, "alienation" is quite the proper word, because the noblemen knew and felt that despite their newly acquired individuality and culture they were a creation of the state. Hence the ambivalence toward state and country, the inescapable need to break loose from the state-nourisher, leading in some cases to the rejection of all authority. All these elements, of course, can be found in the mental makeup of members of the Russian élite in the nineteenth century, whatever their specific political opinions.

The second claim made by the nobility was for recognition of their authority to assume the role of moral guide and teacher to the people. The notion of dedication—which was implicit in the ideal of service—was becoming transferred from the ideal of service to the state to responsibility toward the nobility's fellow men. The nobility demanded that they be allowed to give concrete expression to their sense of obligation to the nation. Denial of this permission (by Catherine the Great) led to drawing away from the very state that had been instrumental in shaping the nobility into a moral and intellectual élite and in creating their self-image. This amalgam of alienation from the state and an orientation to action was to provide the guidelines for the intellectual and moral search of the first generation of the intelligentsia.

FIVE

The Impact
of Western Ideas

WESTERN civilization was adopted by the entire
Russian nobility in the course of the eighteenth
century; its outward manifestations filtered down even to the
estate in the remote provinces. Yet only a minority became
well acquainted with the major intellectual values of the
West, and still fewer assimilated them fully. But in any case,
men whose entire existential framework was determined by
state service and whose home and school experiences fostered
rootlessness and insecurity were bound to perceive and adapt
Western culture and ideas in a particular, idiosyncratic way.
The dynamics and "valence" of these ideas were bound to be
different in the Russian institutional and social environment
from what they had been in the context of the West.

As there was much to choose from in the treasure trove of

Western civilization, there had to be some selectivity, if only because a newcomer needed time to become acquainted with Western offerings and to acquire the tools necessary for a meaningful assimilation of Western ideas. But Russian borrowings from the West were not only selective but also adopted without reference to the context in which the borrowed ideas had first been elaborated. The eighteenth-century Russian intellectual—such as he was—was still too unfamiliar with the reality of Western Europe to understand the framework of the intellectual phenomena that attracted him; he was too uncritical in his desire to imitate the West to make adjustments that would accommodate the shift to the Russian environment. Not until the generation of the Decembrists do we meet with a more realistic understanding of the complexity and significance of Western European conditions and a more sober appraisal of the discrepancy between Western enlightenment and Russian reality. But without the eighteenth-century experience even the contemporaries of Alexander I and Napoleon would not have been able to draw the political conclusions they did from their contact with the West.

Under the circumstances, much of what the West could offer had only a "decorative" function, embellishing life and making social intercourse more pleasant and civilized. Fashions, arts, music, and entertaining belles-lettres, therefore, need not arrest our attention. Other ideas and attitudes, furthermore, were too much bound up with specific institutional and political situations in the West to be readily endowed with a positive function in Russia. A most striking example of this is perhaps "Voltairianism." In the West (France in particular, of course) Voltaire's popularity stemmed largely from his protest against intolerance and injustice and, more specifically, from his fight against the Church as an institution and against religion as an accumulation of superstitions. For the average educated Russian, however, these were not burning issues. As an institution the

Church was unquestionably subordinated to the state that the nobleman served. Nor was the enlightened nobleman concerned about religious superstition, for it had little impact on public and cultural life. True, the peasantry still lived by it, but then the educated nobleman no longer shared a common language and culture with the peasants. Thus "Voltairianism" in Russia meant merely superficial and snobbish irreverence for Church ritual and a provocative philosophical rationalism. Fashionable primarily among the upper circles of the rich nobility in the capital, it had no significant impact on the outlook and life of the majority of educated noblemen. Its foolish excesses merely helped to foster a religious revival among the nobility.

Paradoxical as it may appear at first glance, philosophy was the principal Western intellectual influence on the Russian élite in the eighteenth century. But perhaps it was not such a paradox after all. Institutionally and culturally the Russians were in the process of acquiring the externals of the economic and political patterns and behavior of the West. To consolidate these new acquisitions and permit further progress, there had to be developed a new image of man and a new conception of the relationship between the latter and his social and physical universe.[1] This was no easy matter, because the process of westernization was taking place in the presence of a breakdown of the traditional pattern of human relationships and values. S. Solov'ev may have overstated the case,[2] but there is no question that in the seventeenth century the Russian élite—in relation to both seventeenth-century Europe and eighteenth-century Russia—was less individualized and its members more bound by their family and "clan." There was also a strong attachment to traditional customs of behavior, which did not leave much scope for individualism and "rationalism." When M. M. Shcherbatov decried the corruption of morals in the eighteenth century (a common complaint when one sociocultural pattern is in the process of breaking down), he was in fact bemoaning the rapid spread of individualism and modernity.[3] In this respect eighteenth-century Russia reminds us strongly of Central and Western Europe in the fifteenth and early sixteenth centuries where the traditional conception and image of man had been put in question by the emergence of the individual as an autonomous entity and force. No wonder, therefore, that in Russia —as in Renaissance Italy and Northern Europe two centuries before—ethical and psychological problems held the center of attention, overshadowing by far other branches of philosophy.[4] True enough, some kind of metaphysics would be implicit in any serious discussion of ethics. But in the eighteenth century the Russians were not overly concerned with metaphysics, little prepared as they were by their previous cultural tradition;[5] thus their ethical writings remained superficial and imitative. Little wonder, too, that the Russians did not share the passionate interest in epistemology that played such a vital role in the philosophical speculations and intellectual life of eighteenth-century Western European intellectuals.[6]

In its efforts at establishing social (both public and private) relationships on as rational a basis as possible, eighteenth-century European thought was engaged in discovering and properly defining a notion of man that would accurately picture the individual's "natural" relationship to his world. European thinkers and writers wanted to see what they had learned about man implemented through a more rational organization of society. Man's "reason," of course, was most amenable to "scientific" investigation and capable of providing directives for new rules of social action that would not be based on tradition, superstition, or error. In so doing, eighteenth-century thinkers relied not only on their faith in the fundamental rationality of man (or at any rate on his being accessible to reason), but also on the power of his will. They felt that the individual, freed from the fetters of irrational beliefs, should be able to apply his will to "build" the kind of relationships that made for the greatest happiness for himself and his fellow men. Unavoidably, high value was put on the individual's dignity and worth, for it was he—not irrational forces—who was to create the new society and define his place in the world. Respect for the individual's reason, will, and dignity led in the West to the proclamation of the social and political notions we usually subsume under the terms enlightenment and liberalism.

These aspects of Western European thought and philosophy had a great appeal in Russia. This, indeed, is not surprising, for the Russians were in search of a modern image of man, an image that would suit their new condition, fit their new costume and social behavior, and provide a solid foundation for further progress along the path shown by Peter the Great. For this purpose, eighteenth-century Western writings could provide the ethical *notions* (it would be exaggeration to speak of a comprehensive system) consonant with modern, cultural standards and accomplishments.[7] These notions stressed the dignity and worth of the individual, which, in the long run, of course, served to focus attention on the principal obstacle to their fulfillment in Russia: the autocratic government. The ethics of eighteenth-century Europe also entailed reliance on human will and reason, which could not only bring about the conditions necessary to modern life and culture, but could also help in shaping, even transforming, the individual himself. After all, had the Russian nobleman not been transformed by Peter's will and rational acts? The paeans sung to the memory of Peter the Great expressed a profound psychological truth when they lavishly used images of creation. Peter the Great had initiated the transformation of the Muscovite slave (*rab*) and servant (*kholop*) into a loyal subject and a citizen endowed with his own sense of dignity. The eighteenth-century noble serviceman, not sufficiently acquainted with history to be aware of the deeper roots of the transformation undergone by Russia, thought that Peter the Great was its prime mover. His reign seemed to prove that will and reason could create social reality and set goals for the dynamic drive toward greater progress.[8]

The notions of ethics imported from the West helped to regulate the conduct of individuals who were freed from the fetters of tradition, including those based on religious norms. As an institution the Church had ceased to be a social and intellectual authority for the nobility in Russia (if it ever had been one), for its traditional precepts could hardly satisfy the needs of individuals living in an environment so utterly unlike that of Old Muscovy.[9] This did not necessarily affect the personal side of religious life and feeling, but in questions of daily public life there could no longer be dependence on the Church's authority. Moral questions and human relationships had to be solved on the basis of a respect for the individual's worth and a rational notion of the common good. Reliance on "rational" ethical norms imparted to Russian culture in the eighteenth century a very strong didactic streak, as had been true also of Western culture a century or two earlier. But in Russia this trend was more blatant because the élite was cruder and more self-conscious.[10] It was believed that rational norms were absolutes that could be taught to all in order to transform man, as reflected in the complete reliance on education as a means for constant transformation. Such an attitude imparted a dynamic quality to the self-image and mode of thought of the Russian élite that was bound to clash violently with the socioeconomic and political forces (that is, serfdom and the autocracy) that hampered its full manifestation.

We should also remember the undeniably "Utopian" element in eighteenth-century thought. It was Utopian in that it believed in the possibility of creating a new social reality as part of a comprehensive rational system. The men nurtured on the historical experience of the reign of Peter the Great—eager to transform their own behavior, thinking, and self-image—in short, men whose primary role was in the service of their country and its institutions, readily welcomed these goal-directed elements in Western thought. This is what imparts naïveté and boring didacticism to eighteenth-century literature.[11]

At first, the political conclusions that had been drawn in the West from the notions of the Enlightenment did not arrest the attention of the Russians. Indeed, the Russian élite—men of service in the main—still lacked the affective ingredients capable of transforming a set of diffuse values into a political ideology or creed. That such a transformation was in the making at the end of the eighteenth century is proven by the careers of Novikov, Radishchev, and the works of men like Pnin, Popugaev, etc., who reached maturity at the accession of Alexander I.[12] Because the Western European situation was so different, it is important to stress that in Russia the political implications of eighteenth-century notions were the result of a realization that—under prevailing conditions—the majority of the people did not and could not share in the country's cultural and economic progress. In the West the politicization of the Enlightenment had largely been the consequence of the struggle against the obstacles that the survival of antiquated institutions and traditions put in the path of the élite. In Russia politicization developed out of an ethical and social need to draw the rest of the population into the orbit of modernity. Thus, from the start, the political implications drawn from eighteenth-century thought were in Russia more "positive" and "active" than they had been in the West; not content with merely removing obstacles in the path of an evolution already under way, the Russians wanted to use Western ideas to create a new social reality and a new type of men.[13]

The popularity of natural law in eighteenth-century Russia had similar causes. Natural-law concepts penetrated into Russia in a more systematic and comprehensive manner than did Western ethical notions. The latter were almost accidental by-products gained from reading Western European literature and copying Western ways and fashions. Natural law, on the other hand, came through academic and administrative institutions. This is why the Germans played the major role in disseminating it, for they made up the majority of the professional academics of foreign origin.[14] In Russia, therefore, natural-law notions came in German Protestant rather than in French or English garb. Not only was natural law an important subject in most educational institutions, but it also was widely disseminated through translations, abridgments, and handbooks, while its basic concepts found expression in the literary productions of the time.[15]

In its German Protestant form, natural law stressed will, service (calling, *Berufung*), and social responsibility as the essential elements of the truly good life.[16] It also taught obedience to the powers that be, a precept of practical relevance in eighteenth-century Russia, where the élite still did not believe that open challenge to the political regime was possible. This voluntaristic element in natural-law doctrine went well with the belief in further transformation so popular among the Russians. And the notion of calling (service) and social solidarity obviously found a favorable response in the Russian service nobility. These elements had motivated Peter the Great to introduce natural-law concepts into Russian thought and political practice through the translations of the works of Pufendorf and Grotius he ordered.[17] After Peter's death, the works of other natural-law writers continued to be translated and read under the auspices of government institutions. The Russian rulers reasoned that the ideas of German natural-law writers encouraged unquestioning obedience to the absolute, well-regulated, "creative" state that had been introduced into Russia, while justifying this obedience by rational, secular norms outside the framework of Church tradition.[18] On their side, successive generations of the Russian élite found in natural law the absolute norms justifying their rational activity and striving for progress. The basic notions of natural law were uniformly valid for all times, all places, all peoples—hence their great appeal to people who wanted to see their country part of the Western family of nations.[19]

In institutional terms, natural law exercised great influence on the many efforts made during the eighteenth (and early nineteenth) century at organizing the administration rationally and efficiently, for the "life of the law" had to help form the framework of modern society and enhance the country's further progress and development.[20] The uniform and universal norms based on or derived from natural law stressed the value and dignity of human personality and action, underlined the importance of the free exercise of purposeful and useful activity, and related the individual's station and happiness in this world to his control and enjoyment of the fruits of his labor. Naturally such notions could easily have "subversive" and revolutionary implications in Russia, where sheer political despotism and serfdom prevailed, preventing it from becoming a truly Western nation. Notions of natural law are, therefore, found at the basis of criticism and suggestions for reforms throughout the eighteenth century.[21]

More immediately, natural law influenced the numerous efforts at codification undertaken in the eighteenth century.[22] It was felt that the new Russia and its emerging new man needed for their public life a code more comprehensive than that which outdated tradition or confusing *ad hoc* legislation, issued from case to case, were able to provide. Codification was approached in the systematic spirit of the eighteenth century and with a reliance on rationalism that bore little resemblance to similar efforts in the seventeenth century, both in Muscovy and Western Europe. Of perhaps even greater significance in the long run was the impact that the various legislative commissions, particularly the Commission on Codification called by Catherine in 1767, had on public opinion (*i.e.* that of the educated élite). Catherine's Nakaz (instructions to the Commission) set the tone, leading many a deputy to think in terms of natural-law concepts and the principles of the Enlightenment. Reference to natural law justified criticisms, arguments, and proposals, although at times it lent an abstract character to the debate.[23] The commissions on codification contributed to an uncritical belief that codification had a positive, creative task to perform. At the same time they popularized notions of social responsibility and social service. An entire generation was largely influenced by the concept of natural law; this notion accustomed that generation to giving theoretical justification for its criticism of reality, its proposals for reform, and its eagerness to accept the responsibility of action.

The didactic element so typical of eighteenth-century intellectual life also found expression in the growing interest for history. Historicism—in Meinecke's sense—did have its roots in the eighteenth century, as scholars have lately pointed out.[24] Yet the average educated man had still not made historicism and comparative cultural relativism part of his way of thinking; he still approached history in a didactic (pragmatic) and moralistic way. This was also the way taken by the Russians, for whom history was still a very new discipline.[25] We have mentioned that Russian history was little taught in the schools, and it was poorly known in good society throughout almost the entire century.[26] On the other hand, universal history was better taught and better known, a fact that contributed to the isolation of the educated Russian from the historical experience of his nation. Indeed, the belief in the value of universal history for the educated mind assumes a fundamental universality in the historical evolution of peoples and nations, while the obvious differences (which may even be emphasized) are related to superficial causes only. As the basic universality of human experience alone matters, fortunes and misfortunes, of any country, people, or individual, can and must be used for didactic exemplary purposes.[27] This emphasis focused the mind of the educated Russian on what the processes and events of universal his-

tory could teach him, rather than acquainting him with a
Russian past that he ought to understand and love for its
own sake.[28]

Paradoxically, it was his acquaintance with universal history that led the Russian intellectual to become aware of
his lack of contact with both the Russian tradition and the
Russian people. He began to realize that European writers
and thinkers did not operate in a cultural and social vacuum,
as the Russians seemed to do. However remote he may have
been from the ordinary peasant, the European writer or
thinker appealed to some of the nobility and most of the
bourgeoisie, and from them he derived his strength. But the
Russian élite, because of their foreign educational and intellectual experiences, sadly lacked a factual knowledge of
their country and people. Little wonder that they saw the
solution to specific ills in terms of an all-embracing theoretical
or ideological framework. Their Western heritage only deep-
ened the isolation of the Russian intellectuals from the state
and the people.

The task of Russian nationalism consisted, therefore, in
creating this bond between the élite and the people. It happened that this was the direction advocated by the new
ideas, which spread in the guise of sentimentalism. For the
latter's stress on the emotional bond with the people and
on the spiritual role of the folk and popular traditions found
resonance in the young nobleman as he faced leaving the
protective isolation of his school. In sentimentalism's call for
a return to nature and in its glorification of the simple folk,
the young serviceman heard an echo of his own early years,
when he was in the care of peasant nurses and tutors and
played with village children. Here lay, he felt, a chance for
renewed and even closer contact with the people and an end
to his isolation.[29] Perhaps the young nobleman even remembered his nurse (*niania*) and her unselfish love for him, in
contrast to the neglect frequently shown by his parents. Rediscovery of his nation on emotional rather than rational

grounds might well have helped to recall childhood fancies.

We must not—as is too often done—see Western and national influences on the Russian intellectual in the second half of the eighteenth century as opposed, but rather as a convergence of separate streams.[30] The combination of these influences had a powerful impact, as it occurred in the presence of isolation and rejection.

On one hand, the intellectual influences acting on the educated Russian were varied and profound. They paved the way for a completely new type of Russian man: an individual westernized not only outwardly, but inwardly as well. These individuals were keenly sensitive to their own worth and dignity, eager to share their newly gained traits and accomplishments, easily oriented toward positive social action, and zealous about spreading learning. At the same time, the traditional dedication of the Russian élite to service for the state and ruler was becoming transformed into a desire to help the Russian people (particularly the peasant) and humanity in general. The personal bond between the nobility and the Tsar had been lost through the bureaucratization of governmental authority, and the state was no longer dependent on the nobility for military manpower. As the Russian élite became estranged from the state, it found a feeling of personal closeness to, even worship of, the people.[31] It was this peculiar blending of rational conviction and strong emotional need that would give to Russian social and political thought in the nineteenth century its passionate and dynamic quality.

The popularity of Freemasonry in the eighteenth century was closely related to the intellectual concerns just discussed. The disappearance of the hierarchical world of Muscovy had left the educated individual isolated and craving for bonds with similarly minded individuals. Action-oriented rationalism had undermined simple and naïve faith, as well as revealed theology, and it drove men to seek a more personal and yet "reasonable" religious experience. The official Church could not satisfy this need, partly because of the poor education and low status of its rank-and-file ministers. The implementation of the rationalistic and philanthropic precepts of eighteenth-century ethical thought gave birth to new forms of association based on an emotional urge to do good combined with an approach free from superstition and tradition. For a society that had lost the elements of mystery, privacy, and ceremony, which had been a hallmark of the spiritual and social dedication of the medieval orders of chivalry, Freemasonry provided a welcome substitute. This is not to deny that Masonic lodges were at times based on quackery, sham, and plain stupidity. But these were perversions, for as a rule the Freemasons sought (and largely succeeded) to restore a sense of solidarity, dedication, compassion, and spiritual comfort to the members of a society that felt overwhelmed by the facile triumph of secularism, rationalism, and skepticism.

In Russia, of course, there were some additional reasons for the popularity and success of Freemasonry; not an insignificant part was played by the desire to imitate everything done in Western Europe. The ritual aspect of Masonry appealed to a service nobility that, without the traditions of feudalism or chivalry, was eager to create its own aristocratic code of behavior and set of values.[32] Infatuation with the ceremonial aspect no doubt led to the establishment of lodges of a purely social character, dedicated to entertainment and good living. This was frequently the case in the capitals and residences of the idle and wealthy nobility, for whom the lodges served the same purpose that fraternities and clubs had on the campus of socially select English and American universities. There is no question that in Russia this type of lodge merely served as a screen to corruption, debauchery, and vice.[33] This type of Masonry will not be our concern here, though in its own perverted way it, too, played a role in the westernization of Russia's upper classes.

From the incomplete evidence available, we can infer that

Freemasonry made its appearance in Russia in the first third of the eighteenth century, probably imported by Scotsmen and Englishmen in the service of Peter the Great. But it was not until the second half of the eighteenth century that the serious and intellectually oriented Masonic lodges made their appearance and rapidly took hold among members of the Russian élite. The internal history of the major observances has been adequately described and need not be our concern.[34] We shall limit ourselves to pointing out those intellectual and spiritual elements in Freemasonry that have contributed to the shaping of the attitudes of the Russian élite. It should be noted that this contribution extended beyond the limited confines of the lodges themselves; indeed, some lodges did not hide their activities: moreover, members of the Russian educated élite, being so close to one another, were used to sharing their interests and thoughts; it was unavoidable that many people became acquainted with Masonic ideas and notions purely through casual social contact. Finally, the Masons themselves—witness Schwartz and Novikov—actively sought recruits and proselytized their ideas.[35]

The reasons for joining Masonic lodges were mainly psychological, spiritual (religious), and moral. The first reflected the growing individualism and self-awareness of members of the nobility, their increasing sense of human dignity. The Masonic ideas and practices imported from England and Germany (rather than France) acquainted the average nobleman with the significance of the individual personality. The Masonic hierarchy and code were entirely related to individual merit and accomplishments. It was the Mason's personal performance of his obligations that determined his position in the hierarchy of the lodge. In a sense, in the moral and spiritual spheres Masonry offered a parallel or equivalent to the Table of Ranks in public service. Spiritually it expressed a reaction to the shallow, materialistic, and gross way of life that still prevailed among the upper classes, especially among the provincial and lower service nobility. This reaction was related to a sense of moral crisis arising from the breakdown of traditional beliefs and the inadequacy of the Church in the performance of its task of moral guidance, accompanied by a growing perplexity over the impact of secularism and rationalism. Freemasonry provided a new mold for ethical norms and standards of behavior, norms and standards that were, however, rooted in Christian precepts.

The Freemason assumed a double set of obligations. Toward himself he took on the obligation of leading a "clean," high-minded life. It was his duty to develop his inner resources to the maximum through education and constant study. Conscious of his own human dignity as the creature of a benevolent and rational divine Being, the Mason had to behave responsibly in accordance with this high status: shun vices and corruption, eschew moral laxness and gross hedonism. In the final analysis, the Mason's personal morality was firmly anchored in a profound religious belief: it was not enough that the Freemason follow all the formal requirements of the Church life; he had to become fully aware of the deeper import of his beliefs and actually live by them.[36]

Obligations toward his fellow men naturally occupied a place of prime importance in the life of the conscientious Mason. Rooted in the Christian precepts of love and charity, these obligations gave recognition to the individuals' dignity and worth and imposed the duty to treat them accordingly. In the past Russia had known few instances of private initiative in alleviating social ills.[37] It is true that in its "kenotic" interpretation of Christianity the Russian had a hallowed tradition of help to fellow men. But this help was given on an individual basis only and required that the charitable person demean himself to the level of those he was succoring. It had, therefore, only limited social value, even if it possessed profound personal spiritual meaning. The Freemasons in a sense "socialized" this tradition by making it a public and group enterprise, both for the donors and the recipients.[38] The goal of men like Schwartz, Novikov and Labzin was to bring about broad and effective public action to eliminate social ills and remedy their morally and spiritually baneful consequences. Recognition of the individual's worth and dignity led to the discovery that poverty, ignorance, misery resulted in man's dehumanization. To be effective, therefore, help should not humiliate the recipient, and it should be on a sufficient scale to make a significant impact. Such social action would also prove instrumental in shaping the members of the Russian élite into high-minded moral beings.

In effect, therefore, Freemasonry transferred the notion of service from the State to those in society who were in need of assistance. A genuinely moral and educated person had to assume responsibility for the condition of his fellow men —not only for the beggar or sick man who directly appealed to his pity, but for all those who needed help. The Masons were calling for a "rationalization" and "institutionalization" of the ideal of Christian charity. To perform genuine social service well, an individual (*i.e.* the Mason) had to be properly prepared spiritually. For indeed help was not to be merely in the form of momentary relief (alms, for example); it was to be the first step in "redeeming" the underprivileged, in returning their dignity as human beings to them. Social service, therefore, recognized that the underprivileged, *i.e.* the majority of the Russian people, would not be truly human as long as they remained in their miserable condition. It will be readily seen that this new notion of social service was well in line with the didactic and creative motif underlying much of Russia's institutional and cultural life in the eighteenth century.

One of the aspects of this broad aim of "humanizing" Russian society was to raise the people's educational level, to enlighten them. For this reason educational and literary activities played a major part in the Masons' programs of action. Naturally, their endeavors were not limited to the poor and downtrodden, but included all those in Russia who were culturally still very backward in spite of their relatively high social and economic level. It is of only secondary importance that this cultural and educational effort was intimately connected with the dissemination of the interpretation that the Masons gave to the Christian faith and way of life. Here it is essential to note that it was the first large-scale nongovernmental effort to spread Western ideas among broad strata of society.[39] In so doing they made Western culture, its philosophic learning and its literature, accessible to more people than had ever been possible. No doubt, the Masons' success was in part due to the fact that they hit on a very responsive cord, one that had its source in the Russian kenotic tradition as well as in the great curiosity the Russian had for life.[40] It contained, moreover, a moral element that freed it from association with either personal vanity or state interest.

The ideal of social solidarity had been slow in emerging in Russia, at least in its individual, secular, and rational form. It was quite different from the solidarity that had prevailed within the framework of Muscovite family and clan structure, and which was nothing but personal egoism writ large. In a political sense—on the level of the state—Peter the Great had inculcated the service nobility with a sense of social solidarity and responsibility. But he failed to endow it with that personal element required to make it fully effective; Russia's political and social structure in the eighteenth century, on the other hand, foreclosed the nobility's awareness of its solidarity with and responsibility to the people. This was the gap that the Masons tried to breach by stressing the universality of human nature, the need to respect its dignity and worth. Man had been created by God for happiness and joy, and it was every Christian's duty to give concrete form to this purpose.[41]

The Russian nobility was a profoundly divided class; comprising many conflicting interests, it had never achieved the sense of solidarity we observe in the West that might have enabled it to resist the autocracy's monopoly of political and social leadership. It is true that in the eighteenth century Western culture, and a modern way of life, enabled noblemen to experience a degree of solidarity that they had not previously known. The Masonic lodges reinforced this spiritual and cultural foundation by their secrecy, rituals, and sense of mission. But as Masonic activities were viewed with suspicion and hostility, especially in the 1780's and 1790's, the sense of solidarity its members felt also contributed to reinforce their isolation vis à vis both government and the remainder of society. Acutely conscious of their special position as crusaders for a spiritually better life and a more just society, the Masons foreshadowed the mood and psychology of the secret societies and Decembrists in the reign of Alexander I.[42] At the same time they helped to establish an acceptance in Russia of the equality of all those educated and enlightened. As the latter were few in number and alienated from the people, they came to share the Masons' sense of solidarity, which played such a powerful role in the life of the Russian intellectual élite that the intelligentsia came to be equated with a select order of chivalry.[43]

The basic notions of Freemasonry were rationalistic, and derived directly from the scientific discoveries of the seventeenth and eighteenth centuries. But in stressing the individual's worth and his personal relation to God and his fellow men, the Masons made room for feeling and emotion. Much of the popularity that Freemasonry enjoyed in the West and in Russia was due to its revolt against the desiccating effects of excessive rationalism. Freemasonry endeavored to re-emphasize the life of the heart, for good deeds were not good merely because they were reasonable and required by properly understood self-interest, but mainly because they restored a sense of dignity and a true God-given personality to the afflicted and humiliated. Only the involvement of the heart,

sentiment, made any activity genuinely human and benef-
icent. This psychological insight made the best Freemasons
particularly receptive to the suffering of the Russian people,
especially the serfs. As they pondered the condition of the
serfs, they themselves felt humiliated and debased, and their
sense of shame gave its emotional force to the emerging
"populism" of the Russian élite. They developed an urge to
help the serf, not only because their reason (or clearly conceived self-interest) dictated it, but because they could not
stand the gnawing feeling of guilt or resist the exaltation
of missionary fervor.[44]

The new role of the heart was closely related to the personal religious experience common to most of the Masons.
This was no isolated phenomenon peculiar to Russia; on the
contrary, it reflected a broad movement—especially in Protestant countries—of religious restoration. After all, the eighteenth century was not only the century of the Enlightenment
and of Goddess Reason, but also that of Pietism, Methodism,
and many other spiritualistic movements, which did not leave
Russia unaffected.[45] The impact of Western Europe's religious revival on Russia was indirect, for there never was
any attempt, let alone threat, to convert the Russians away
from Greek Orthodoxy.[46] But the Pietists' rediscovery of the
individual spiritual experience, as well as their concern for
the social implications of Christ's teachings, found a favorable response among westernized Russians. Nor did Russia
escape the effects of the European revival of mysticism. Much
of the literature translated and published with the assistance
of Masonic groups consisted of the classics of Protestant
Pietism and Western mysticism. That mysticism answered
a need can be inferred from the fact that its devotional
literature circulated widely and was eagerly read.[47] The
literature helped to prepare the ground for the explosion of
religious passion and mysticism in the first quarter of the
nineteenth century, after the Napoleonic Wars. The same
spirit also found some of its best-known expressions in the

sentimental literature of the end of the eighteenth century
(which owed as much to Pietist German models as it did to
Rousseau and the English forerunners of Romanticism).

The burden of our analysis has been to show that in his
adoption of the intellectual goods of the West, the Russian
nobleman was a neophyte. Unlike the Western European,
whose intellectual development took place within the framework of institutions and attitudes shaped by several generations, the Russian élite tended to convert Western ideas and
notions into absolutes whose validity was not to be ques-
tioned. This tendency was accentuated by all the nobleman's
institutional and existential experiences, centering on service.
In service, he was engaged in westernizing and modernizing
his country and people according to the scheme initiated by
Peter the Great. Given the lack of opposing, independent
institutions, the Russian élite was thus prepared to implement Western ideas directly and completely. They were
helped by the assent of the state on one hand and the absolute power they wielded over the serf population on the
other. In short, they easily acquired the "Utopian" attitude
that man and society could be transformed according to a
theoretical blueprint. Ideas became guides to action, rather
than merely tools of analysis and reflection. The educated
individual could create "the good society." Man, as Ivan
Pnin put it, "dictates his laws to the world; he is on earth
what God is in the universe." [48]
With such an attitude, the noble serviceman was fated to
clash with the autocratic state, which prevented him from
living according to his self-image. The Petrine state had
created helpmates who were no longer content with their
role and who wanted to give life to their own conception
of westernization and of social and spiritual progress. They
did not merely wish to satisfy selfish interests (although they
did that too). The educated élite of servicemen aimed at

grounding all of Russia's institutional life on the rational and moral principles they had acquired as a result of their westernization. The autocracy, however, was interested only in preserving its monopoly of authority within the Empire and its position of power outside. The demand of the élite for moral and material progress, as well as their claim to a greater and more independent role in this process, ran counter to the concepts of indivisible sovereignty and central state guidance held by the Autocrat and his officials. As the people and the individual, rather than the state, increasingly became the object of the élite's notion of service, the autocracy and the enlightened nobility parted ways. By the end of the eighteenth century this shift had affected only a select group. But by the middle of the nineteenth century, thanks to the effort of these few, the new orientation had taken hold of most truly educated Russians.

This cleavage, however, did not yet signify a complete rejection of the state and its institutional framework. On the contrary, conscious of their basic rootlessness and alienation from the people, the élite of the nobility hoped to give a new meaning to their function in the state without abandoning the tradition of service, which was *the* stable element of their existence. The men who reached adulthood in the first fifteen years of the nineteenth century shared the characteristic intellectual and psychological traits of the eighteenth-century nobility. But they were the first to give those traits full scope in their public and private lives. In this respect they were but following in the footsteps of A. Radishchev, who had first drawn the practical conclusions of the élite's relationship to the state that had nurtured it and their cultural obligation and moral responsibility to the people. In reading about the early nineteenth-century literary circles and discussion groups formed by young students in Moscow and later continued by officials and officers in service, in following the careers and spiritual development of those who participated in the wars against Napoleon,[49] we en-

counter an educated élite without specific ties to a particular
region or system of traditions; they craved service, but they
wanted to serve the people, not just the state. Their mental
horizon was defined entirely by their reading of Western
literature and their study of modern European thought. It
is true that they made efforts to Russify their classical and
European mental baggage, but the results were rather artificial. More so than their fathers, of course, they had felt
the impact of the revolution in the life of emotion that had
found expression in sentimental literature and budding Romanticism.

Quite naturally, the men of this generation tried to find a
synthesis between the eighteenth-century pattern of relationships to state and people and the new interests and emotional commitments generated by the French Revolution and
the Napoleonic Wars. They had become conscious of the
great variety of possibilities in human affairs, and they
wanted to be able to develop this hidden potential in their
own country. This was the new meaning they attached to
westernization. Laws and institutions designed to give members of society full scope to develop their potential talents—
be it in the service or in pursuit of cultural and economic
progress—were advocated by the young Alexandrine generation.[50] Their "program" implied paying greater attention
to the realities of Russian life, as well as to Russia's historical
experience and the traditions of its people (however badly
they may have been understood). In spite of this shift of
emphasis, the state was not left out of the picture. On the
contrary, the young men of Alexander I's time believed that
they would enlist the active support of the state, for they
still thought in eighteenth-century terms of state leadership
and were great advocates of national power.

After four years of Paul's repressive rule, the early years
of Alexander's reign held out the promise of a fulfillment of
these hopes, at least in the opinion of contemporaries. Reforms were talked about and planned; a few social and po-

litical improvements were actually made. Of even greater significance was the fact that Russia had to fight Napoleon's domination, both in Europe and at home. Participation in the war gave the young generation a feeling of commitment and usefulness, and the hint at reform made by the government during the struggle seemed to hold out the promise that after the conflict implementation of their suggestions would be permitted.[51] It is well known that the Napoleonic Wars stimulated romantic exaltation and national fervor. This only increased the disillusionment when after the peace was signed even the limited improvements of an earlier day were undone by the repressive policies of the *Arakcheev-shchina*. These policies produced a sense of alienation that turned to rebellion because they barred the young noblemen from living according to the very ideas and attitudes with which their family, school, and service experience had imbued them.

Frustrated and exasperated, the generation of the 1820's turned to the organization of secret societies and staged the abortive revolt of December 14, 1825. Their failure, as is well known, created an irrevocable gulf between the élite and the state—the one institution that through service had been an anchor for the educated class since Peter the Great. The élite had not yet overcome its isolation from the people, and now its ties to the state were cut too. Left alone and adrift, its members turned their energies to find new roots, using the mental and spiritual traits that had been developed during the eighteenth century. Lacking solid roots in their family, their region, or their people, the new generation of the élite sought meaning for their life in thought and action aimed at transforming the men and society surrounding them, and at creating another—better, modern, "Western," or "Slavic"—cultural, economic, and political environment.[52] The intelligentsia was coming into being.

The members of the intelligentsia combined the moral and intellectual tenets of the eighteenth-century servicemen with the fervor and emotional commitment to action of the Decembrists. As Alexander Herzen well saw, the first generation of the intelligentsia, to which he himself belonged, were the younger brothers of the men of 1812 and 1825. But this meant that they were also the sons of the Russian noblemen of the eighteenth century. From their fathers they acquired a cast of mind and a moral and psychological temper that predisposed them to theories and absolutes. To overcome their alienation from both the people and the state, whose creation after all they were, they put all their energies and will power into ideas and doctrines aimed at bringing about a radical transformation of reality.

A straight line of spiritual and psychological filiation connects the servicemen of Peter the Great to the revolutionaries of the nineteenth century.

Notes

Abbreviations used in this section

Bolotov: Andrei T. Bolotov, *Zhizn' i prikliucheniia Andreia Bolotova, opisannye samim im dlia svoikh potomkov 1738–1793* (4 vols., Saint Petersburg, 1870).

Chteniia: *Chteniia v Moskovskom obshchestve istorii i drevnostei rossiiskikh pri Moskovskom universitete* (Moscow, 1846–1918).

KM: A. N. Filippov, ed., "Bumagi Kabineta Ministrov imperatritsy Anny Ioannovny 1731–1740," *Sbornik IRIO*, CIV, CVI, CVIII, CXI, CXIV, CXVII, CXX, CXXIV, CXXVI, CXXX, CXXXVIII, CXLVI.

PSZ: *Polnoe Sobranie Zakonov Rossiiskoi Imperii* (1st series [Saint Petersburg, 1830]).

Sbornik IRIO: *Sbornik imperatorskogo russkogo istoricheskogo obshchestva* (Saint Petersburg, 1867–1916).

UK 1767: D. Polenov, V. Sergeevich, N. Chechulin, eds., "Istoricheskie svedeniia o Ekaterininskoi kommissii dlia sochineniia Proekta Novogo Ulozheniia," *Sbornik IRIO*, IV, VIII, XIV, XXXII, XXXVI, XLIII, LXVIII, XCIII, CVII, CXV, CXXIII, CXXXIV, CXLIV, CXLVII.

VTS: N. F. Dubrovin, ed., "Protokoly, zhurnaly i ukazy Verkhovnogo Tainogo Soveta 1726–1730 gg.," *Sbornik IRIO,* LV, LVI, LXIII, LXIX, LXXIX, LXXXIV, XCIV, CI.

Zh. M. N. Pr.: *Zhurnal Ministerstva Narodnogo Prosveshcheniia* (Saint Petersburg, 1834–1917).

Zh. S.: A. N. Filippov, ed., "Zhurnaly Pravitel'stvuiushchego Senata za 1737 g.," 2 parts, *Zapiski Moskovskogo Arkheologicheskogo Instituta,* III (1910), XII (1911).

1. Introduction

1. All dates in this book are given according to the Julian Calendar (in force in Russia until 1918), which lagged behind the Gregorian Calendar by eleven days in the eighteenth century and twelve days in the nineteenth.

2. Cf. R. Pipes, ed., *The Russian Intelligentsia* (New York: Columbia University Press, 1961 [first as Summer, 1960, issue of *Daedalus*]). While the literature on the history of ideas held by the intelligentsia is too large to be cited here, the most significant general works are those by T. G. Masaryk, V. V. Zenkovskii, P. Scheibert, A. von Schelting, and P. N. Miliukov.

3. A particularly brilliant treatment of the foremost prototype of the intelligentsia, A. Herzen, is M. Malia, *Alexander Herzen and the Birth of Russian Socialism 1812–1855* (Cambridge, Mass.: Harvard University Press, 1961).

4. Naturally, the makeup of a social group or class changes over a period of time. Thus the Russian intelligentsia changed in the course of the nineteenth century; for example, we have an important influx of children of non-noble origin in the 1860's and 1870's. But essentially the values and "ethos," the mentality and psychology, of the group are worked out and set by the first generation. In the case of the intelligentsia it was the men of the 1830's who were of noble

origin; the *raznochintsy* (*i.e.* not belonging to any of the official "ranks" and "classes" recognized by the state, *e.g.* children of priests, soldiers, etc.) added a few elements, perhaps, and stressed some aspects at the expense of others, but they did not modify the basic character of this vital element of the Russian élite.

5. For example, Adeline Daumard, *La bourgeoisie parisienne de 1815 à 1848* (Paris, 1963). Genealogical records and studies can only provide background information and do not reveal much about attitudes and behavior of members of the group. Cf. N. von Preradovich, *Die Führungsschichten in Oesterreich und Preussen 1804–1918* (Wiesbaden, 1955 [Veröffentlichungen des Instituts für Europäische Geschichte, Mainz, Bd. II]). For Russian genealogy see L. M. Savelov, *Bibliograficheskii ukazatel' po istorii, geral'dike i rodosloviiu rossiiskogo dvorianstva* (2nd ed.; Ostrozhek, 1897); V. K. Lukomskii and S. Troinitskii, *Ukazatel' k Vysochaishe utverzhdennomu obshchemu gerbovniku* (Saint Petersburg, 1910); *Opyt bibliograficheskogo ukazatelia pechatnykh materialov dlia genealogii russkogo dvorianstva 1785–1885* (Saint Petersburg, 1885); A. Bobrinskoi, *Dvorianskie rody vnesennye v Obshchii gerbovnik* (Saint Petersburg, 1890).

6. K. D. Muratova, ed., *Istoriia russkoi literatury XIX v.— Bibliograficheskii ukazatel'* (Moscow, 1962).

7. Being interested in the underlying phenomena of the "collective mind," we could reach meaningful conclusions on the basis of only a sampling of eighteenth-century Russian publicistic writings, for not all surviving material is readily accessible to the scholar in the West.

8. *E.g.*, it was felt unnecessary to repeat the evidence culled from the Complete Collection of Russian Laws (*PSZ*) on the legal status of the nobility that has been fully summarized in A. Romanovich-Slavatinskii, *Dvorianstvo v Rossii ot nachala XVIII veka do otmeny krepostnogo prava* (2nd ed.; Kiev, 1912), and to which the reader must be referred if he wishes to follow the vagaries of Russian legislation.

9. All Russian words, names, and titles in this book are transliterated according to the Library of Congress system, slightly simplified on the basis of modern spelling. Whenever pos-

sible, the transliteration is made from the nominative singular form of the word in modern spelling.

10. Exemption from personal taxation was not exclusively the privilege of the nobility, for it was shared by the clergy and a few other small groups of the population. The nobility did not have a monopoly on the ownership of land, although for a brief period (in the reign of Catherine the Great) it did enjoy the monopoly of possession of cultivated and settled estates.

11. A Soviet historian recently attempted a comprehensive survey of all non-nobles who could be counted among the intelligentsia at the end of the eighteenth century. The result is not very impressive. M. M. Shtrange, *Demokraticheskaia intelligentsiia Rossii v XVIII veke* (Moscow, 1965).

2. *The Noble Serviceman in Muscovite Russia*

1. M. D'iakonov, *Ocherki obshchestvennogo i gosudarstvennogo stroia drevnei Rusi* (3rd ed.; Saint Petersburg, 1910); V. O. Kliuchevskii, *Istoriia soslovii v Rossii* (2nd ed.; Moscow, 1914); N. P. Pavlov-Sil'vanskii, "Feodalizm v udel'noi Rusi," *Sochineniia* (Saint Petersburg, 1910), III; V. Sergeevich, *Russkie iuridicheskie drevnosti* (3 vols.; Saint Petersburg, 1890–1903).

2. It is true that the formerly independent and appanaged princes also had their own service nobles, their own boyars. But when the princes entered the service of Moscow their retinue came along and merged with the lesser Muscovite service nobility.

3. A. I. Markevich, *Istoriia mestnichestva v Moskovskom gosudarstve v XV–XVII v.* (Odessa, 1888), pp. 185–86.

4. *Ibid.*, p. 167; *UK 1767*, XLIII, 139.

5. S. B. Veselovskii, *Issledovaniia po istorii oprichniny* (Moscow, 1963).

6. Provisions were also made for temporary possession and

usufruct of at least a portion of a *pomestie* by widows and minor children. Cf. N. Pavlov-Sil'vanskii, *Gosudarevy sluzhilye liudi—proiskhozhdenie russkogo dvorianstva* (Saint Petersburg, 1898).

7. *Ibid.*, p. 227; Markevich, *op. cit.*, pp. 177, 179.

8. *Ibid.*, pp. 168, 170; Sh., "Dvorianstvo v Rossii (istoricheskii i obshchestvennyi ocherk)", *Vestnik Evropy*, XXII (April, 1887), 539, note 1 with reference to the decree of 1653 threatening those *dvoriane* and *deti boiarskie* who refused to join the military with deprivation of noble service status and demotion to the status of tillers of the soil. Narezhnyi's picaresque novel, *Rossiiskii Zhil'blaz*, gives a nice caricatured picture of such *zakhudalye* noblemen.

9. For example, the relatives of M. Danilov, *Zapiski napisannye im v 1771 g (1733–1762)* (Moscow, 1842), p. 16.

10. On the much-debated question of feudalism in medieval Russia, cf. Pavlov-Sil'vanskii, "Feodalizm v udel'noi Rusi," *loc. cit.*; Marc Szeftel in R. Coulborn, ed., *Feudalism in History* (Princeton, N.J.: Princeton University Press, 1956). For a summary of the Soviet view, see *Ocherki istorii SSSR (XIV–XV and XV–XVII centuries)* (Moscow, 1953–1955).

11. "Servant" is a more accurate rendering than "slave," a word sometimes found in English historical literature.

12. Of course, court etiquette and ceremonial were mainly of Byzantine origin, and the source for the humbling of those approaching the *basileus* was oriental and religious. In Muscovy, however, this humbling was not a matter of mere etiquette and symbolism; it actually reflected concrete human and social relationships.

13. The pride and independence of Western nobles found expression in such characteristic (even if apocryphal) remarks as *"Qui t'as fait roi?"* in early Capetian times or the alleged motto of the Rohan family, *Roi ne puis, prince ne daigne, Rohan suis* in the France of the Bourbon kings.

14. O. Brunner, *Adeliges Landleben und europäischer Geist* (Salzburg, 1949); J. M. J. Vicomte de Marsay, *De l'âge des privilèges au temps des vanités* (Paris, 1946); O. Brunner, *Land und Herrschaft (Grundfragen der territorialen Verfassungsgeschichte Oesterreichs im Mittelalter)* (4th ed.;

Wien-Wiesbaden, 1959); P. de Vaissière, *Gentilshommes campagnards de l'ancienne France* (2nd ed.; Paris, 1925).

15. This receives the fullest treatment in Markevich, *op. cit.* See also the very interesting and suggestive article by S. O. Shmidt, "Mestnichestvo i absoliutizm (Postanovka voprosa)" in *Absoliutizm v Rossii XVII–XVIII vv.: Sbornik statei k semidesiatiletiiu so dnia rozhdeniia i sorokapiatiletiiu nauchnoi deiatel'nosti B. B. Kafengauza* (Moscow, 1964), pp. 168–205.

16. See example cited by Markevich, *op. cit.*, pp. 458–59, of the decline of the Viazemskii family in the seventeenth century.

17. The argument in favor of the *mestnichestvo's* role as a limitation on autocracy was most fully developed by V. Val'denberg in *Drevnerusskie ucheniia o predelakh tsarskoi vlasti* (Petrograd, 1916). S. O. Shmidt, "Mestnichestvo i absolutizm (Postanovka voprosa)," *loc. cit.*, argues (quite convincingly to my mind) the opposite. For a balanced conclusion that stresses the role of the Tsar's discretion because of the service character of the nobleman see A. E. Presniakov, *Moskovskoe tsarstvo (Obshchii ocherk)* (Petrograd, 1918), p. 94 ("The Tsar does not grant family status, but in the absence of the sovereign's grant [of rank] the family is threatened with decline, while [the sovereign's] power may create a new family status [*poroda*]").

18. *"Tsar zhaluet chinom, ne rodom."*

19. Markevich, *op. cit.*, p. 458; Sh., "Dvorianstvo v Rossii," *loc. cit.*, XXII (May, 1887), 208. The ambiguous nature of the *mestnichestvo* made its abolition in 1682 unavoidable and easy.

20. The enjoyment of an estate's revenues derived from established dues in money, kind, or services. Possession, by contrast, gave rights to the actual management of the estate—*i.e.* making changes in dues and operations.

21. This state of affairs received its legal sanction when early in the eighteenth century the distinction between *pomestie* and *votchina* types of possession was abolished. Cf. Decree of March 23, 1714, *PSZ*, #2789. Yet the distinction did not disappear immediately, as witness the entry in the

Minutes of the Senate for January 27, 1737 (No. 365), *Zh. S.*, Part I, pp. 64–65.

22. S. Kniaz'kov, "Dvorianstvo vremen Petra Velikogo," *Ocherki iz istorii Petra Velikogo i ego vremeni* (2nd ed.; Saint Petersburg, 1914), p. 363; A. A. Tankov, ed., *Istoricheskaia letopis' kurskogo dvorianstva* (Moscow, 1913), I, 387, 403.

23. Tankov, *op. cit.*, p. 387; M. M. Bogoslovskii, *Oblastnaia reforma Petra Velikogo (Provintsiia 1719–1727 gg.)* (Moscow, 1902), pp. 410–11.

24. M. M. Bogoslovskii, "Smolenskoe shliakhetstvo v XVIII v.," *Zh. M. N. Pr.*, CCCXX (1899), Part III, 25–61, and the sources cited in M. Raeff, "Staatsdienst, Aussenpolitik, Ideologien," *Jahrbücher für Geschichte Osteuropas*, VII, No. 2 (1959), pp. 168–69.

25. Markevich, *op. cit.*, p. 157 ("Tsar Boris Fedorovich [Godunov] raised a certain Filatov from servant to the rank of boyar's child and then again returned him to servant rank"). Also S. Kniaz'kov, *op. cit.*, p. 346.

26. *"Ne kazn' strashna, strashna tvoia nemilost'."*

27. It is enough to recall the family feuds and disgraces during the minorities of Theodore, Ivan V, and Peter the Great. The anonymous contributor to the journal *Sobesednik* (I [1783], No. 1, 18), remembered this insecurity when he wrote: "Some were afraid to go to bed in olden times, so as not to suffer for someone else's guilt the next morning" (*"Inye spat' lozhas' boialis' v starinu, chtob utrom ne stradat' za ch'iu nibud' vinu . . ."*).

28. True enough, in some instances (especially in the case of military operations in defense of the southern and eastern frontiers of Russian settlement) there also was a feeling of serving the country, of fulfilling an obligation or duty vis à vis the Orthodox Christian people of Russia.

29. There are no comprehensive studies of the nature of notions of kingship in Russia. For a provocative introduction to the problem see M. Cherniavsky, *Tsar and People*, (New Haven: Yale University Press, 1961).

30. Cf. S. F. Platonov, *Lektsii po russkoi istorii* (Saint Petersburg, 1904); also articles by N. V. Ustiugov ("Evoliutsiia prikaznogo stroia Russkogo gosudarstva v XVII v.") and

N. F. Demidova ("Biurokratizatsiia gosudarstvennogo apparata absoliutizma XVII–XVIII vv.") in *Absoliutizm v Rossii,* cited earlier.

31. See the suggestive comments on the effect of single-minded concern for unity of sovereignty in R. Kosellek, *Kritik und Krise, Ein Beitrag zur Pathogenese der bürgerlichen Welt* (Freiburg, 1959), and C. Schmitt, "Soziologie des Souveränitätsbegriffs und politische Theologie" in M. Palyi, ed., *Erinnerungsgabe für Max Weber* (München-Leipzig, 1923), II, 1–35.

32. For a description of contrasting trends in Western and Central Europe see O. Hintze, "Staatenbildung und Kommunalverwaltung," in his *Staat und Verfassung (Gesammelte Abhandlungen zur allgemeinen Verfassungsgeschichte)* (Leipzig, 1941), pp. 206–31, and H. Rosenberg, *Bureaucracy, Aristocracy, and Autocracy—The Prussian Experience 1660–1815* (Cambridge, Mass.: Harvard University Press, 1958).

33. There were some exceptions, of course. The best known was the economically minded boyar B. I. Morozov in the reign of Alexis. Cf. J. Blum, *Lord and Peasant in Russia from the ninth to the nineteenth century* (Princeton, N.J.: Princeton University Press, 1961), Chap. 12. Soviet historians have endeavored to show how far from the natural economy stage Russia had progressed in the seventeenth century. But their evidence does not affect the picture of the average landowner-serviceman drawn here. For a summary of the Soviet point of view, cf. *Ocherki istorii SSSR —XVII v.* (Moscow, 1955). For an interesting picture of a seventeenth-century serviceman's career and home life, see N. N. Selifontov, *Ocherk sluzhebnoi deiatel'nosti i domashnei zhizni stol'nika i voevody XVII stoletiia, Vasiliia Aleksandrovicha Daudova* (Saint Petersburg, 1871).

34. Intense religious concerns, rare among the active servicemen, could be a source of satisfaction to only a few; and these concerns tended to remove them from involvement in worldly matters. Cf. *Zapiski Danilova,* pp. 1–20; Bolotov, I, 147.

3. The State and Service in the Eighteenth Century

1. K. Griewank, *Der neuzeitliche Revolutionsbegriff. Entstehung und Entwicklung* (Weimar, 1955). For a nicely balanced treatment of the reign of Peter the Great and a penetrating discussion of its "revolutionary" character, see Reinhard Wittram, *Peter I Czar und Kaiser* (*Zur Geschichte Peter des Grossen in seiner Zeit*) (2 vols.; Göttingen: Vandenhoeck & Ruprecht, 1964). The book appeared too late to be used for detailed citation. Also cf. the poem by the student A. Fialkonskii "Tsvetushchee sostoianie Rossii" in *Rastushchii Vinograd*, II (January, 1786), 6–13, which well illustrates the notion commonly held in Russia that the country's "new beginning" dates from the reign of Peter the Great.

2. It was, primarily, a "negative" view of the function of government, *i.e.* to prevent harm and injustice from befalling the land. Bogoslovskii gives a good summary of it in the first chapter of *Oblastnaia reforma Petra Velikogo* (*Provintsiia 1719–1727 gg.*) (Moscow, 1902).

3. They called it *otechestvo*, *i.e.* "fatherland."

4. M. M. Shcherbatov, "Razmyshleniia o zakonodatel'stve voobshche," *Sochineniia*, I (Saint Petersburg, 1896), 390 ("In the first place I think that inasmuch as the monarch is not the patrimonial lord, but the governor and protector of his state . . .").

5. As O. Hintze has defined it, the absolute monarchical state existed for its own sake and set as primary goal for its institutional, economic, and cultural activities the perpetuation and extension of its own power. Cf. *Staat und Verfassung* (*Gesammelte Abhandlungen zur allgemeinen Verfassungsgeschichte*) (Leipzig, 1941), *passim*.

6. I. I. Nepliuev, *Zapiski Ivana Ivanovicha Nepliueva 1693–1773* (Saint Petersburg, 1893), p. 110. Cf. also F. Hartung, "L'état, c'est moi," *Historische Zeitschrift*, CLXIX (1949), 1 ff.

7. Cf. Nashchokin's report of Peter's words at the signing of the peace of Nystad, D. Iazykov, ed., *Zapiski Vasiliia A. Nashchokina* (Saint Petersburg, 1842), p. 12. Also the

sentiments about Peter expressed by a deputy to the Commission of 1767 (UK 1767, LXVIII, 556), which, in spite of their panegyric tone, clearly indicate the belief that the greater power of the Russian state would result in the greater happiness of the Russian people as a whole. For an analysis and discussion of the contradictions implicit in this belief of eighteenth-century absolute monarchies see Kurt Wolzendorf, *Der Polizeigedanke des modernen Staates* (Breslau, 1918 [Abhandlungen aus dem Staats- und Verwaltungsrecht, Heft 35]), chap. 1.

8. The best known expression of this belief is Peter's order of the day to the army on the eve of the battle of Poltava, *Pis'ma i bumagi Petra Velikogo* (Moscow, 1950), IX, No. 1, p. 226 (No. 3251). Peter's most recent biographer correctly points out that although this version of the Tsar's order of the day is a later formulation, it accurately reflects Peter's thinking. Reinhard Wittram, *op. cit.*, I, p. 312 and p. 468, note 122.

9. Nepliuev, *op. cit.*, p. 122. The very exaggerations of Feofan Prokopovich's funeral oration are characteristic of this mood (Feofan Prokopovich, *Sochineniia* [Moscow-Leningrad, 1961], pp. 126–29).

10. E. Shmurlo, *Petr Velikii v otsenke sovremennikov i potomstva* (Saint Petersburg, 1912), I.

11. PSZ, #2467 (January 16, 1712).

12. *Ibid.*, #3890 (January 24, 1722).

13. Under the system of equal inheritance that prevailed throughout the eighteenth century (with the exception of a few years after 1714), a title, too, was inherited by all male members of a family. This alone contributed to the rapid devaluation of the title. At the time of its award, and for the individual so distinguished, the title was the culminating expression of a series of rewards for services that the monarch had wanted to recompense more particularly. But the title lost this meaning in the next generation; and if the children of the first holder failed to gain distinction in service, their inherited title conferred them no distinction and carried little value in the eyes of society.

There is some evidence that a titled person possessed of

great wealth cut a better figure in high society in the first quarter of the nineteenth century. But in the final analysis it was wealth *and* service, not the mere title, that were the determining factors. L. Tolstoi very well noted this feature of Russian society in drawing the figure of Pierre Bezukhov.

14. S. N. Glinka, *Zapiski Sergeia Nikolaevicha Glinki* (Saint Petersburg, 1895). Everybody in the eighteenth century took it as a matter of course that access to nobility through service did not extend to the serf population (although a serf who became a soldier could, in theory, rise through the ranks to personal noble status. But such cases were extremely rare.)

15. The most dramatic and symbolic instance—and admittedly one of the most galling ones—was the rise of Aleksandr D. Menshikov. The son of a simple tradesman or artisan (pie baker was the most frequently mentioned profession) became Most Serene Prince (*sviatleishii kniaz'*) and the most important personage in the state. If this had been an exceptional occurrence it would have stirred comment, but not become ground for deep-seated resentment. But Menshikov's career was in fact only the most successful example of a very common phenomenon.

16. Statistical information on the eighteenth century is very scant and not very reliable. Some idea of the increase in the number of officials can be obtained from N. F. Demidova, "Biurokratizatsiia gosudarstvennogo apparata absoliutizma v XVII–XVIII vv.," *Absoliutizm v Rossii* (Moscow, 1964), pp. 206–42. On vital statistics for the eighteenth century cf. V. M. Kabuzan, *Narodonaselenie Rossii v XVIII—pervoi polovine XIX v. (po materialam revizii)* (Moscow, 1963).

17. It was a similar process of individualization, heightened by social and psychological insecurity, and the aspiration to a meaningful role in society, that accounts for the transformation of many members of the Western European bourgeoisies into "*philosophes*" and prototypes of an intelligentsia. Taine and Tocqueville remain the most stimulating writers on this question. See also T. Geiger, *Aufgaben und Stellung der Intelligenz in der Gesellschaft* (Stuttgart, 1949).

18. Bolotov, I, 78.
19. Iu. V. Got'e, *Istoriia oblastnogo upravleniia ot Petra I do Ekateriny II* (Moscow, 1913), I, 183; Gavril Iv. Dobrynin, "Istinnoe povestvovanie ili zhizn' G. Dobrynina im samim pisannaia, 1752–1827," *Russkaia Starina*, III (1871), 567–68.
20. *Zh. S.*, I, 116; *KM*, CXXX, 602.

Ukaz of H. M. the Emperor and Autocrat of All Russia to Soldier Afanasii Diurdin and his aides of the provincial chancelry of Uglich: "You will proceed to the Uglich district, to various estates and patrimonies listed below, and after arrival there send out to Moscow for review all retired noblemen and officers and take a written pledge from them. . . . And if these nobles are not to be found at home, take their children, servants, and peasants and bring them to Uglich . . ." (F. V. Taranovskii, ed., *Akty Uglichskoi provintsial'noi kantseliarii [1719–1726 gg]* [Trudy Iaroslavskoi gubernskoi uchenoi arkhivnoi komissii, kn. V (Moscow, 1909)], II, 63, 72, see also 86–90).

21. *VTS*, LXIII, 37, 182; *ibid.*, LXIX, 254; Bolotov, II, 132, 269.
22. A few typical examples from the innumerable cases found in published sources may serve to illustrate the preceding paragraphs:

Petition of 1727 requesting a raise in rank (*VTS*, LXIII, 232–33):

I am serving Y. I. M. from the year 700 [*i.e.* 1700], first in the Swedish war where I was in the regular army and in combat . . . And in 1722 . . . I was taken out of the regiment as a major and assigned to the College of Justice as procurator, and from that time on I have been in this office without interruption and without home leave. And in 1705 my father was killed in Astrakhan, and the few miserable villages that I inherited and those I owned have deteriorated completely as I could not supervise them, and from this I have been ruined and fallen ill . . .

Petition of 1726 requesting retirement because of age and sickness (*VTS*, LVI, 339–40):

He [Procurator of the College of Commerce Sylvester Gur'ev] has served Their Majesties . . . in the year 204 [*i.e.* 7204 or 1696] in Moscow, and from 1703 on in the regular army as dragoon, and was in combat and has been wounded; from 1722 . . . taken from the rank of major into the Senate as *ekzekutor,* and from there assigned as procurator to the College of Commerce with a colonel's rank . . . where is still serving today.

The Senate suggests that the applicant be given sick leave, but return every year for certification, and be reassigned to the Senate as soon as well enough.

Vasilii Anichkov has served since 7187 (1679) in the army, from 1704 to 1726 on various civil assignments. He is sixty-seven years old, has bad memory. Has two sons, both serving as captains. Senate appoints him as assessor to College of Justice (*VTS,* LXIX, 81).

Report of Senate, 1732: Major Iurii Fedorovich Eropkin released from the army in 1726 for illness, transferred to care of Heraldry. Is to be assigned to civil affairs, and given a one-year leave to cure himself (*KM,* CIV, 250).

Other interesting cases are cited in: *Zh. S.,* I, 53, 338; *VTS,* LVI, 58–60, 386–403, 571–72; *VTS,* LXIX, 111–12, 185–92, 782–83, 786; *ibid.,* XCIV, 244–46; *KM,* CIV, 133–34, 192–93, 232–33, 289–90; *ibid.,* CXVII, 1–2; *ibid.,* CXX, 418–19; *ibid.,* CXXXVIII, 99, 305. Also Bolotov, II, 583; P. G. Liubomirov, "Rod Radishcheva," *A. N. Radishchev— Materialy i issledovaniia* (Moscow, 1936), p. 329; *Po- khozhdenie nekotorogo Rossianina* (Moscow, 1790), p. 2; V. Tatishchev, *Testament de Basile Tatistcheff* (Paris, 1860), p. 31; kn. P. A. Viazemskii, *Fon Vizin* (Saint Petersburg, 1848), p. 180.

23. On occasion, and with great reluctance, some decentralization was permitted, for example the commissions of review set up in Moscow and Saint Petersburg under the local commander-in-chief in the 1720's; cf. for example *VTS,* LXXIX, 130; *KM,* CXI, 88. Records of *smotry* of young noblemen (minors in the sense indicated, *nedorosli*) in the minutes of the Supreme Privy Council, Cabinet of Ministers, and Senate are too numerous to be mentioned here, but cf. for example *KM,* CXIV, 135, 341, 387, 525, 544; CVI, 25–27, 44. There is a reference to Ukaz of July 13, 1732, which put the *smotry* under Cabinet of Ministers in *KM,* CXXX, 14; and an example of the Senate ordering servicemen to be

sent to it for review of their status in *Zh. S.*, I, 245 ff., and II, 54. The Supreme Privy Council on occasion delegated the function to the Senate (*VTS*, CI, 362–63).

". . . Under penalty of natural and political death the Master of Heraldry is to account for all nobles at all times, so that if any person is needed by the Senate he can be presented immediately . . ." (S. Kniaz'kov, "Dvorianstvo vremen Petra Velikogo," *Ocherki iz istorii Petra Velikogo i ego vremeni* [2nd ed.; Saint Petersburg, 1914], p. 355).

". . . we are convinced of the high meaning of this legislation [*i.e.* system of ranks] which gave the Autocracy such a powerful weapon which, as long as it remains in the hands of the rulers, will hardly make it possible to shake the autocratic power based on it" (S. S. Uvarov, "O sisteme chinov v Rossii" [February, 1847, memorandum to Nicholas I] in V. A. Evreinov, *Grazhdanskoe chinoproizvodstvo v Rossii—istoricheskii ocherk* [Saint Petersburg, 1887], Appendix No. 5, p. 83).

24. E. N. Shchepkina, *Starinnye pomeshchiki na sluzhbe i doma, iz semeinoi khroniki* (1578–1762) (Saint Petersburg, 1890), p. 114.

25. On scattered land grants, cf. the papers of the *VTS, KM*. Also "Zapiski Dmitriia Borisovicha Mertvago 1760–1824," *Russkii Arkhiv*, V (1867), Appendix, 37; F. P. Pecherin, "Zapiski o moikh predkakh i o sebe, na pamiat' detiam v 1816 g. sdelannye," *Russkaia Starina*, LXXII (1891), 613; P. G. Liubomirov, "Rod Radishcheva," *loc. cit.*, p. 337; V. Nashchokin, *op. cit.*, p. 110.

26. The picture changed drastically for many only after 1861.

27. In this respect Bolotov is not quite typical. Contrast to the situation in France, Robert Forster, "The Nobility of Toulouse in the Eighteenth Century, a Social and Economic Study," *Johns Hopkins University Studies in Historical and Political Sciences* (Series LXXVIII, No. 1 [Baltimore: Johns Hopkins University Press, 1960]). Also R. Shackleton, *Montesquieu* (New York: Oxford University Press, 1961).

28. P. Viazemskii, "Moskovskoe semeistvo," *Russkii Arkhiv*, 1877, p. 307. Also the works of Karnovich.

29. It has been noted that there never developed in modern

Russia the habit of taking one's family name from the name of one's estate. E. P. Karnovich, *Rodovye prozvaniia i tituly v Rossii* (Saint Petersburg, 1886), pp. 28–29. Contrast this to the French attitude (Valéry Larbaud, *A. O. Barnabooth —ses oeuvres complètes* [2nd ed.; Paris, 1948], p. 235):

Vous connaissez le dicton français: noblesse oblige. Eh bien, c'est toute la définition de la noblesse: elle oblige et ne fais pas autre chose. Elle obligeait celui qui l'avait à n'être que l'homme d'une terre et le vassal de qui avait l'hommage de cette terre. Et aujourd'hui çà n'est pas fini. C'est comme si nous n'avions pas de noms. C'est la terre qui nous prête son nom indéstructible qui passera à d'autres après nous, soit par succession, soit par alliance. Pas d'espérance de nous faire un nom: on l'a déjà fait pour nous . . . .

Cf. also Romanovich-Slavatinskii, *Dvoriantsvo v Rossii ot nachala XVIII veka do otmeny krepostnogo prava* (2nd ed.; Kiev, 1912), pp. 171–72; N. Belozerskaia, "Vliianie perevodnogo romana i zapadnoi tsivilizatsii na russkoe obshchestvo XVIII v.," *Russkaia Starina*, LXXXIII (January, 1895), 132.

30. On settlement in the border areas, cf. S. Aksakov and Bolotov.

31. On the scattered nature of estates, see the memoirs of Derzhavin and—again—Bolotov. Cf. also C. Danilov, *Zapiski napisannye im v 1771 g (1733–1762)* (Moscow, 1842), p. 97; P. I. Poletika, "Vospominaniia Petra Iv. Poletika," *Russkii Arkhiv*, November, 1885, p. 306.

32. Even S. Aksakov, who came from a patriarchal and tightly knit family, spent all his adult life away from the region of his birth and childhood. This fact was noted by P. Chaadaev, who in his first so-called "Philosophical Letter," says, *"Nous sommes tous des voyageurs."* Cf. also *Dnevnaia zapiska Fedora Kozel'skogo 1771 g* (Saint Petersburg, 1774), p. 31.

33. Bolotov, II, pp. 577, 611; N. Karamzin, "Pis'mo sel'skogo zhitelia," *Sochineniia* (1848), III, p. 569.

34. In Muscovite Russia civil functions were not in a separate category (except for clerkships), and administrative assignments were given and carried out by regular military per-

sonnel. It was also easier to rise in rank and receive rewards for military deeds of courage and enterprise.

35. Grigorovich, "Kantsler kniaz' Aleksandr Andreevich Bez-borodko, v sviazi s sobytiiami ego vremeni," *Sbornik IRIO* (Saint Petersburg, 1879), XXVI, 70; *KM*, CXXXVII, 82–83; M. Raeff, "Home, School, and Service in the Life of the Eighteenth-Century Russian Nobleman," *The Slavonic and East European Review*, XL, No. 95 (June, 1962), 295–307.

36. I. U. Dolgorukov, *Povest' o rozhdenii moem, proiskhozhdenii i vsei zhizni—Zapiski kn. I. M. Dolgorukova* (Petrograd, 1916), p. 344; *KM*, CVIII, 24, on the priority given to rank in Guards regiments in citation of official titles.

37. Bolotov, IV, 113–14; *VTS*, LV, 405.

38. Dolgorukov, *op. cit.*, p. 40. Extreme examples of such transfer of habits to the civilian realm would be Governor General of Siberia I. B. Pestel (cf. M. Raeff, *Siberia and the Reforms of 1822* [Seattle: University of Washington Press, 1956]) or the older brother of the Decembrist N. Krivtsov (M. Gershenzon, *Dekabrist Krivtsov i ego brat'ia* [Moscow, 1914]).

39. Peter's practice of a mechanical and numerical (based on population) division of the empire was followed by Catherine the Great and maintained itself into the nineteenth century.

40. M. Raeff, "The Russian Autocracy and its Officials," *Harvard Slavic Studies*, IV (1957), pp. 77–91, and *idem.*, "L'état, le gouvernement et la tradition politique en Russie impériale avant 1861," *Revue d'histoire moderne et contemporaine*, October-December, 1962, pp. 295–307.

41. True enough, the relative geographic and social uniformity of the Empire mitigated this situation somewhat. But the harm of a global and uniform approach to administrative practices was very real and serious, as the constant complaints from the provinces clearly show.

42. The bureaucratic vocabulary of the time contains many words and expressions conveying the idea of movement of papers (*bumagi postupaiut, dvizhenie bumag*, etc.)

43. The absence of independent or autonomous *corps* inter-

médiaires was a contributing factor. The uniformity of the nobility was enhanced by the *smotry* introduced by Peter, which had broken up home ties and local loyalties (Bogoslovskii, *Oblastnaia reforma,* pp. 277, 300).

The theoretical and educational literature stressed the same orientation. Cf. Rozhdestvenskii, *Ocherki po istorii sistem narodnogo prosveshchenia v Rossii v XVIII–XIX vv.* (Zapiski istoriko-filologicheskogo fakul'teta, CIV [Saint Petersburg, 1912]), 207; the popular handbook on natural law (Strube de Piermont, *Ébauche des loix naturelles et du droit primitif* [nouv. éd.: Amsterdam, 1744], p. 31) repeated the point of view. Kurganov, *Pis'movnik,* (5th ed.; Saint Petersburg, 1793) II, 130–31; I. V. Lopukhin, *Blagost' i preimushchestvo edinonachaliia* (Moscow, 1795), p. 4. The curious attitude toward reliance on custom and abstract concepts is well illustrated in the debates of 1767: *UK 1767,* IV, 39; VIII, 152; XXXVI, 23.

44. On the plight and shortage of civil employees, see the memorandum presented by the Duke of Holstein to the Supreme Privy Council in *VTS,* LV, 189.

45. N. Pavlov-Sil'vanskii, *Gosudarevy sluzhilye liudi—proiskhozhdenie russkogo dvorianstva* (Saint Petersburg, 1898), p. 274. For examples of the back-and-forth movement from civil to military assignments, cf: *KM,* CVI, 429–32, 484–87, 557–60; *KM,* CVIII, 340–41, 349–50; KM, CXXXVIII, 49; *Zh. S.,* I, 19–20. For personal testimonies and reminiscences, see *Zapiski Danilova,* pp. 24, 32, 37; Dolgorukov, *op. cit.,* p. 224; Bolotov, I, 695, and III, 727.

On the problem of equivalences of rank between the military and civil branches in case of transfers or mutations, see *Zh. S.,* I, 114, 377, and II, 8–9. For further discussions and decisions in individual cases see *VTS,* LV, 180; *ibid.,* LXXIX, 335; *KM,* CXVII, 602–603; *ibid.,* CXXIV, 126.

A separation between civil and military careers was advocated by V. Tatishchev, *op. cit.,* p. 36.

46. On the nobility's preference for the military for economic reasons, see "Mnenie grafa A. I. Ostermana o sostoianii i potrebnostiakh Rossii v 1740, soobshcheno im zhe," *Pamiatniki novoi russkoi istorii* (Saint Petersburg, 1873), III, 270.

47. Chr. Becker, "Raznochintsy: The Development of the Word and of the Concept," *American Slavic and East European Review*, XVIII, No. 1 (February, 1959), 63–74. Cf. Got'e, *op. cit.*, p. 144; for interesting examples, see *KM*, CXXX, 622–23, and Dobrynin, "Istinnoe povestvovanie ili zhizn' G. Dobrynina im samim pisannaia 1752–1827," *loc. cit.*, p. 570. Also S. A. Tuchkov, *Zapiski Sergeia A. Tuchkova* (Saint Petersburg, 1906), p. 23, and Vigel', *Zapiski*, S. Ia. Shtraikh, ed., I (Moscow, 1928), 174.

48. A borderline case was presented by the petty Ukrainian (Cossack) nobility, whose children were educated in ec-clesiastical schools and then entered government service. Cf. A. F. Shafonskii's observation (*Topograficheskoe opisanie Chernigovskogo namestnichestva*, 1786), cited in M. I. Demkov, *Istoriia russkoi pedagogiki* (2 vols.; Saint Peters-burg, 1897), II, 133–34. Cf. also VTS, LXIX, 7–8; *UK 1767*, XLIII, 10; Bolotov, I, 741, 748, 879; and Gr. Vinskii, "Moe vremia. Zapiski malorossianina o Rossii v tsarstvovanie Ekateriny II (1760–1793)," *Russkii Arkhiv* (1877), *passim.*

49. See the instructions of the Senate and of the Office of the Master of Heraldry to the Commission on Legislation of 1767, in *UK 1767*, XLIII, 15 and 141. This was also the conclusion of the historian Müller (Miller), in Gerhard Friedrich Mueller, *Izvestie o dvorianakh rossiiskikh . . .* (Saint Petersburg, 1790), p. 306. Cf. also Ustimovich, *Mysli i vospominaniia pri chtenii zakonov o dvorianstve* (Moscow, 1886), and the memorandum of the jurist A. I. Kniazev, dated March 3, 1776, and presented to the special committee appointed by Catherine the Great to elaborate statutes for the main classes of the Russian nation, cited by A. N. Filippov, "K voprosu o pervoistochnikakh 'Zhalo-vannoi gramoty dvorianstva,'" *Izvestiia AN SSSR* (6th series; 1926), XX, Nos. 5–6, 430.

50. The best and most concise statement of this is in Shcher-batov, "Primechaniia vernogo syna otechestva na dvorianskie prava na manifest," *Sochineniia*, I (1896), 269–334, in par-ticular 328.

51. Mueller, *op. cit.*, p. 308; V. Nashchokin, *op. cit.*, p. 93.

52. P. de Vaissière, *Gentilshommes campagnards de l'ancienne*

France (2nd ed.: Paris, 1925); M. Bloch, "Sur le passé de la noblesse française: quelques jalons de recherche," *Annales d'histoire économique et sociale,* VIII (1936), 366–78. Cf. also V. A. Grigor'ev, *Reformy oblastnogo upravleniia pri Ekateriny* II (Saint Petersburg, 1910).

53. Bolotov, II, 127. The literary expressions of these attitudes toward Elizabeth and Catherine the Great are too numerous to be cited.

54. Although an echo of this erotically tinged relationship is found again in the reign of Alexander I—as witness the exaltations of Karazin (and their literary equivalent in Tolstoi's Nicholas Rostov).

55. *VTS*, LXIX, 406; *KM*, CXX, 125–26.

56. This is well described, and its political-administrative implications spelled out, in Count Nikita P. Panin's memorandum to Catherine the Great (December 28, 1762), *Sbornik IRIO*, III (1871), 202–17.

57. See Cherniavsky, *Tsar and People* (New Haven: Yale University Press, 1961), the chapter on the "Sovereign Emperor." It meant also an attempt at by-passing the bureaucracy—a course advocated by all traditionalists: Shcherbatov and Karamzin at the turn of the eighteenth century, K. Aksakov and A. Khomiakov in the middle of the nineteenth.

58. The whole idea of the monarch as the *deus ex machina* in solving the problems of his subjects that we find in eighteenth-century novels, comic operas, social criticism, and Utopias (Shcherbatov's and Radishchev's, for example) also fitted well into the notions of enlightened absolutism and state paternalism.

59. Cf. C. Schmitt, "Soziologie des Souveränitätsbegriffs und politische Theologie," *Erinnerungsgabe für Max Weber* (München, 1923), II.

60. As we shall see, however, alienation did set in at the end of the eighteenth century, and it reached its full development in the second quarter of the nineteenth. Nicholas I's Third Section was an attempt, admittedly clumsy and outdated, to restore the lost personal relationship between ruler and subjects. S. Monas, *The Third Section. Police and*

Society in Russia under Nicholas I (Cambridge, Mass.: Harvard University Press, 1961).

61. A curious eighteenth-century attempt at "calculating" the rate of change in Russia and Peter's part in it was M. M. Shcherbatov, "Primernoe vremiaischislitel'noe polozhenie, vo skol'ko by let, pri blagopoluchneishikh obstoiatel'stvakh, mogla Rossiia sama soboiu bez samovlastiia Petra Velikogo, doiti do togo sostoianiia, v kakom ona nyne est' v rassuzhdenii prosveshcheniia i slavy," *Sochineniia*, II (1898), 13–22.

62. This was the burden of the argument made by P. N. Miliukov in his classic *Gosudarstvennoe khoziaistvo v pervoi chetverti XVIII stoletiia i reforma Petra Velikogo* (2nd ed.: Saint Petersburg, 1905). Soviet historians have vigorously contested this thesis: cf. *Ocherki istorii SSSR, XVIII v. (pervaia chetvert')* (Moscow, 1954); E. Zaozerskaia, *Manufaktura pri Petre I,* (Moscow-Leningrad, 1947); E. Spiridonova, *Ekonomicheskaia politika i ekonomicheskie vzgliady Petra I* (Moscow, 1952).

63. *"Il n'est pour bien voir que l'oeil du maître."*—La Fontaine.

64. In addition, greater demands on the productive capacity of the estates had been created because part of the produce had to be sent to the absentee nobleman or marketed for cash to enable the landlord to buy articles needed in service, as well as to pay taxes. The testimony of Bolotov on this is very eloquent. Cf. also the findings of Soviet historians, best summarized in P. K. Alefirenko, *Krest'ianskoe dvizhenie i krest'ianskii vopros v Rossii v 30–50kh godakh XVIII veka* (Moscow, 1958); or N. L. Rubinshtein, *Sel'skoe khoziaistvo Rossii vo vtoroi polovine XVIII v. (istoriko-ekonomicheskii ocherk)* (Moscow, 1957).

65. The best description of this state of affairs is in a memorandum of Biron's (V. Stroev, *Bironovshchina i kabinet ministrov* [Saint Petersburg, 1910], Part II, Vyp. 1, p. 68):

Weiln auff Allerhöchsten Kayserl. Befehl Biss anhero alle von Adel von 15-ten Jahre an, Theils zu Schulen, Theils zu Kriegsdiensten enrolliret und eingeschrieben und dadurch allesambt von Ihren Güthern entfernt werden. Dachero dann sie die Administra-

tion von Ihren Güthern den Prikaschcziken und Starosten über-
lassen, welche mit ihrer übeln Wirtschaft nicht allein das herr-
schaftliche, sondern auch zugleich die Bauern totaliter ruiniren,
wodurch denn viele Edelleuthe in solchen armseligen zustand
gerathen, dass Sie ihre familien ohnmöglich wieder aufhelfen
können; und die Bauern werden nicht nur ruiniret, sondern auch
die Einkünfte des Reiches, durch sothane schlechte Wirthschaft
gegen die sonst gehörige Einnahme sehr vermindert . . .

See also P. I. Iaguzhinskii, "Zapiska o sostoianii Rossii,"
Chteniia (1860), Bk. IV, p. 271.

66. In 1737, in support of his petition for retirement, the sixty-
three-year-old Il'ia Isaev declared that he had been in service
for thirty years, ". . . and for twenty-five years I have been
away from my home, and for this reason deprived of [my]
possessions . . ." *KM*, CXVII, 1–2. See also *ibid.*, CIV, 74–
75; *ibid.*, CXXXVIII, 249–55; *ibid.*, CXLVI, 336; *VTS*,
LXIII, 617–18; *ibid.*, LXIX, 234–35. For further illustrations see Bolotov, I, 26–27, 147, 975; II, 294, 331, 562, 566;
IV, 59. See also I. F. Lukin, "Zhizn' starinnogo russkogo
dvorianina," *Russkii Arkhiv*, III (1865), No. 8, 901. Pertinent
legislation is summarized in A. Romanovich-Slavatinskii, *op.
cit.*, pp. 65–66.

The evidence on retirement for economic reasons is not
conclusive, for frequently noblemen returned to service in
order to make ends meet. Neledinskii-Meletskii, *op. cit.*, p.
254; Grigorovich, *Aleksandr Andreevich Bezborodko, loc.
cit.*, XXVI, 172 (letter on the occasion of the death of
Kochubei's father); S. A. Tuchkov, *op. cit.*, p. 37; A. L.
Del'vig, *Polveka russkoi zhizni—Vospominaniia A. I. Del'-
viga (1820–1870)* (Leningrad, 1930), I, 28; P. G. Liubomirov, "Rod Radishcheva," *loc. cit.*, pp. 308, 331.

67. ". . . but he [father of writer] was so tied to service that
he did not once even go to glance at his possessions. They
remained without any supervision, and during this time one
of the neighbors . . . arbitrarily seized a large amount of
. . . land; and even though the old bailiff, a serf, repeatedly
wrote to my father concerning the unjust claims of the con-
queror, my father did not answer these letters for the same

reason, *i.e.*, that he did not think of anything else but service" ("Byt russkogo dvorianina v raznye epokhi ego zhizni," *Biblioteka dlia chteniia* [Saint Petersburg, 1848], XC, 122). Also Lukin, "Zhizn' starinnogo russkogo dvorianina," *loc. cit.*, p. 911; Bolotov, II, 304, 308.

68. VTS, LV, 218–19, 227 (in 1727, arrears of salary for 1721–24 to be paid out of goods in the College of Foreign Affairs); LXIII, 34–36 (case of 700 rubles of travel expenses incurred during a mission to the Turkish Vizier not paid out for more than ten years), 91, 191. See also *KM*, CIV, 263–64; CVIII, 152–53; CXVII, 84–85 (all the staff of the College of Commerce to be paid in "Siberian goods" and not in cash, except foreigners under contract). See also *Zh. S.*, I, 323, 328; and also Got'e, *op. cit.*, p. 188.

69. Bolotov, I, 178; II, 139–40.

70. "Zapiski Dmitriia Borisovicha Mertvago 1760–1824," *loc. cit.*, p. 156.

71. It may be worthy of note that the initiative in the Supreme Privy Council was taken by foreign dignitaries and councilors (VTS, LXIII [Nos. 78, 79]). Curiously, too, the full decree was never published (Bogoslovskii, *Oblastnaia reforma*, p. 485). Cf. also VTS, LV, 363, 404, 474–75.

72. Peter's law on single inheritance (*PSZ*, #2789) might have provided a satisfactory foundation for the service nobility's economic security. But it was honored mainly in the breach and abolished early in the reign of Anne.

73. Bolotov, I, 630; *Zapiski Danilova*, pp. 34–35.

74. Iaguzhinskii, "Zapiska o sostoianii Rossii," *loc. cit.*, p. 271; *KM*, CXXXVIII, p. 305 (with reference to the decree of 1736 limiting service obligation to twenty-five years). The papers of the Cabinet of Ministers are filled with instances of recall to *smotry* or to duty.

75. Upon the death of Peter II in January, 1730, members of the Supreme Privy Council, led by Prince D. M. Golitsyn, tried to impose "conditions" on Anne of Courland, whom they had elected to the throne. These conditions spelled a limitation of the ruler's autocratic power for the benefit of the Supreme Privy Council. Taking advantage of the rank-

and-file service nobility's opposition to the Supreme Privy
Council, Anne "was pleased to tear up the conditions" and
assume unlimited autocratic power.

The most comprehensive account of this attempt to limit
the autocracy, with reproduction of major documents, is still
D. A. Korsakov, *Votsarenie imperatritsy Anny Ioannovny*
(Kazan, 1880). Cf. also P. Miliukov, "Verkhovniki i shliakhetstvo," *Iz istorii russkoi intelligentsii* (Saint Petersburg,
1903), pp. 1–51 (in French "Les hommes d'en haut et la
noblesse" in *Le Mouvement intellectuel russe*, trad. de J. W.
Bienstock [Paris, 1918], pp. 5–86); W. Recke, "Die Ver-
fassungspläne der russischen Oligarchen im Jahre 1730 und
die Thronbesteigung der Kaiserin Anna Ivanovna," *Zeitschrift für Osteuropäische Geschichte*, II (1911), 11–64 and
161–203; H. Fleischhacker, "1730. Das Nachspiel der
petrinischen Reform," *Jahrbücher für Geschichte Osteuropas*,
VI (1941), 201–74. Selections from the main petitions of
1730 will be found in translation in M. Raeff, *Plans for
Political Reform in Imperial Russia 1730–1905* (Englewood
Cliffs, N.J.: Prentice-Hall, 1966), pp. 41-52.

Recently, a Soviet scholar reviewed the archival evidence
and reached the conclusion, first stated by Recke, that Prince
D. M. Golitsyn had no constitutional plan to complement the
"conditions" imposed on Anne. G. A. Protasov, *Konditsii i
proekty 1730g.* (Avtoreferat dissertatsii na soiskanie stepeni
kandidata istoricheskikh nauk, Moskovskii Oblastnoi Peda-
gogicheskii Institut) (Moscow, 1955); *idem*, " 'Konditsii'
1730 g. i ikh prodolzhenie," *Uchenye Zapiski Tambovskogo
Pedagogicheskogo Instituta*, fasc. XV (1957), 215-31.

76. The strong dissenting voice was that of typical Petrine serviceman Artemii Volynskii, who warned that a turbulent
praetorian guard would develop (he recalled the Russian
precedent of the *streltsy*) if the nobility were not forced to
serve ("Delo Salnikeeva," *Chteniia*, 1868, No. 3, Miscellany
p. 29).

77. High ranks were given very sparingly until approximately
the middle of the eighteenth century. There are numerous
instances of long and honorable service careers ending with
the grade of sergeant or lieutenant. A perusal of the *curricula*

vitae in the papers of the *VTS, KM,* and *Zh. S.* will confirm this general statement.

78. This was particularly true of the navy and artillery (with their technical knowhow) and—in the absence of schools of law and administration—of the civil administration.

79. Bolotov, I, 735, 746.

80. Complaints on the role of the *raznochintsy* can be found in *UK 1767,* VIII, 449, and XLIII, 10. See also *VTS,* LXIII, 725–27; *KM,* XXVI, 413–16; *Zh. S.,* I, 102, 151, for examples of ways in which the government dealt with the situation. Also S. A. Maevskii, "Moi vek (1779–1831)," *Russkaia Starina,* VIII (1875), 130. A satirical summary of a service career by Prince A. A. Gundurov (N. P. Likhachev, "Genealogicheskaia istoriia odnoi pomeshchich'ei biblioteki," *Russkii Bibliofil,* 1913, No. 5, p. 65):

> *Byl nekogda pistsom*
> *Bukhgalterom, sekretarem,*
> *Uezdnym striapchim, ofitserom,*
> *V pekhote, v konnitse sluzhil,*
> *I tselyi mesiats byl,*
> *O rok! v Kazane gazeterom . . .*

81. *VTS,* LV, 190; *UK 1767,* XLIII, 10; A. Kulomzin, ed., "Pervyi pristup v tsarstvovanie Ekateriny II k sostavleniiu Vysochaishei Gramoty dvorianstvu rossiiskomu" in N. Kalachov, *Materialy dlia istorii russkogo dvorianstva* (Saint Petersburg, 1885), II, 40. Other illustrations of this feeling are found in the comic operas written and performed in the eighteenth century (cf. *Rossiiskii Featr*).

82. For instance "Matiushkin's project," Korsakov, *op. cit.,* Appendix, pp. 9–11; "Grekov's project" in V. Kashpirev, ed., *Pamiatniki novoi russkoi istorii—sbornik istoricheskikh statei i materialov,* I (Saint Petersburg, 1871), Part II, 4–5; "Outline submitted to the rank-and-file nobility," in *ibid.,* pp. 7–8. These demands, incidentally, are not given much prominence and are phrased in the most general and vague way.

83. The preference was dramatically illustrated when Elizabeth ennobled all soldiers of the Guards units that helped her to the throne in 1741.

84. *PSZ,* #5811, dated July 29, 1731—which also spells out the

relation of Cadets to Guards and school obligation for service. V. A. Evreinov, *Grazhdanskoe chinoproizvodstvo v Rossii—istoricheskii ocherk* (Saint Petersburg, 1887), pp. 38–39.

85. It is fair to assume that the nobles did not think at all of the peasantry in 1730. The only commoners who could benefit from this attitude were those who might gain access to the nobility—foreigners, children of the clergy, and, on occasion, wealthy merchants.

86. Bolotov, II, 603, 604. Cf. also Ukaz of 1726 ordering nobility to retain in retirement the "civilized" dress acquired in service (Bogoslovskii, *Oblastnaia reforma*, p. 9).

87. Although regimental and garrison schools were established to train the children of soldiers, subaltern officers, and townspeople. *Zh. S.*, I, 226; *VTS*, LVI, 316, 318–19.

88. *VTS*, LXIX, 176–77; *KM*, CIV, 419; *ibid.*, CXIV, 402; *Zh. S.*, I, 20; *UK 1767*, IV, 217.

Among the numerous memoir literature on this point, we may cite: Bolotov, I, 25, 985; I. M. Dolgorukov, *op. cit.*, p. 16; P. I. Poletika, "Vospominaniia Petra Iv. Poletiki," *loc. cit.*, p. 320; N. G. Levshin, "Domashnii pamiatnik Nikolaia Gavrilovicha Levshina," *Russkaia Starina*, VIII (December, 1873), 842 (cites the saying: "Military service is the soul of everything, one is taught everything there"); S. A. Tuchkov, *op. cit.*, p. 3; V. A. Bibikov, *Zapiski o zhizni i sluzhbe Aleksandra Il'icha Bibikova* (Saint Petersburg, 1817), p. 152; "Byt russkogo dvorianina . . .", *loc. cit.*, p. 15; *Zerkalo liubopytstva*, 1791, p. 11.

89. The most famous example is the great poet Gavril R. Derzhavin; see his *Zapiski* (Moscow, 1860). A later instance was the soldier poet Denis Davydov (cf. Vl. Orlov, "Denis Davydov," *Puti i sud'by, literaturnye ocherki* [Moscow-Leningrad, 1963], pp. 61–101).

90. Quartering fell on the bourgeois homes of the Baltic provinces. The German nobility was particularly suspicious of the Russians and wary of making contacts. Cf. Bolotov; also *Pokhozhdenie Rossianina*, 1790, Part I, pp. 29–30, 59–60.

91. Bolotov's memoirs are the most complete record of the experiences of someone who benefited from the military campaign abroad to better himself. For a description of the

whole picture, cf. Georg von Frantzius, *Die Okkupation Ostpreussens durch die Russen im Siebenjährigen Kriege, mit besonderer Rücksichtigung der russischen Quellen* (Berlin, 1916). Cf. also Protas'ev, "Stranitsy starogo dnevnika," *Istoricheskii Vestnik*, 1887, No. 11, p. 410; S. A. Tuchkov, *op. cit.*, p. 6–7.

92. Ukaz of May 31, 1726 (*PSZ*, #4893).

93. *KM*, CXXIV, 207; CXLVI, 479–80. A. Veselovskii, *Prosvetitel'nyi vek i Aleksandrovskaia pora* (Moscow, 1916), p. 90.

94. "*Otechestvo nam Tsarskoe Selo.*"

95. On the question of rootlessness and new attachments, see also M. Raeff, "Staatsdienst, Aussenpolitik, Ideologien," *Jahrb. für Gesch. Osteuropas*, VII–2 (1959), 147–81, and *idem, The Decembrist Movement* (Englewood Cliffs, N.J.: Prentice-Hall, 1966), Introduction.

96. D. Mornet, *Les origines intellectuelles de la Révolution française 1715–1787* (5th ed.; Paris, 1954); P. Grosclaude, *La vie intellectuelle à Lyon dans la deuxième moitié du XVIIIe siècle* (Paris, 1933); L. Trénard, *Lyon de "l'Encyclopédie" au préromantisme* (Paris, 1958); Forster, *op. cit.*, Shackleton, *op. cit.*

97. And they were combined with efforts at reproducing Western city conditions on the estate. The mixture, with interest for Western inspiration predominant, can be seen in Bolotov's activities as steward of an imperial domain.

98. This helps to explain the great resentment against laws that restricted foreign travel (especially in the reign of Paul I).

99. The best known cases are those of Fonvizin and Karamzin. On this question, cf. H. Rogger, *National Consciousness in Eighteenth-Century Russia* (Cambridge, Mass.: Harvard University Press, 1960).

100. This is not to deny that—especially in the first three quarters of the eighteenth century—many poorly educated and not very successful noblemen yearned to return to their homes and shed the appurtenances of Western civilization. In point of fact, however, few did completely. Only in their pattern of entertainment do we notice a preservation of traditional customs, probably because they involved the peasantry and domestics as well as the masters.

101. For example, the role of Derzhavin as governor of Tambov (I. I. Dubasov, "Tambovskii krai v kontse XVIII i nachale XIX stoletiia," *Istoricheskii Vestnik*, XVIII [1884], 134). Also B. L. Modzalevskii, ed., "Zapiski P. S. Baturina 1780–1798," *Golos Minuvshego*, 1918, No. 1, pp. 74 ff; Dolgorukov, *op. cit.*, p. 277; S. N. Glinka, *op. cit.*, p. 14; A. Artem'ev, "Kazanskie gimnazii v XVIII v.," *Zh. M. N. Pr.*, CLXXIV (July, 1874), 20; G. Gukovskii, *Ocherki po istorii russkoi literatury XVIII v.* (Moscow-Leningrad, 1936), p. 10; V. Semennikov, "Literaturnaia i knigopechatnaia deiatel'nost' v provintsii v kontse XVIII i v nachale XIX vv," *Russkii Bibliofil*, 1911, Bk. VI, pp. 15, 21.

102. Jacob Fries, *Beschreibung der Stadt Weliki Ustiug (1791)* (Manuscript, G. von Asch Collection), No. 163, p. 32; *Drammaticheskii Slovar'* (Moscow, 1787), Introduction, p. 4; Semennikov, "Literaturnaia i knigopechatnaia deiatel'nost' . . . ," *loc. cit.*, p. 32; Artem'ev, "Kazanskie gimnazii v XVIII v.," *loc. cit.*, May, 1874), p. 66; *UK 1767*, IV, 205; and the injunction of *O dolzhnostiakh cheloveka*, p. 127.

103. A. Veselovskii, *Prosvetitel'nyi vek i Aleksandrovskaia pora* (Moscow, 1916), p. 90; Semennikov, "Literaturnaia i knigopechatnaia deiatel'nost' . . . ," *loc. cit.*, p. 20; E. I. Rubinshtein, "Knigopechatanie v russkoi provintsii XVIII v.," *400 let russkogo knigopechataniia (1564–1917)*, (Moscow, 1964), I, 200–209; *UK 1767*, IV, 160.

104. The education received in ecclesiastical schools also emphasized the "rational" and universal point of view. This explains the easy success that graduates of these schools had in government service (cf. Raeff, *M. M. Speransky—Statesman of Imperial Russia* (The Hague, 1957), Chap. 1, and *idem*, "L'état, le gouvernement, et la tradition politique," *loc. cit.*). Cf. also A. Kartashev, *Ocherki po istorii tserkvi* (Paris, 1959), II, 540.

105. The creative role of Peter was emphasized not only by the generation that had known him (cf. I. I. Nepliue, *op. cit.*, for example), but throughout the eighteenth century. Some illustrations are cited in Raeff, "L'état, le gouvernement et la tradition politique," *loc. cit.*; also *Rastushchii Vinograd*, II (January, 1786), 6–13.

106. On the *Kulturträger* role of the retired serviceman, see Bolotov, II, 605, 661; III, 754; IV, 513, 708. Also, Ia. P. Shakhovskoi, *Zapiski, pisannye im samim* (3rd ed.; Saint Petersburg, 1872), p. 184; Ia. O. Otroshchenko, "Zapiski generala Otroshchenko," *Russkii Vestnik*, September, 1877, p. 127; S. V. Drukovtsev, *Ekonomicheskoe nastavlenie dvorianam. . . . ,* (Saint Petersburg, 1781), p. 14; *UK 1767*, VIII, 507; L. B. Svetlov, " 'Obshchestvo liubitelei rossiiskoi uchenosti' pri Moskovskom universitete," *Istoricheskii Arkhiv*, V (1950), 304.

107. For a brief summary, see J. Blum, *Lord and Peasant in Russia from the Ninth to the Nineteenth Centuries* (Princeton, N.J.: Princeton University Press, 1961), Chaps. 19–22; also M. Confino, *Domaines et seigneurs en Russie vers la fin du XVIIIe siècle (Étude de structures agraires et de mentalités économiques)* (Paris, 1963 [Collection historique de l'Institut d'Études slaves, XVIII]). The vast Soviet literature on serf economy and exploitation can be located with the help of the *Istoriia SSSR, Ukazatel' sovetskoi literatury 1917–1952* (2 vols.; Moscow, 1956) as well as the books by Alefirenko and Rubinshtein cited earlier. The standard pre-Soviet monographs are by V. I. Semevskii, *Krest'iane v tsarstvovanie imperatritsy Ekateriny II* (2 vols.; Saint Petersburg, 1903) and *Krest'ianskii vopros v Rossii v XVIII i pervoi polovine XIX veka* (2 vols.; Saint Petersburg, 1888).

108. Cf. Confino, *Domaines et seigneurs* . . . ; N. L. Rubinshtein, *Sel'skoe khoziaistvo*, Chap. 3, sect. 1 (and bibl. references therein).

109. Dobrynin, "Zapiski . . . ," *loc. cit.*, pp. 567–68; Bolotov, II, 723–24.

110. The decree of May 31, 1726, cited in Bogoslovskii, *Oblastnaia reforma*, p. 9, required that German garb and uniforms be worn while on leave and during retirement. Uniforms were designed for all noblemen according to area. (Collection of G. von Asch, Universitätsbibliothek, Goettingen, No. 187, 42 plates of uniforms for nobility.) The uniforms were cut identically, but the color and ornamental details varied from area to area. Thus there were three colors for the coat: blue (for North and Northeast), red (for

central and central-western regions), and brown (for the Ukraine). It is interesting to note that the areas were vaguely and arbitrarily defined. When noblemen gathered for common business, they devised procedures copied from the military (Bolotov, III, 225; *UK 1767*, IV, 397).

111. Bolotov, II, 342; III, 66; IV, 30. Rozhdestvenskii, *Ocherki istorii sistem* . . . , p. 95.

112. The situation did not exclude occasional instances of strong personal bonds and attachments between master and serf; but even in these cases the crucial element of mutual understanding was lacking (*e.g.* Oblomov and his Zakhar, or Bolotov's serf tutor—the parallel to the ante-bellum South is striking).

113. Bolotov, III, 1110; see also Bolotov's well-known account of Pugachev's execution (III, 488–91, 496). Cf. also Alefirenko, *op. cit.*, and V. V. Mavrodin, *Krest'ianskaia voina v Rossii v 1773–1775—Vosstanie Pugacheva* (Leningrad, 1961), I.

114. Bolotov, II, 746; *Zapiski Danilova*, pp. 42–43; V. N. Zinov'ev, "Zhurnal puteshestvii po Germanii, Italii, Frantsii i Anglii 1784–88," *Russkaia Starina*, XXIII (1878), 104 (note).

115. This realization first took the form of protective and authoritarian paternalism toward the peasants. Cf. Bogoslovskii, *Oblastnaia reforma*, p. 517; E. Dashkova, "Bumagi kn. E. R. Dashkovoi," *loc. cit.*, p. 137; M. Confino, "La politique de tutelle des seigneurs russes envers leurs paysans vers la fin du XVIIIe siècle," *Revue des Études Slaves*, XXXVII (1960), 39–69. Marshall S. Shatz has prepared an article on the notions of paternalism toward serfs and peasants displayed in eighteenth-century comic operas.

116. Notions like those of Boulainvilliers in France that the nobility came from a racially different and superior stock found no echo in Russia (most probably because of the well-known ethnically mixed origin of most Russian noble families).

117. When reference to family was made, it was to stress the favorable milieu that a noble family provided for the education and spiritual development of their children. This was the view defended most ardently by Prince M. M. Shcherba-

tov, especially at the Commission on Legislation of 1767 (cf. M. M. Shcherbatov, *Sochineniia*, I [1896], 1–218).

118. These beliefs found their fullest expression during the eighteenth century in the project of a charter of the nobility elaborated by a committee of the Commission on Legislation of 1767, cf. in particular *UK 1767*, XXXII, p. 579. Also P. I. Shuvalov, "Predlozhenie Pravitel'stvuiushchemu Senatu general fel'dtsekhmeistera grafa P. I. Shuvalova ob uchrezh-denii artilleriiskoi i inzhenernoi shkol" *Artilleriiskii Zhurnal*, 1885, No. 5, pp. 479–80.

119. "Cherty nravov sto let tomu nazad," *Russkii Arkhiv*, V (1867), p. 190; S. A. Tuchkov, *op. cit.*, p. 23.

The aspiration for special status for the nobility is illus-trated by Bolotov's admiration of the "civilized" way of life he witnessed in Königsberg (Bolotov, I, 861). Later, he made his own a notion of nobility based on honor, virtue, and a sense of duty toward his society (*idem*, I, 827; III, 105; and his poem IV, 1210–1212).

The term *kholop* used by noblemen in addressing the Tsar in Muscovy was replaced by *rab* in 1702, and not until 1786 did Catherine the Great abolish this custom and order that all nobles refer to themselves as *vernopodannyi* (loyal). The nobility was referred to as "noble" only since the Ukaz of 1754 (*PSZ*, #10 558). Cf. Romanovich-Slavatinskii, *op. cit.*, pp. 74, 542; Evreinov, *op. cit.*, p. 9, note; Bogoslovskii, *Byt i nravy russkogo dvorianstva v pervoi polovine XVIII v.* (Moscow, 1906), p. 51; V. Surin, *Lichnost' i gosudarstvo v russkoi literature vtoroi poloviny XVIII v.* (Kharkov, 1910), p. 4, 8. For repercussions in educational policy and practice, cf. *VTS*, LV, 119; M. I. Demkov, *op. cit.*, II, 187–88 (in-stead of corporal punishment, a punished student should be dressed in peasant's garb). On the basis of this high notion of the honor of the nobility, Count S. R. Vorontsov objected to various edicts concerning the right to display of luxury "Zapiska grafa S. R. Vorontsova o dvorianstve," *Arkhiv kn. Vorontsova*, XVI (Moscow, 1880), p. 297.

The matter received the widest repercussion at the Com-mission on Legislation of 1767. Catherine the Great in her Nakaz (Bk. XV, § 360) had defined nobility as an honorable title. The deputies expatiated on this theme, citing specific examples or raising particular demands to justify such a definition: cf. *UK 1767*, IV, 148, 152, 288; VIII, 107, 495; XXXVI, 15.

120. The expression current at the time, *"byt' v sluchae"* (*i.e.* be in a favorable situation, have a chance) well expresses the accidental, chance character of the connection, as everywhere and always the favorites' energies were completely absorbed by efforts to secure the maximum personal, material advantages while "chance" lasted.

121. Nepliuev said: "This monarch brought our fatherland to the level of other countries; he taught us to recognize that we too are human beings; in short, whatever you see in Russia has its beginning in him, and whatever will be done in the future will be taken from him." This well-known remark of his, on hearing the news of the death of Peter the Great, is cited in Nepliuev, *op. cit.*, p. 122. Also Tatishchev's preface to his history (V. N. Tatishchev, *Istoriia Rossiiskaia*, A. I. Andreev, S. N. Valk, M. N. Tikhomirov, eds. [Moscow-Leningrad, 1962], I, 87).

122. It is only in the acts of 1775 and 1785 that we may detect the indirect influence of Baltic patterns and practices. Even the discussions of 1762 and 1767 provide no evidence that the Baltic model was present in the minds of the Russians. Cf. Ia. Zutis, *Ostzeiskii vopros v XVIII veke* (Riga, 1946).

123. We are reminded of R. Redfield's concepts of "great" and "small" tradition that live simultaneously in a society undergoing rapid cultural transformation. In Russia, as eighteenth-century literature kept stressing, the new norms ("great" tradition) pertained to public and intellectual life, while the old patterns ("small" tradition) still prevailed within the framework of family and private relations. Nor is the presence of a double standard very surprising among new men who, like the *nouveaux riches* of other times and places, arrogantly display their recently acquired self-assertion at the expense of those at their mercy.

124. This was particularly true of the Ukraine. Cf. also Bolotov, I, 879; II, 778.

125. As a means for educational and cultural achievement, money

and service opportunities were much more important than either birth or family origins.

126. The same factors explain the easy acceptance of educated bastard children, for example I. Betskoi, I. Pnin, V. Zhukovskii, etc.

127. Bolotov, I, 741, 939; *Zh. S.*, I, 102; and the discussions at the Commission on Legislation for illustration of the stress on and role of education (*UK 1767*, IV, 246; XIV, 495).

128. Belles-lettres would provide the best illustration (Fonvizin, Narezhnyi, Derzhavin, Radishchev). Also, V. A. Stoiunin, "Nasha sem'ia i ee istoricheskie sud'by," *Pedagogicheskie Sochineniia* (3rd ed.; (Saint Petersburg, 1911), p. 22; Dolgorukov, *op. cit.*, p. 124; *UK 1767*, IV, 216–17.

129. Ustimovich, *Mysli i vospominaniia pri chtenii zakonov o dvorianstve* (Moscow, 1886), pp. 47–48; Kulomzin, "Pervyi pristup . . ." *loc. cit.*, gives the comments of N. Panin and the conclusion of the committee appointed to study the effects of the Act of 1762 and draft a statute for the nobility (pp. 36, 38, 39, 40, 49, 64). Cf. also Lukin, "Zhizn' starinnogo dvorianina," *loc. cit.*, p. 924; Rozhdestvenskii, *op. cit.*, p. 353; N. Bulich, *Iz pervykh let Kazanskogo universiteta 1805–1819* (2d ed.; Saint Petersburg, 1904), p. 42; *Drammaticheskii slovar'* (Moscow, 1787), Preface; Strube de Piermont, *Lettres russiennes* (n. pl., 1760), p. 232–33; *Sobesednik liubitelei rossiiskogo slova*, I, No. 1 (1783), 151, and II, No. 3, 182. In his announcement of a course in natural law, the historian Christian Schlötzer describes his auditors in Göttingen: *"Tous les auditeurs étaient anoblis par le désir commun de former leur esprit et d'acquérir des connaissances utiles"* and sets them up as models for the Russian noble youth (Chrétien de Schlötzer, *Adresse à la jeune noblesse russe* [Moscow, September, 1804], p. 1).

130. Among the higher bureaucracy, discussion of a new definition of the nobility and its privileges had been initiated in 1763. Cf. the decree of February 11, 1763, and the Report of the Commission on the Rights and Privileges of the Russian Nobility in *Sbornik IRIO*, VII (1871), 232, 238 ff. The essentials of the report were later incorporated in the Charter of 1785.

131. Besides the minutes of the discussions published in the *Sbornik IRIO,* the secondary literature on the Commission summarizes the instructions given to the deputies from the nobility by their electors (A. Presniakov, "Dvorianskii i krest'ianskii vopros v nakazakh" and "Dvorianskii i krest'ianskii vopros v Ekaterininskoi komissii," *Velikaia Reforma* (Moscow, 1911) I, II; V. N. Bochkarev, *Voprosy politiki v russkom parlamente XVIII v.* (Tver', 1923).

132. *UK 1767,* VIII, 107; XXXII, 203, 209, 578; LXVIII, 363–64. It may be interesting to note, as it is characteristic of the political simple-mindedness of the nobility, that the debate rarely turned to these general issues, but dealt only with superficial, technical matters involved in the award and proof of nobility.

133. *UK 1767,* IV, 149, 150; XXXII, 180–82, 184.

134. Of course, the arguments were made *ad usum delphini;* they had to hide arrogant claims and defend selfish interests. But such a defense had to be conducted in ways acceptable to contemporaries and in terms that reflected their basic outlook, their system of values. And state service was a key element of this value system. When tracing the history and development of political attitudes and ideologies, it is as important to pay attention to the manner in which selfish interests are camouflaged as it is necessary to know the nature of these interests themselves.

135. Besides the opinions of Shcherbatov referred to earlier, see also those of Kurakin in V. N. Aleksandrenko, *Russkie diplomaticheskie agenty v Londone v XVIII v.* (Warsaw, 1897), I, 378, note 5.

136. *UK 1767,* XXXVI, 15, 16, 17; Kulomzin, "Pervyi pristup . . ." *loc. cit.,* pp. 49–50; also *O dolzhnostiakh cheloveka i grazhdanina* (Saint Petersburg, 1783), p. 135 (the book was commissioned by Catherine the Great, and she may have helped to edit it). N. Karamzin, as usual, gave expression to this change of orientation in his "Rytsar' nashego vremeni" and "O novom obrazovanii narodnogo prosveshcheniia v Rossii," both in his *Sochineniia,* A. Smirdin, ed. (Saint Petersburg, 1848), III, 263, 352.

137. *UK 1767,* XXXII, Appendix II, 575 ff.

138. On the impact of the service orientation on discussions and proposals for corporate status of the nobility, cf. A. Kulomzin, "Pervyi pristup . . ." *loc. cit.*, pp. 13–71, and N. Panin, "Formy manifestu, kakoi rassuzhdaiutsia, ne mozhet li byt' ugoden k izdaniiu pri zakonnom po predopredeleniiu Bozheskomu vozshestvii na Prestol Naslednika" (1784) in E. S. Shumigorskii, *Imperator Pavel I—zhizn' i tsarstvovanie* (Saint Petersburg, 1907), Appendix, pp. 22–35.

139. *VTS*, LXIII, 596–97, 658–59; LXIX, 716–20, 856; CI, 311–12. Also *KM*, CIV, 450; CXVII, 650–52; CXXX, 181–83. Also the petitions in 1730 in Korsakov, *op. cit.*, and Kulomzin, "Pervyi pristup . . . ," *loc. cit.*, pp. 29, 32–34, 58, 59. For contemporary reactions, see Bolotov, II, 75; "Poslanie k slovu tak," *Sobesednik liubitelei rossiiskogo slova*, I, No. 1 (1783), 18, and for the end of the eighteenth century, Vigel', *op. cit.*, I, 70, note.

On the police in the eighteenth century, cf. V. I. Veretennikov, *Iz istorii tainoi kantseliarii 1731–1762 (ocherki)* (Kharkov, 1911); N. B. Golikova, "Organy politicheskogo syska i ikh razvitie v XVII–XVIII vv.," *Absoliutizm v Rossii*, pp. 243–80 (and the literature cited therein). See also G. Esipov, *Liudi starogo veka (Rasskazy iz del Preobrazhenskogo i Tainogo Prikazov)* (Saint Petersburg, 1880).

140. Cf. Dolgorukov, *op. cit.*, p. 16, for a contrast with the situation in Western Europe. *Ächtung*, for ex., was a moral condemnation that did not change the individual's legal status and necessarily affect his property. O. Brunner, *Land und Herrschaft (Grundfragen der territorialen Verfassungsgeschichte Oesterreichs im Mittelalter)* (4th ed.; Wien-Wiesbaden, 1959), Chap. I.

141. *UK 1767*, XXXVI, 360 ff.

142. Bolotov, II, 567, 637, 681–82, 693, 754, 866, 911, 932.

143. Likhachev, "Genealogicheskaia istoriia biblioteki," *loc. cit.*, p. 38; Ustimovich, *op. cit.*, pp. 78, 101.

144. A. Filippov, "K voprosu o pervoistochnikakh 'zhalovannoi gramoty dvorianstva'," *loc. cit.*; I. I. Ditiatin, "K istorii 'zahlovannykh gramot' dvorianstvu i gorodam 1785 g.," *Russkaia Mysl'*, 1885, Nos. 4–6, (also in his *Stat'i po istorii russkogo prava* [Saint Petersburg, 1896], pp. 49–152); A. V.

Florovskii, "K istorii teksta zhalovannoi gramoty dvorianstvu 1785 g.," *Russkii Istoricheskii Zhurnal,* 1917, Bks. III–IV, pp. 186–94.

145. See Narezhnyi's satirical picture in his *Rossiiskii Zhil Blaz.* Also Neledinskii-Meletskii, *Khronika nedavnoi stariny—iz arkhiva kn. Obolenskogo-Neledinskogo-Meletskogo* (Saint Petersburg, 1876), p. 254.

146. Cf. the definition of landowner in *Zemledel'cheskii Zhurnal* for 1821, as cited in M. Aleksandrov, *Gosudarstvo, biurokratiia i absoliutizm v istorii Rossii* (Saint Petersburg, 1910), p. 58.

147. In fact, albeit indirectly, it became the nobility's exclusive privilege only in the reign of Catherine the Great. But already under Alexander I this monopoly status was infringed. There are some interesting remarks on this in G. Sacke, "Aufhebung des Grundbesitzmonopols des russischen Adels," *Jahrbücher für Geschichte Osteuropas,* VI (1941), 92–105.

148. It may not be amiss to recall in this connection Pokrovskii's argument that the capitation tax (*podushnaia*) on the serfs was in fact a tax levied on their owners (who were responsible for its payment to the state). Pokrovskii quotes the definition of a contemporary foreign diplomat that "the *podushnaia* was a tax paid by every *pomeshchik* on his serfs" (M. N. Pokrovskii, *Russkaia istoriia s drevneishikh vremen, v 4kh tomakh* [Moscow, 1933], III, 45).

149. These features may help to explain the survival—and in many cases even the strengthening—of the role, including police functions, played by the village commune in peasant life.

150. In short, the Russian nobleman had secured the rights of *proprietas* without ever obtaining those of *potestas.* Very much like a modern farmer, but in contrast to the West European feudal lord, he was a proprietor and a master (*barin, gospodin*), but not a lord (*gosudar'*) in the eyes of his peasants.

151. Cf. Hans Rosenberg, *Bureaucracy, Aristocracy, and Autocracy—The Prussian Experience 1660–1815* (Cambridge, Mass.: Harvard University Press, 1958). There is also a great contrast with the position of the planters in ante-

bellum Southern states. As in Russia, the planters' rights over his slaves stopped at the border of his estate; but in America the plantation owner also controlled all means of coercion and political sovereignty in the state governments. The Russian noble had no such power over the Emperor's administration.

152. Kulomzin, "Pervyi pristup . . . ," *loc. cit.*, pp. 31–32, as well as the opinions of M. L. Vorontsov (*Arkhiv kn. Vorontsova*, IV) and N. Panin in Kulomzin, "Pervyi pristup . . ." *loc. cit.*, and in Shumigorskii, *op. cit.*

153. *PSZ*, #14 392 and #16 187.

154. Some obscurities remained, however, especially with respect to the legal definition of nobility. These were eliminated only by the Svod Zakonov.

155. Romanovich-Slavatinskii, *op. cit.*, pp. 53–55.

156. The name of the office changed a great deal throughout the nineteenth century, although its functions did not.

157. Baron S. A. Korf, *Dvorianstvo i ego soslovnoe upravlenie za stoletie 1762–1855 godov* (Saint Petersburg, 1906).

158. Only the *zemstvo* legislation, under quite different circumstances, took decisive steps in that direction, but even then the effort was ultimately cut short in the reign of Alexander III and the events of the first years of the twentieth century. Without the acts of 1775 and 1785, however, even the limited success of the *zemstvo* reform would have been unlikely. Cf. G. Fischer, *Russian Liberalism: From Gentry to Intelligentsia* (Cambridge, Mass.: Harvard University Press, 1958); V. Leontovitsch, *Geschichte des Liberalismus in Russland* (Frankfurt a. Main, 1957); A. Vucinich, "The State and the Local Community," *The Transformation of Russian Society—Aspects of Social Change since 1861*, C. E. Black, ed. (Cambridge, Mass.: Harvard University Press, 1960), pp. 191–209.

159. Bolotov, IV, 1294; Dolgorukov, *op. cit.*, pp. 74, 277.

160. Bolotov, for example, viewed his estates in the steppe region like colonies to which he had no genuine ties (Bolotov, III, 1124). He was also reluctant to participate in local elections—a reluctance shared by many, as witness the decline of participants in these elections over the years follow-

ing 1775 (cf. *Sobranie sochinenii, vybrannykh iz mesia-tseslovov na raznye gody*, IV [1790], 209).

161. In addition to S. A. Korf, *op. cit.*, see also V. F. Zheludkov, "Vvedenie gubernskoi reformy 1775 goda," *Uchenye zapiski* (Leningradskogo gosudarstvennogo pedagogicheskogo insti-tuta imeni A. I. Gertsena) (Leningrad, 1962), CCXXIX, 197–226.

162. The Emperors Paul I, Alexander I, and Nicholas I never disguised their scorn for elected local officials and gave preference to the appointed governors in case of conflict. For the average nobleman's disdain of elective offices, cf. Bolotov, IV, 1289.

163. "Vospominaniia S. V. Skalon," *Istoricheskii Vestnik*, XLIV (May-June, 1891), 606.

164. Dolgorukov, *op. cit.*, p. 249; Bolotov, III, 721; A. T. Bolotov, *Pamiatnik protekshikh vremen, ili kratkie istoricheskie zapiski o byvshikh proisshestviiakh i o nosivshiesia v narode slukhakh* (Moscow, 1875), pp. 2–3, 64.

165. The obvious exception to this pattern was the marshal of the nobility who was simultaneously a high dignitary with good connections and interests in Saint Petersburg.

166. In fact, there was little security even in the formal exemp-tions, for an imperial decree (obtained by God knows what means) or judicial decision could deprive an individual of nobility and subject him to corporal punishment.

167. E. R. Dashkova, "Bumagi kniagini E. R. Dashkovoi (urozh-dennoi grafinei Vorontsovoi)," *Arkhiv kn. Vorontsova*, XXI, 138.

168. It was not truly "aristocratic," for it included several high dignitaries who were almost *homines novi* themselves, and it did not stress the element of birthright or tradition, but rather wealth and education.

169. N. Panin's proposal in *Sbornik IRIO*, III (1871), pp. 202–17. See the objections to the plan by Quartermaster General Villebois in K. L. Blum, *Graf Jakob Johann v. Sievers und Russland zu dessen Zeit* (Leipzig-Heidelberg, 1864), pp. 44–45.

170. For a summary, see M. Raeff, "Le climat politique et les

projets de réforme dans les premières années du règne d'Alex-andre Ier," *Cahiers du Monde Russe et Soviétique*, II, No. 4 (Octobre-Décembre, 1961), 415–33, and *idem, M. M. Speransky*, Chap. 2.

171. It may be worthy of note that the assumptions underlying the proposals of the "aristocratic orientation" at the end of the eighteenth century were revived—in a somewhat mod-ernized form—by the Slavophiles of the middle nineteenth century. In both cases there was a desire to develop a body of "intermediaries" between people and Tsar that could be entrusted with the responsibility of administration and eco-nomic progress on the local level. In both instances the proposals aroused the successful opposition of service nobles and officials, as well as the distrust of the Emperor. When Alexander III finally adopted this point of view it was too late, and its intent was interpreted as an effort at bolstering a class in decline.

172. M. Confino, "Seigneurs et intendants en Russie aux XVIIIe-XIXe siècles," *Revue des Études Slaves*, XII, Nos. 1–4 (1962), 61–91; *idem*, "La comptabilité des domaines privés en Russie dans la seconde moitié du XVIIIe siècle," *Revue d'Histoire Moderne et Contemporaine*, I, No. 3 (1961), 5–34.

173. In a sense, this would encourage a return to the pattern of regional loyalties and corporate solidarities that had begun to emerge in northeastern Russia in the seventeenth century and had been cut short by the reforms of Peter the Great.

174. For a frank opinion, see Grand Duc Nicolas Mikhailovitch, *Le Comte Paul Stroganov* (Paris, 1905), II, 37–38.

175. In the category of non-noble officials we may also include the small, poor, and low-born nobles (Cossacks) from the Ukraine and the southwestern borderlands who had gone through ecclesiastical schools (see note 48).

176. Max Weber's formulation of the "ideal type" of the bu-reaucracy can be found in his *Wirtschaft und Gesellschaft* (Tübingen, 1956, Chap. 9, section 3 (pp. 559–87); M. Raeff, "The Russian Autocracy and Its Officials," *loc. cit.*

For an introductory discussion of the Russian bureaucratic thought pattern, see Frederick I. Kaplan, "Tatiščev and

Kantemir, Two Eighteenth-Century Exponents of a Russian Bureaucratic Style of Thought," *Jahrbücher für Geschichte,* XIII, No. 4 (December, 1965), 496–510.

177. Even when he was given estates for his services, the low-born official remained more interested in his salary and service rank (Speranskii, for example). Of course, the difference between Russia and the West is striking; in the West officials were drawn from the bourgeoisie and tended to become landowning members of the nobility with local ties and roles. (In Russia, of course, there was no bourgeoisie that was endeavoring to become part of the "aristocracy" as the *noblesse de robe* had been in France.) On the Western situation, cf. H. Rosenberg, *op. cit.,* O. Hintze, *op. cit.,* as well as Robert Forster, *op. cit.*

178. In a way, mainly by virtue of their education, this group in Russia could be compared to the *légistes* of Capetian France, rather than to the *noblesse de robe*. (Cf. A. Kartashev, *op. cit.*), II, 527.

179. A contributing factor to this development was the shift from *zasluga* (merit) to *vysluga* (seniority) as the basis for promotion in the Table of Ranks. For a very perceptive and thorough description and history of the Russian bureaucracy from the end of the eighteenth to the middle of the nineteenth centuries see Hans-Joachim Torke, *Das russische Beamtentum in der ersten Hälfte des 19. Jahrhunderts* (In-augural-Dissertation, Philosophische Fakultät an der Freien Universität Berlin, 1966).

180. *PSZ,* #11 444. The history of this important act is still shrouded in mystery. If Vernadsky's hypothesis that it was the work of the Vorontsov group is correct, then he is also right in stressing the influence of Masonic ideas of personal honor (G. V. Vernadskii, "Manifest Petra III o vol'nosti dvorianskoi i zakonodatel'naia komissiia 1754–1756 gg," *Istoricheskoe Obozrenie,* XX [1915], 51–59). N. L. Rubin-shtein, on the other hand, denies the role of the Vorontsov clique, making the Act of 1762 mainly the work of Glebov ("Ulozhennaia komissiia 1754–1766 gg i ee proekt novogo ulozheniia 'O sostoianii poddannykh voobshche,'" *Istoricheskie Zapiski,* XXXVIII (1951), 208–51.

The act came as a surprise and was greeted with some suspicion at first by many. After a short period of joy at the possibility of "vacations," the majority of the nobles returned or stayed in service. See Bolotov, II, 245; IV, 1168, 1173 (Bolotov could not see any other pattern than service for his children and grandchildren, although he himself had been one of the few most enthusiastic about retiring from service in 1762). Also Dolgorukov, *op. cit.*, p. 204; Lukin, "Zhizn' starinnogo dvorianina," *loc. cit.*, p. 911; D. B. Mertvago, "Zapiski Dmitriia B. Mertvago 1760–1824," *loc. cit.*, V, 1867, Appendix, 157, 312; D. Neledinskii-Meletskii's account of his relative, Prince Alexander P. Obolenskii, *op. cit.*, p. 88. For attitudes to service after 1762 based on the notion of honor, cf. Dolgorukov, *op. cit.*, p. 368; A. M. Fadeev, *Vospominaniia Andreia Mikhailovicha Fadeeva, 1790–1867* (Odessa, 1897), p. 95.

Only the Svod Zakonov of 1833 explicitly stated that a nobleman retained his privileged status even if he did not serve; the Act of 1762 had made no such provision. P. Ustimovich, *op. cit.*, p. 151. Also V. N. Latkin, ed., *Proekt Novogo Ulozheniia, sostavlennyi zakonodatel'noi kommissiei 1754–1766 gg* (*Chast' III "o sostoianiiakh poddannykh voobshche"*) (Saint Petersburg, 1893. Chap. 22, §12).

181. In fact, the government still could—and did—recall noblemen into service; it would seem that only in 1820 did this practice lose its legal compulsory force (*PSZ*, #28 368); cf. Romanovich-Slavatinskii, *op. cit.*, p. 149, Got'e, *op. cit.*, I, 357. The reality of this threat is confirmed by Bolotov, who many times feared he would be recalled to service or compelled to accept some official assignment (*e.g.* II, p. 740); see also the instructions of Smolensk nobility (*UK 1767*, XIV, 416). The passport system and the duty of registering with the government for service and then obtaining leave to study or remain at home does not seem to have disappeared throughout the entire eighteenth century. A. Artem'ev, *Kazanskaia gimnaziia v XVIII v.* (Saint Petersburg, 1874), p. 95, cites such a case from a petition (with reference to relevant legislation). Such an eloquent spokesman for the rights of the nobility as Prince M. M. Shcherba-

tov took the pattern of service—and its desirability—for granted ("Primechaniia vernogo syna otechestva na dvorianskie prava na manifest," *Sochineniia*, I [1896], 306). An illustration of the continuing practice of service and its relationship to education can be found in S. P. Pisarev, ed., "Instruktsiia o vospitanii 1772–1775 (Mikhail Lebedev smolenskii pomeshchik)" *Russkaia Starina*, XXXI (1881), 656 and *passim;* M. Erhard, *Joukovski et le préromantisme russe* (Paris, 1938), p. 42; S. I. Gamaleia, *Pis'ma S. I. G.* (2nd ed.; Moscow, 1836), I, 14; "Dnevnik kurskogo pomeshchika I. P. Annenkova," *Materialy po istorii SSSR* (Dokumenty po istorii XVIII veka [Moscow, 1957]), V, 794–823 *passim*. To serve as long as one was useful, was also the rule propounded by Starodum in Fonvizin's play (expressing the opinions of the author, which in turn reflected those of the educated nobility) (P. Viazemskii, *Fon Vizin* [Saint Petersburg, 1848], pp. 217–18).

182. This orientation found expression in the acts of Catherine the Great—foundation of the Free Economic Society, the general land survey, the abolition of internal duties, etc. Note also the growing concern for the serfs and peasants—at least in economic terms—which foreshadows the turning from the interests of the state (as an abstraction) to increasing attention to the welfare of the people and the nation. P. Struve has argued that this policy was a means for turning the nobility from political problems and making them forget their efforts in 1730 ("Istoricheskii smysl russkoi revoliutsii," in *Sotsial'naia i ekonomicheskaia istoriia Rossii* [Paris, 1952], pp. 310–16, originally published under the title *Razmyshleniia o russkoi revoliutsii* [Sofia, 1921]). See also Gr. Gukovskii, *Ocherki po istorii russkoi literatury XVIII v—Dvorianskaia fronda v literature 1750kh-1760kh godov* (Moscow-Leningrad, 1936), p. 70. Some of these questions are touched upon by N. L. Rubinshtein, "Ulozhennaia komissiia 1754–1766 . . . ," *loc. cit.* We find signs of this new orientation in the draft project of a new code (V. N. Latkin, ed., *op. cit.*, Chap. 22, §§18, 20, 24).

183. *"Der Mohr hat seine Schuldigkeit getan, der Mohr kann gehen"* (Schiller).

184. S. N. Glinka, *op. cit.*, p. 137, Bolotov, I, 695 ff.
185. In the literature of the period the only references I have
come across are those to service duty and obligation, of acting as good administrator and "governor" toward serfs, on
behalf of the state. For the people, the noble was primarily
the agent and delegate of the Tsar; witness the usage of the
term *boiarin* in referring to one's master.
186. The documentation on this point is very extensive. For a
few representative illustrations: "Zapiski Dmitriia B. Mertvago, 1760–1824," *loc. cit.*, p. 38; V. Nashchokin, *op. cit.*,
p. 250 (note 49) cites the decree of October 1, 1748, establishing equivalencies between Guard and regular army
ranks. See N. Grigorovich, *Aleksandr Andreevich Bezborodko, loc. cit.*, I, 55, for the illustration of a rumor sug-
gesting that the right to distill alcohol be related to rank.
Also I. M. Dolgorukov, *op. cit.*, pp. 54, 55, 85, 105, 135.
A. M. Fadeev, *op. cit.*, I, 12; Neledinskii-Meletskii, *op. cit.*,
p. 123; Vigel', *op. cit.*, I, 86, 106. See the proposal of M. M.
Shcherbatov to reward with rank those merchants or others
who, during a period of starvation, will have been of particular help in feeding the people ("Rassuzhdenie o ny-
neshnem v 1787 g. pochti povsemestnom golode v Rossii,
o sposobakh onomu pomoch' i vpred predupredit' podobnoe
neschastie," *Sochineniia*, I [1896], 659). The draft of a
charter to the nobility, worked out in a committee of the
Commission on Legislation of 1767, gave precedence to the
serving nobleman over all others (*UK 1767*, XXXII, 584),
as well as distinguishing dress and ornaments (*ibid.*, XLIII,
309–10). Bolotov, as usual, provides many curious illustrations (II, 604; III, 136, 139, 592, 1062; IV, 70, 233, 242,
266). Dobrynin put the matter tersely in answer to an offer
of a position in the provinces: "Your Excellency knows that
in Russia a man without rank is, so to speak, a man without
name" ("Istinnoe povestvovanie . . . ," *loc. cit.*, IV (1871),
9. In 1847, S. S. Uvarov repeats the same idea in a memorandum for Nicholas I, "O sisteme chinov v Rossii," in
Evreinov, *op. cit.*, pp. 83–85.
187. N. A. Penchko, ed., *Dokumenty i materialy po istorii Moskovskogo Universiteta vtoroi poloviny XVIII veka, tom I*

(*1756–1764*) (Moscow, 1960), p. 123 (No. 110). Lomonosov attempted to secure automatic promotion to ranks for staff and graduates of schools attached to the Academy of Sciences and the University (S. V. Rozhdestvenskii, *op. cit.*, p. 184).

188. Kulomzin, "Pervyi pristup . . . ," *loc. cit.*, pp. 20–22; Panin, "Formy manifestu . . . ," *loc. cit.*, p. 26; "Zapiska gr. S. R. Vorontsova o dvorianstve," *loc. cit.*, p. 297; S. V. Skalon (née Kapnist), "Pamiat' o rodine (XVIII v.—1830 g.)," *Istoricheskii Vestnik*, June, 1891, p. 606.

189. See S. Aksakov, D. Fonvizin, as well as descriptions of the survival of this state of affairs into the nineteenth century in N. Gogol' and I. Turgenev.

190. Bolotov, II, 256, and IV, 513; Grigorovich, *Aleksandr Andreevich Bezborodko, loc. cit.*, XXVI, 236.

191. VTS, LXIX, 253–54, provides a curious illustration of the consequences of this obligation to build a house in the capital.

192. Nonagricultural physical labor was considered improper, and so was petty retail trade. But while these were frowned upon, they did not disqualify the individual involved from noble status. VTS, LV, 407, illustrates a borderline case. On Western *dérogeance*, see Marc Szeftel, "La vie exemplaire de la noblesse et l'évolution sociale de la France de l'Ancien Régime," *Revue de l'Institut de Sociologie Solvay*, XVI, No. 3 (Bruxelles, Septembre, 1936), 603–10.

193. *UK 1767*, XXXVI.

194. M. M. Shcherbatov, Rassuzhdenie . . . golode," *loc. cit.*, p. 636; *idem, Neizdannye Sochineniia* (Moscow, 1935), p. 93.

195. This was a conception that V. Tatishchev had formulated a generation earlier (*Testament de Basile Tatistcheff, passim*) and hinted at in his "Razgovor dvukh priatelei o pol'ze nauk i uchilishch, 1733" (*Chteniia* [1887], I, 1–171). On Shcherbatov's ideology, cf. M. Raeff, "State and Nobility in the Ideology of M. M. Shcherbatov," *American Slavic and East European Review*, XIX, No. 3 (October, 1960), 363–79.

196. On the organization of the Free Economic Society and its

efforts in this direction, cf. M. Confino, *Domaines et seigneurs . . .*

197. The decree of June 28, 1782 (*PSZ*, #15 447), giving the right to subsoil resources, was confirmed by the Charter to the Nobility of 1785 (*PSZ*, #16 187). The general survey of land holdings ordered September 19, 1765 (*PSZ*, #12 474) laid the foundation for stable landownership rights. Bolotov, II, 627, records the great impression made on contemporaries by this act. Bolotov also gives amusing illustrations of the way it was implemented. On the basis of it, Lukin advises that children of the nobility be given some knowledge of agriculture and estate management ("Zhizn' starinnogo dvorianina," *loc. cit.*, p. 927); Betzky, *Les plans et les statuts des différents établissements ordonnés par SMI Catherine II pour l'éducation de la jeunesse et l'utilité générale de son empire* (Amsterdam, 1775), II, 5; N. G. Kurganov, *op. cit.*, II, 30. An argument against involvement in economic affairs was made at the Commission of Codification in connection with the proposal of elective local functions for the nobility (*UK 1767*, VIII, 505).

198. Bolotov is a mine of information on this point, supplementing the analysis of M. Confino. For example, see Bolotov, III, 524–25, and IV, 783–84, on the ambivalent feelings of those who participated actively in the work, study, and improvements suggested by the Free Economic Society.

199. For most the transformation did not become significant before 1861. Cf. M. Confino, *Domaines et seigneurs . . .*, on the "economic mentality" (or lack of it) of the average Russian nobleman.

Serfdom, of course, played a major role in determining the Russian nobleman's attitude toward economic enterprise; cf. the stimulating suggestions in A. Gerschenkron, "The Problem of Economic Development in Russian Intellectual History of the Nineteenth Century," *Continuity and Change in Russian and Soviet Thought*, E. J. Simmons, ed. (Cambridge, Mass.: Harvard University Press, 1955), pp. 11–39.

200. A. Goodwin, ed., *The European Nobility in the Eighteenth Century* (London, 1953); W. Görlitz, *Die Junker* (*Adel und*

Bauer im deutschen Osten) (Glücksburg/Ostsee, 1956);
also, for somewhat later conditions, see *Explorations in
Entrepreneurial History*, VI (1953–1954), Nos. 2 and 3.

201. Since the medical profession did not enjoy high status, only
poor noblemen (or those from the Ukraine) could be found
to go into it rather readily (S. A. Tuchkov, *op. cit.*, p. 34;
Poletika, "Vospominaniia," *loc. cit.*, p. 307; Ia. Grot, "Ivan
Khemnitser" in *Russkaia poeziia*, S. A. Vengerov, ed., III
[Saint Petersburg, 1893], 454, note 3). See also "Catalogus
omnium Professorum scholae Medico-Chirurgica Caesareae
—Catalogus omnium alumnorum Imperialis Medico-Chi-
rurgicae scholae" (May 20, 1796, in Russlandsammlung
Georgs von Asch, Universitäts-Bibliothek, Goettingen, manu-
script item no. 230). On medicine and members of the
profession in Russia in the eighteenth century, see A. Buch-
holz, *Die Göttinger Russlandsammlung Georgs von Asch*
(Giessen, 1961) (Giessener Abhandlungen zur Agrar- und
Wirtsschaftsforschung des Europäischen Ostens Bd. 17),
Chap. 4. For the most recent account of the Russian med-
ical profession see Roderick E. McGrew, *Russia and the
Cholera 1823–1832* (Madison, Wisc.: The University of
Wisconsin Press, 1965), chaps. 2 and 3.

202. The majority of technical personnel were foreigners or peasants and craftsmen risen to positions of some importance.
Soviet literature on this point is too vast to be adduced
here. For a few examples of recruitment and reward of
technical personnel in government service, cf. *KM*, CXI, 147;
CXIV, 41; CXXX, 99. Also M. Vladimirskii-Budanov, *Gosudarstvo i narodnoe obrazovanie v Rossii XVIII veka* (Iaroslavl', 1874), p. 186. Also the information in M. Confino,
"Maîtres de forges et ouvriers dans les usines métallurgiques
de l'Oural aux XVIIIe–XIXe s.," *Cahiers du Monde russe et
soviétique*, I, No. 2 (January–March 1960), 238–84, and R.
Portal, *L'Oural au XVIIIe siècle* (Paris, 1950 [Collection
historique de l'Institut d'Études slaves, XIV]).

203. In 1729 the historian Müller was complaining: *"Da die
grössesten Gelehrten ohne Rang waren, und das in einem
Reiche wo alle Vorzüge nach dem Range bestimmt sind,
wo einer, der keinen Rang hat, bei keiner öffentlichen*

Gelegenheit erscheinen kann . . . ," cited in D. Tolstoi, *Das akademische Gymnasium und die akademische Universität im XVIII. Jahrh.* (Saint Petersburg, 1886), p. 149. To counteract this situation, the statutes of the Imperial Academy of Arts (1774) provided, *"Nous voulons et ordonnons, une fois pour toujours, que tous ceux qui dépendent de cette Académie, fassent Corps avec les différentes classes de nos sujets . . ."* and the President of the Academy was given fourth rank, the rector sixth, the professors eighth rank, and all the graduates of the Academy were to be free with their descendants (I. Betzky, *Plans et Statuts,* II, 11). See also A. Artem'ev, "Kazanskie gimnazii v XVIII v.," *Zh. M. N. P.,* CLXXIV (June, 1874), 8; for insight into the position of the academicians in the eighteenth century, see K. Stählin, *Aus den Papieren Jacob von Stählins* (Königsberg i. Pr, Berlin, 1929) and E. Winter, ed., *August Ludwig von Schlözer und Russland* [Berlin, 1961] (Quellen und Studien zur Geschichte Osteuropas, IX).

204. For example the careers of V. Tatishchev, I. Betsky, M. Danilov, not to mention those of Sumarokov, Kheraskov, and Radishchev. One is again reminded of conditions in Western Europe at the time of the Renaissance.

205. Only the old titles of *kniaz'* and *boiarin* competed with "general" in the people's vocabulary. But it is interesting to note that *kniaz'* had an undertone of affection, while "general" (and also to a large degree *boiarin*) implied awe.

206. There is a very suggestive psychological portrait of G. Potemkin (Catherine the Great's favorite), which stresses this element of rootlessness and insecurity, by S. V. Eshevskii ("Ocherk tsarstvovaniia Elizavety Petrovny," *Sochineniia po russkoi istorii* [Moscow, 1900], p. 9 [also in his *Sochineniia* (Moscow, 1870), I, and *Otechestvennye Zapiski,* 1868, Nos. 5–7].

207. Neledinskii-Meletskii, *Khronika nedavnei stariny,* pp. 123–24; Vasil'ev, *Dnevnik Vasil'eva,* p. 85; see also Kurganov, *op. cit.,* II, p. 40; and for a somewhat later expression, P. N. Sakulin, *Iz istorii russkogo idealizma. Kn. V. F. Odoevskii* (Moscow, 1913), I, Part 1, 72, note.

208. M. Aleksandrov, *op. cit.*, p. 58, cites the definition of landowner as a police agent.
209. Evidence is readily found in the difficulties experienced by the Free Economic Society; cf. the testimony of Bolotov and M. Confino, *Domaines et seigneurs.* . . .
210. The dichotomy had been well put by Artemii Volynskii in 1730 ("Delo Salnikeeva," *Chteniia,* 1868, Bk. III, Miscellany, p. 29 [note]):

> One still hears that there will be freedom from service. And it is true that to serve under constraint (*v nevole*) is very difficult. But if one were to give complete freedom, you know that our people are not very ambitious and rather lazy. So that if there were not some compulsion, obviously those who are satisfied to sit at home and eat rye bread only will not wish to obtain either honor or better sustenance through their labor.

4. Home and School

1. Dolgorukov, *Povest' o rozhdenii moem, proiskhozhdenii i vsei zhizni—Zapiski kn. I. M. Dolgorukova* (Petrograd, 1916), p. 21; F. P. Pecherin, "Zapiski o moikh predkakh i o sebe, na pamiat' detiam v 1816 g. sdelannye," *Russkaia Starina,* LXXII (1891), 594; "Vospominaniia S. V. Skalon," *Istoricheskii Vestnik,* XLIV (May-June, 1891), 346; Bolotov, II, 294; *ibid.,* III, 352.

   See the advice of Lukin on the proper upbringing of noble children, in I. F. Lukin, "Zhizn' starinnogo dvorianina," *Russkii Arkhiv,* III (1865), No. 8, 921–30. Also the memoirs of Danilov, *Zapiski napisannye im v 1771 g.* (*1733–1762*) (Moscow, 1842), for the older generation.
2. This was the case of the mothers of Bolotov, A. E. Labzina, and—in later times—of I. Turgenev and S. Aksakov. See also S. N. Glinka, *Zapiski Sergeia Nikolaevicha Glinki* (Saint Petersburg, 1895), pp. 36, 138; V. Stoiunin, "Nasha sem'ia i ee istoricheskie sud'by," *Pedagogicheskie Sochineniia* (3rd ed.; Saint Petersburg, 1911), p. 13.

3. Women close to court circles and the life of the capitals were, of course, moving away from this situation. The most striking, albeit somewhat exceptional, example being Princess Dashkova. For the situation in the provinces, see Dolgorukov, *op. cit.*, pp. 124–25; M. A. Dmitriev, *Melochi iz zapasa moei pamiati* (2nd ed., Moscow, 1869), p. 17.

4. A book of rules and etiquette for domestic life enunciated and practiced in Muscovite Russia.

5. *diad'ka*—servant in charge of young boy of noble family. He took care of the young master after the latter had left the nurse and before he was entrusted to a tutor or governor. Sometimes the *diad'ka* continued to look after the physical needs of his charge for many years, while the young master was at school or under the supervision of a tutor. This was the case of Bolotov, for example.

6. One can't help think of James Baldwin's point about the Negro mammy's love in *The Fire Next Time*.

7. V. N. Zinov'ev, "Zhurnal puteshestvii po Germanii, Italii, Frantsii i Anglii 1784–88," *Russkaia Starina*, XXIII (1878), 229.

8. Although somewhat idealized and fictionalized, Russian literature is the best source of illustrations for this point. S. Aksakov's psuedo-memoirs come most readily to mind.

9. Does this not perhaps account for the rosy, idealized, unreal qualities attributed to the *muzhik* by many a writer from the nobility in the eighteenth and even nineteenth centuries?

10. V. N. Zinov'ev, "Zhurnal puteshestvii . . . ," *loc. cit.*, p. 229; S. Rozhdestvenskii, "Proekty uchebnykh reform v tsarstvovanie imper. Ekateriny II do uchrezhdeniia komissii o narodnykh uchilishch," *Zh. M. N. Pr.*, XII (new series [December, 1907]), 176; Betsky, *Les plans et les statuts des différents établissements ordonnés par SMI Catherine II pour l'education du la jeunesse et l'utilité générale de son empire* (Amsterdam, 1775), I, 114. (Also in P. M. Maikov, *Ivan Ivanovich Betskoi—opyt ego biografii* [Saint Petersburg, 1904], p. 139); S. V. Rozhdestvenskii, *Ocherki po istorii sistem narodnogo prosveshcheniia v Rossii v XVIII–XIX vv.* (Zapiski istoriko-filologicheskogo fakul'teta, CIV [Saint Peters-

burg, 1912]), 382; Ph. H. Dilthey gives an opinion on this matter in A. I. Kirpichnikov, "Pedagogi proshlogo veka," *Istoricheskii Vestnik*, XXI (1885), 439. S. Aksakov gives similar testimony on the basis of his own upbringing.

11. N. Karamzin, "Flor Silin—blagodetel'nyi chelovek," *Sochineniia*, A. Smirdin, ed. (Saint Petersburg, 1848), III. Cf. also V. V. Sipovskii, *Ocherki iz istorii russkogo romana* (Saint Petersburg, 1910), I, Part II, 737; Bolotov, IV, 1210 ff.

12. My seminar students also perceived this element of play in the constitutional projects of the Decembrists (especially the Constitution of the Union of Welfare). For a fictionalized picture, see the *povest'* of P. Mel'nikov-Pecherskii, "Starye gody" in *Russkie povesti XIX veka 60-kh godov*, I (Moscow, 1956), 27–101.

13. Bolotov, III, 79–80.

14. *VTS*, LXXXIV, 682; *Rasstushchii Vinograd*, III (July, 1786), 1. Bolotov confirms this picture, as does—indirectly —the whole *corpus* of satirical literature in the reign of Catherine the Great.

15. The papers of the *VTS*, *KM*, and the Senate are full of records of *smotry* of young noblemen in connection with enrollment into service and leaves for further education. The "Dnevnik kurskogo pomeshchika I. P. Annenkova," *Materialy po istorii SSSR* (Dokumenty po istorii XVIII veka [Moscow, 1957]) also lists numerous instances of measures taken by Annenkov to secure education for his children. In addition, A. P. Butenev, "Vospominaniia o moem vremeni," *Russkii Arkhiv*, III (1881), 6; *Zapiski Danilova*, pp. 15, 121; I. I. Dmitriev, *Vzgliad na moiu zhizn'* (Moscow, 1866), p. 12; L. N. Engel'gardt, *Zapiski L'va Nikolaevicha Engel'gardta* (Moscow, 1868), pp. 5, 6, 7, 9. V. S. Khvostov, "Zapiski Vasiliia Sem. Khvostova," *Russkii Arkhiv*, VIII (1870), 552–53; N. V. Lopukhin, "Zapiski nekotorykh obstoiatel'stv zhizni i sluzhby d.t.s. senatora N. V. Lopukhina," *Chteniia*, 1860, Bk. II, p. 1; "Vospominaniia S. Skalon," *loc. cit.*, p. 341; S. A. Tuchkov, *Zapiski Sergeia A. Tuchkova* (Saint Petersburg, 1906), pp. 3, 5, 6, 101. Vigel', *Zapiski*, S. Ia. Straikh, ed. (Moscow, 1928), I, 51; Bolotov, IV, 828.

P. I. Poletika, "Vospominaniia Petra Iv. Poletiki," *Russkii Arkhiv*, November, 1885, p. 307.

16. Protas'ev, "Stranitsy iz starogo dnevnika," *Istoricheskii Vestnik*, 1887, No. 11, p. 409; N. K. Piksanov, *Griboedov i staroe barstvo* (Moscow, 1926), p. 65; L. N. Maikov, "Vasilii Maikov," in S. A. Vengerov, *Russkaia poeziia*, II (1893), 266.

17. Mitronanushka, the hero of Fonvizin's *Nedorosl'*, is a caricature, of course, but his situation and attitudes are basically typical of his milieu.

18. S. Aksakov's case was exceptional perhaps, but not quite untypical; cf. Bolotov, IV, 1011.

19. M. S. Nikoleva, "Cherty starinnogo dvorianskogo byta," Russkii Arkhiv, XXXI (1893), 116; P. Puzanov, *Sukhoputnyi shliakhetskii kadetskii korpus* (Saint Petersburg, 1907), p. 15.

20. The most extreme case was that of young S. Aksakov, as he reports it in his "memoirs."

21. "Zapiski Dmitriia B. Mertvago 1760–1824," *Russkii Arkhiv*, appendix to V (1867), 156.

22. We need only remind the reader of Pushkin's well-known poem to the Tsarskosel'skii *litsei* of which he himself was a graduate. See also the testimony of V. Raevskii, the "first Decembrist," in P. E. Shchegolev, *Pervyi Dekabrist Vladimir Raevskii* (Saint Petersburg, 1905), p. 7.

23. We need only think of Bolotov, the Turgenev family, the Slavophiles (Aksakov, Samarin, Khomiakov), and their elders, like Stankevich.

24. In using Russian fiction of the nineteenth century as evidence for the family patterns among the nobility (Tolstoi, Turgenev, Chekhov), it is well to keep in mind that they refer to a much more settled and harmonious mid-nineteenth-century situation. This was not the usual condition in the eighteenth century.

25. The standard histories of Russian education deal at some length with the reign of Peter the Great: S. Rozhdestvenskii, *Ocherki po istorii sistem*, M. Vladimirskii-Budanov, *Gosudarstvo i narodnoe obrazovanie v Rossii XVIII veka* (Iaro-

slavl'-Saint Petersburg, 1874); M. L. Demkov, *Istoriia russkoi pedagogiki* (Saint Petersburg, 1897), Part II; P. F. Kapterev, *Istoriia russkoi pedagogiki* (2nd ed.; Petrograd, 1915); E. N. Medynskii, *Istoriia russkoi pedagogiki do velikoi oktiabr'skoi sotsialisticheskoi revoliutsii* (2nd ed.; Moscow, 1938); N. Konstantinov and V. Struminskii, *Ocherki po istorii nachal'nogo obrazovaniia v Rossii* (Moscow, 1953); in addition, P. Pekarskii, *Nauka i literatura v Rossii pri Petre Velikom* (2 vols., Saint Petersburg, 1862); P. N. Miliukov, *Ocherki po istorii russkoi kul'tury*, II, Part II (Paris, 1931), and III (Paris, 1930); for summaries in English see N. Hans, *History of Russian Educational Policy* (London, 1931); Wm. H. E. Johnson, *Russia's Educational Heritage* (Pittsburgh, Pa., 1950); A. Vucinich, *Science in Russian Culture—A History to 1860* (Stanford, Calif.: Stanford University Press, 1963). Cf. also *VTS*, LVI, 318–32 on proposals and measures to continue Peter's educational work.

26. On ecclesiastical schools in general, cf. I. Smolitsch, *Geschichte der Russischen Kirche 1700–1917* (Leiden, 1964), I, Chap. 5; M. Raeff, *M. M. Speransky—Statesman of Imperial Russia* (The Hague, 1957), Chap. 1; P. Znamenskii, *Dukhovnye shkoly v Rossii do reformy 1808 g.* (Kazan, 1881). On the orientation of state schools under Peter the Great see also L. Beskrovnyi, "Voennye shkoly v Rossii v pervoi polovine XVIII v.," *Istoricheskie Zapiski*, XLII (1953), 285–300.

The ecclesiastical schools, to the extent that they were professionally oriented, rated much lower than the secular schools in the opinion of the nobility, although they were an important means for acquiring education in the provincial backwaters (and the Ukraine). It was the absence of a sense of cultural and moral duty that put the average *bursak* in an inferior status vis à vis his noble classmates (who may have been as poor as he). But if the graduate of the ecclesiastical school overcame his inferiority by acquiring this sense of social commitment and displayed it through literary or administrative activities (like Speransky, Martynov, Slovtsov, etc.), he was fully accepted in the ranks of the progressive and educated élite.

27. Demkov, *op. cit.*, II, 133.

28. B. E. Raikov, *Akademik Vasilii Zuev—ego zhizn' i trudy* (Moscow, 1955), pp. 206, 209.

29. This is abundantly confirmed by contemporary memoirs, as well as satirical literature.

30. K. V. Sivkov, "Chastnye pansiony i shkoly Moskvy v 8okh godakh XVIII v.," *Istoricheskii Arkhiv*, VI (1951), 315–23. Cf. the request of the Academy of Sciences to be entrusted with the supervision of private education in its "Instruction" to the Commission of 1767, *UK 1767*, XLIII, 371–72. An exception, with limited impact, were the Jesuit schools under Paul I. M.-J. Rouët de Journel, *Un Collège de Jésuites à Saint Petersbourg, 1800–1816* (Paris, 1922); J. T. Flynn, *Educational Reform Policies in the Reign of Alexander I* (Unpublished Ph.D. dissertation, Clark University, 1964).

31. The obligation was pointedly confirmed in the so-called Manifesto on the "freedom of the nobility," February 19, 1762 (*PSZ*, #11 444, §7. Also explained at length in Chap. 4 ("O dolzhnosti roditel'skoi") of *Proekt Novogo Ulozheniia, sostavlennyi zakonodatel'noi kommissiei 1754–1766 gg*, V. N. Latkin, ed. (Saint Petersburg, 1893), pp. 19–28 *passim*.

32. The references to examinations given to young nobles are too numerous in the papers of the *VTS*, *KM*, and Senate to be cited here. Cf. V. Nashchokin, *op. cit.*, pp. 14, 157–58, "Dnevnik kurskogo pomeshchika Annenkogo," *loc. cit.*, *passim*; Rozhdestvenskii, *Ocherki po istorii sistem*, p. 202, note.

33. *VTS*, LXIII, 323; *KM*, CIV, 32 (with reference to *PSZ*, #5888); *Zh. S.*, I, 101–102, 285. The same approach was advocated by Count P. I. Shuvalov in 1761, "Predlozhenie Pravitel'stvuiushchemu Senatu general fel'dtsekhmeistera grafa P. I. Shuvalova ob uchrezhdenii artilleriiskoi i inzhenernoi shkol," *Artilleriiskii Zhurnal*, 1855, No. 5, p. 483.

34. For examples of the plight of superannuated students, see *VTS*, LXXXIV, 682–87; F. F. Veselago, *Ocherk istorii morskogo kadetskogo korpusa* (Saint Petersburg, 1852), p. 73.

35. *E.g.* VTS, LXXXIV, 682–87.

36. N. V. Sushkov, ed., "Ob'iavlenie o blagorodnom pansione," *Moskovskii universitetskii blagorodnyi pansion* (Moscow,

1858), p. 45; S. Shevyrev, *Istoriia imperatorskogo Moskovskogo Universiteta* (*1755–1855*) (Moscow, 1855), p. 22.

37. N. Pavlov-Sil'vanskii, *Proekty reform v zapiskakh sovremennikov Petra Velikogo* (Saint Petersburg, 1897) (Zapiski
istoriko-filologicheskogo fakul'teta imp. SanktPeterburzh-
skogo universiteta, XLII); I. N. Tikhanov, ed., "Propozitsii Fedora Saltykova (ob uchenii)," *Pamiatniki drevnei
pis'mennosti*, LXXXIII (1891), No. 5; P. Efremov, ed.,
*Sochineniia, pis'ma i izbrannye perevody kn. Antiokha
Kantemira* (Saint Petersburg, 1867) (especially the satires
on learning and education, also in recent Soviet edition,
Bol'shaia biblioteka poeta [Leningrad, 1956]); V. N.
Tatishchev, "Razgovor dvukh priatelei o pol'ze nauk i
uchilishch (1733)," *Chteniia*, 1887, Part I, pp. 1–171;
Feofan Prokopovich, *Pervoe uchenie otrokam . . .* , (Saint
Petersburg, 1720).

38. Cf. the proposals submitted by rank-and-file noblemen in
1730 (in Korsakov, *Votsarenie imp. Anny Ioannovny*
[Kazan, 1880], Appendix).

39. *UK 1767*, XXXII, 457, 521. In addition, cf. studies on the
Commission of 1767, for example Ia. Abramov, "Soslovnye
nuzhdy, zhelaniia i stremleniia v epokhu Ekaterininskoi
komissii," *Severnyi Vestnik*, Nos. 4, 5 (1886); V. Bochkarev,
"Kul'turnye zaprosy russkogo obshchestva nachala tsarstvovaniia Ekateriny II po materialam zakonodatel'noi komissii
1767 g.," *Russkaia Starina*, January–May, 1915; M. Bogoslovskii, "Dvorianskie nakazy v Ekaterininskoi komissii 1767 g.,"
Russkoe Bogatstvo, Nos. 6, 7 (1897); L. D. Pisarzhevskaia,
"Dvorianskie deputaty i dvorianskie nakazy ekaterininskogo
vremeni," *Vsemirnyi Vestnik*, August, 1905; for contrast, see
also Artem'ev, *Kazanskie gimnazii v XVIII v.* (Saint Petersburg, 1874), p. 39.

40. I. N. Tikhanov, ed., "Propozitsii Fedora Saltykova (ob
uchenii)," *loc cit.;* cf. also E. Likhacheva, *Materialy dlia
istorii zhenskogo obrazovaniia v Rossii* (Saint Petersburg,
1890–1893), I, II.

41. I. Betzky, "Institution de la Communauté des Demoiselles
& de celle des Bourgeoises," *Plans et Statuts*, II (Amsterdam,
1775), 249–367; on I. Betskoi, the prime mover of this

institution, P. M. Maikov, *Ivan Ivanovich Betskoi—opyt ego biografii* (Saint Petersburg, 1904); E. Likhacheva, *op. cit.*, I.

42. N. Penchko, ed., *Dokumenty i materialy po istorii Moskovskogo Universiteta vtoroi poloviny XVIII v.*, I (Moscow, 1960), Nos. 72, 93, 106, 110, 116, 122; *KM*, CXXIV, 367; the observations of Inspector C. F. Moderach in D. Tolstoi, *Das akademische Gymnasium und die akademische Universität im XVIII. Jahrh.* (Saint Petersburg, 1886), p. 128; N. G. Levshin, "Domashnii pamiatnik Nikolaia Gavrilovicha Levshina 1780–1804," *Russkaia Starina*, VIII (December, 1873), 842; A. P. Butenev, "Vospominaniia o moem vremeni," *Russkii Arkhiv*, 1881, p. 27; A. I. Del'vig, *Polveka russkoi zhizni—Vospominaniia A. Del'viga 1820–1870* (Leningrad, 1930), I, 56, 90; Artem'ev, *op. cit.*, pp. 8, 10.

43. The specific ranks varied throughout the period. On the demands for direct relationship between rank and education put forth at the Commission of 1767, cf. *UK 1767*, XXXII, 212–13; XLIII, 143. D. Tolstoi, *op. cit.*, p. 162, cites the regulations of the Academy on this matter. Also "Nechto ob ekzamene, byvshem v S.Peterburgskoi gubernskoi gimnazii i nekotorye podrobnosti o sem zavedenii," *Otechestvennye Zapiski*, V (1821), p. 109; P. Sakulin, *Iz istorii russkogo idealizma. Kn. V. F. Odoevskii* (Moscow, 1913), I, Part I, 11.

44. M. Shugurov, "Uchenye i ucheniki v XVIII v (po povodu biografii A. Ia. Polenova)," *Russkii Arkhiv*, IV (1866), No. 3, 311–12; N. Bulich, *Iz pervykh let Kazanskogo Universiteta 1805–1819* (2nd ed.; Saint Petersburg, 1904), I, 53; N. Piksanov, *Griboedov i staroe barstvo* (Moscow, 1926), pp. 62–65.

45. Bulich, *op. cit.*, I, 344–46 (of course the flight from school was partly determined by the patriotic and warlike exaltation of the Napoleonic period, of which Tolstoi has given a beautiful description in *War and Peace*).

46. Cf. N. M. Chentsov, *Vosstanie Dekabristov—Bibliografiia* (Moscow-Leningrad, 1929); M. V. Nechkina, ed., and R. G. Eimontova, compiler, *Dvizhenie Dekabristov—Ukazatel' literatury 1928–1959* (Moscow, 1960).

47. I. A. Geim (Heym), *Ueber den Zustand der Wissenschaften in Russland unter Paul dem Ersten* (Moscow, 1799), p. 4.

48. This was the case of Bolotov, Karamzin, Derzhavin, Danilov, and most Decembrists.

49. This is the subject of much of Russian eighteenth-century satirical literature, especially Novikov's and Fonvizin's. On this element of the nobility, see the material gathered by V. A. Gol'tsev, *Zakonodatel'stvo i nravy v Rossii XVIII v.*, (2nd ed.; Saint Petersburg, 1896); N. Chechulin, *Russkoe provintsial'noe obshchestvo vo vtoroi polovine XVIII v.* (Saint Petersburg, 1889) (also *Zh. M. N. Pr.*, March–June, 1889); N. F. Dubrovin, "Russkaia zhizn' v nachale XIX v.," *Russkaia Starina*, December, 1898–August, 1899.

50. E. S. Kots, *Krepostnaia intelligentsiia* (Leningrad, 1926); A. N. Korsakov, "Dela davno minuvshikh let," *Istoricheskii Vestnik*, XXXIV (October, 1888), pp. 176–201; S. Slovutinskii, *General Izmailov i ego dvornia* (Moscow, 1937).

51. These activities offered an "aesthetic" by-product in the form of love for regularity, order, etc., which we have noted earlier.

52. Graf Minikh, "Raport o kadetskom korpuse (7 January 1733)," *Chteniia*, 1862, Bk. I, p. 172; S. P. Pisarev, ed., "Instruktsiia o vospitanii 1772–1775," *Russkaia Starina*, XXXI (1881), 660–61.

53. N. Sushkov, *op. cit.;* D. F. Kobeko, *Imperatorskii Tsarskosel'skii litsei* (Saint Petersburg, 1911); A. Rubets, *Stoletie imperatorskogo Aleksandrovskogo litseia* (Saint Petersburg, 1911); J. T. Flynn, *op. cit.;* G. N. Teplov, "Proekt k uchrezhdeniiu universiteta Baturinskogo 1760 g," *Chteniia*, 1863, Bk. II, Part V, pp. 67–85.

54. One is reminded of the Renaissance curriculum nicely described and spoofed by Rabelais. See Graf Minikh, "Raport . . . ," *loc. cit.;* G. N. Teplov, "Proekt k uchrezhdeniiu universiteta Baturinskogo," *loc. cit.*, p. 80; S. Pisarev, "Instruktsiia . . . ," *loc. cit.;* Pekarskii, *op. cit.*, I, 61; Sushkov, *op. cit.*, p. 28; *Sobranie sochinenii vybrannykh iz mesiatseslovov*, IV (Saint Petersburg, 1790), 211–12.

55. S. P., "Pis'mo o poriadke obucheniia nauk," *Ezhemesiachnye*

sochineniia k pol'ze i uveseleniiu sluzhashchie, February, 1757, p. 128.

56. *Sobranie staraiushcheesia o perevode inostrannykh knig.*

57. S. A. Tuchkov, *op. cit.,* p. 29; M. Antonovskii, "Zapiski Mikhaila Ivanovicha Antonovskogo (nachatye v 1806 g)," *Russkii Arkhiv,* XXIII (1885), No. 2, 155; Gukovskii, *Ocherki po istorii russkoi literatury XVIII v.—Dvorianskaia fronda v literature 1750kh–1760kh godov* (Moscow-Leningrad, 1936), p. 30; also M. I. Sukhomlinov, *Istoriia Rossiiskoi Akademii* (Saint Petersburg, 1880); V. Bogoliubov, *N. I. Novikov i ego vremia* (Moscow, 1916); G. Makogonenko, *Nikolai Novikov i russkoe prosveshchenie XVIII veka* (Moscow-Leningrad, 1952); V. P. Semennikov, *Sobranie staraiushcheesia o perevode inostrannykh knig* (Saint Petersburg, 1913); *idem., Knigoizdatel'skaia deiatel'nost N. I. Novikova i tipograficheskoi kompanii* (Saint Petersburg, 1921) (additions to this bibliographical guide will be forthcoming as the *Svodnyi katalog russkoi knigi XVIII veka 1725–1800* [Moscow, 1962 ff.] is completed in five vols.); L. B. Svetlov, " 'Obshchestvo liubitelei rossiiskoi uchenosti' pri Moskovskom universitete," *Istoricheskii Arkhiv,* V (1950), 300–22. Also the information in J. S. G. Simmons, "Samuel Johnson 'on the Banks of the Wolga,' " *Oxford Slavonic Papers,* XI (1964), 28–37.

58. *Nastavlenie znatnomu molodomu gospodinu . . .* (Saint Petersburg, 1778) (Artillery and Engineering Noble Cadet Corps), p. 12; Tolstoi, *op. cit.,* p. 30. For the notion of demeaning labor, cf. H. Arendt, *The Human Condition* (Chicago: University of Chicago Press, 1958).

59. A. Kantemir mentions this orientation in his poetic work. Cf. Vladimirskii-Budanov, *op. cit.,* p. 145; Rozhdestvenskii, *Ocherki po istorii sistem,* p. 351.

60. I. F. Timkovskii, "Moe opredelenie na sluzhbu," *Moskvitianin,* 1852, No. 5, Section IV, p. 30; E. Winter, ed., *August Ludwig von Schlözer und Russland* (Berlin, 1961); Quellen und Studien zur Geschichte Osteuropas, Bd. IX); E. Amburger, *Beiträge zur Geschichte der deutsch-russischen kulturellen Beziehungen* (Giessen, 1961) (Giessener Ab-

handlungen zur Agrar-und Wirtsschaftsforschung des europäischen Ostens, Bd. 14). Also S. Belokurov and A.
Zertsalov, "O nemetskikh shkolakh v Moskve v pervoi
chetverti XVIII v.," *Chteniia*, CCXX, Bk. I (1907), pp. 1–
244. The testimony of the Decembrists confirms this gener-
alization.

61. The Jesuit influence and "aristocratic" orientation of education culminated in the reign of Alexander I. But it did not
enjoy much favor or play a significant role outside the
highest court circles.

62. Betzky, *Plans et Statuts,* and general histories of Russian
education. It is interesting to note that for the common
people education was to remain primarily practical, and
emphasized factual (encyclopedic) knowledge.

63. S. Rozhdestvenskii, "Proekty uchebnykh reform . . . , *loc.
cit.*, p. 176; Vladimirskii-Budanov, *op. cit.*, p. 198; S. N.
Glinka, *op. cit.*, p. 13; as well as Betzky, *Plans et Statuts.*

64. Sushkov, *op. cit.*, and the biographies of Zhukovskii, Radishchev. Also V. Orlov, *Russkie prosvetiteli 1790–1800kh
godov* (Moscow, 1950); *idem, Puti i sud'by—literaturnye
ocherki* (Moscow-Leningrad, 1963) (chapters on P. Katenin,
D. Davydov); A. Fomin, "Andrei I. Turgenev i Andrei Serg.
Kaisarov," *Russkii Bibliofil*, January, 1912, pp. 7–39, and
idem, "Andrei Sergeevich Kaisarov, 1782–1813," *Russkii
Bibliofil*, April, 1912, pp. 5–33; V. M. Istrin, "Druzheskoe
literaturnoe obshchestvo 1801 g.," *Zh. M. N. Pr.* (new
series, XXVIII [August, 1910]), 273–307. This common
experience at school became the seedbed for the romantic
attachments among the generation of the reign of Alexander
I, culminating in the Secret Societies of the future Decembrists. (At times one has a sense of possible homosexual
undercurrents, but our evidence is too fragmentary and reti-
cent to permit more than occasional suspicion.)

65. F. Valjavec, *Geschichte der abendländischen Aufklärung*
(Wien-München, 1961); R. Ruyer, *L'utopie et les utopies*
(Paris, 1950) (particularly Part I); R. Mucchielli, *Le mythe
de la cité idéale* (Paris, 1960); P. Francastel, ed., *Utopie et
institutions au XVIIIe siècle* (*Le pragmatisme des Lumières*)
(Paris-La Haye, 1963).

66. The Russian Church did not play the mediating role that the Church and its cultural orientation had played in the West —and to which the eighteenth-century secular culture was partly a dynamic reaction. To the extent that the members of the Church did play a role in shaping Russian culture in the eighteenth century, it was through accepting secularism and the primacy of the state (as did, for example, Feofan Prokopovich).

67. As had been true of Western culture in the sixteenth century, there was frequently an identification of Russian and Western classical heroes. V. Sipovskii, *Ocherki iz istorii russkogo romana* (2 vols.; Saint Petersburg, 1910), furnishes many illustrations. Cf. also H. Rogger, *National Consciousness in Eighteenth-Century Russia* (Cambridge, Mass.: Harvard University Press, 1960), and M. Raeff's review of it in *Jahrbücher für Geschichte Osteuropas*, VIII, No. 4 (1960), 445–48.

68. For geographical-statistical information, cf. *Sobesednik liubitelei rossiiskogo slova*, I, No. 2 (1783), 72–74 and IV, No. 8 (1783), *passim*. Also *Sobranie sochinenii vybrannykh iz mesiatseslovov*, III (1789); VI (1790); and VII (1791). On the difficulty in assessing the impact of such readings, cf. Lemberg, *Die nationale Gedankenwelt der Dekabristen* (Köln-Graz, 1963).

69. *Zerkalo liubopytstva* (Saint Petersburg, 1791), LI, 123–28. For a more ambivalent point of view, *Sobesednik liubitelei rossiiskogo slova*, VI (1784), 120.

70. There is no connection with Boris Godunov's ill-fated attempt a century earlier.

71. *E.g.* Desnitskii at Edinburgh. Cf. V. Aleksandrenko, "Iz zhizni russkikh studentov v Oksforde v tsarstvovanie imper. Ekateriny II," *Zh. M. N. Pr.*, CCLXXXV (January, 1893), 1–14; N. Hans, "Russian students at Leyden in the eighteenth century," *Slavonic and East European Review*, XXXV (June, 1957), 551–62; J. Stremooukhoff, "Les russes à Strasbourg au XVIIIe siècle," *Revue d'Alsace*, LXXXI (1934), 3–21; E. J. Simmons, *English Literature and Culture in Russia 1553–1840* (Cambridge, Mass.: Harvard University Press, 1935). The literature on Radishchev and his

friends is too large to be cited here; for a superficial summary in English, see D. M. Lang, *The First Russian Radical, Alexander Radishchev 1749–1802* (London, 1959), Chap. 2. For a more searching discussion of the Western intellectual experiences and influences, see A. McConnell, *A Russian Philosopher—Alexander Radishchev 1749–1802* (The Hague: Martinus Nijhoff, 1964).

72. On occasion similar attitudes are to be found among Western European travelers of the time, but the Russians (like the Americans of the late nineteenth and early twentieth centuries) were always more naïve, zestful, and earnest. Cf. V. Zinov'ev, "Zhurnal puteshestvii," *loc. cit.;* the children of Princess Dashkova as per the account of their mother, E. Dashkova, "Bumagi kn. E. R. Dashkovoi," *Arkhiv kn. Vorontsova*, XXI, and the well-known travel notes of Fonvizin and Karamzin.

73. It is true that Western Europe was not very overtly conscious of its own cultural roots and traditions, although such an appreciation was stronger in the German universities (to which the Russians went) than in Parisian salons. What appealed to the Russians, of course, was the eighteenth-century emphasis on the rationality and uniformity of human nature.

74. Although superficially successful, the career of Radishchev is the most dramatic illustration of this situation.

75. The Legislative Commission of 1767, the project for a coronation manifesto drawn up by N. I. Panin for Grand Duke Paul, and the acts of 1762 and 1785 always referred to and stressed the "noble way of life" (in the sense of education and culture) as the *basis* for the freedom of the nobility from service and its claims to various rights and privileges. This contrasts sharply with the Western nobility's self-image—there the "noble way of life" was the *consequence* of privileges and special legal status; it was the illustration, not the justification of their establishment. The notion of cultural responsibility made the Russian nobility a relatively open class, for anyone who had achieved the desired level of education could lead the proper way of life and, therefore, demand acceptance into its ranks. (In the

nineteenth century a commoner who had acquired education was in fact easily admitted into the ranks of the nobility, both legally and socially.)

Furthermore, this notion of cultural responsibility gave the noblemen a sense of cultural solidarity and a missionary spirit, allowing them to disown those who did not live up to their expectations and standards; hence their hatred and contempt for men like Arakcheev and the notorious torturers of serfs. In Russia the sense of honor—the mainstay of the Western European nobility—was strongly infused with a big dose of cultural and social responsibility.

76. Besides the satirical literature, cf. the memoirs of Bolotov and Dolgorukov.

77. There were occasional exceptions, but even then the traditional institutional pattern remained a strong force in the background (*e.g.* Prince Khvorostinin, Archpriest Avvakum). For a brilliant picture of the cultural atmosphere of Muscovite Russia, P. Pascal, *Avvakum et les débuts du Raskol— La crise religieuse au XVIIe siècle en Russie* (Paris, 1938), Chap. 1.

78. We must keep in mind that Western European culture in the eighteenth century—especially in France and England —was no longer predominantly oriented toward the state. Even in Germany there was a growing movement of independence from both church and state. Everywhere in the West the emphasis was on the progress of the individual and of society (the sum total of individuals in a nation), rather than on the institutions.

5. *The Impact of Western Ideas*

1. For a recent general summary of Russian cultural trends in the second half of the eighteenth century, see H. Jablonowski, "Die geistige Bewegung in Russland in der zweiten Häalfte des 18. Jhs." (Rapport présenté au Colloque slavistique sur

le thème "Le mouvement des idées dans les pays slaves pendant la seconde moitié du XVIIIe siècle," Uppsala 20–21 août 1960, Commission International des Etudes Slaves, Comité International des Sciences Historiques, edizioni di *Richerche Slavistiche*), pp. 1–19 (separate offprint).

2. S. Solov'ev, *Istoriia Rossii s drevneishiskh vremen* (Saint Petersburg, n.d.), XIII, Chap. 1.

3. M. M. Shcherbatov, "O povrezhdenii nravov v Rossii," *Sochineniia*, II (1898), 133–246. Cf. M. Raeff, "State and Nobility in the Ideology of M. M. Shcherbatov," *American Slavic and East European Review*, XIX, No. 3 (October, 1960), 363–79.

4. Stoicism was a significant philosophical undercurrent in eighteenth-century Russia. As little attention has been paid by scholars to the philosophic interests of laymen in the eighteenth century, only a few preliminary observations can be made within the context of our discussion. The revival of interest in Stoicism in Western Europe in the seventeenth century produced a lively philosophical literature and influenced belles-lettres and popular writing as well. These became available in Russia when the most important and popular Western books were translated or imitated. The Stoic element, of course, was also present in eighteenth-century academic philosophy, and found its way into Russia through the ecclesiastical schools and university, mainly by means of popular textbooks of philosophy by Chr. Wolff, F. C. Baumeister, etc.

Stoicism appealed to the Russians because it was a universalistic moral philosophy that—as had been the case in the Roman Empire—attracted people who wished to become part of the universal Western civilization. Moreover, the Stoics emphasized the primacy of the individual's character, will, and free choice in determining both private and public conduct and in shaping the moral society. This could not fail to appeal to members of a society that was breaking the fetters of traditions and loyalties based on family and clan ties. Lastly, Stoicism offered a system of norms based on reason and natural laws rather than the authority of custom and religion.

The popularity of Stoicism may be gauged from the fact that one of the most widely read educational books, N. Kurganov's *Pis'movnik* (5th ed.; Saint Petersburg, 1793), contained several substantial selections from Epictetus and Seneca, while journals designed to enlighten the general public and the younger generation, *Utrennii Svet* (1777–1780) and *Rastushchii Vinograd*, for instance, carried translations from Seneca, Galba, and Diogenes Laertius.

5. G. Fedotov, *Novyi Grad* (New York, 1952) (especially Chap. 1); V. Zen'kovskii, *Istoriia russkoi filosofii* (Paris, 1948–1950).

6. This was particularly true of France and England. But as E. Cassirer has so convincingly shown in his *Philosophy of the Enlightenment* (Boston: Beacon Press, 1955), the epistemological interest was far from being as exclusive as often claimed in earlier historiography.

7. Throughout the present discussion only the facets relevant to the Russian situation are taken into consideration. We are, therefore, omitting the "existentialist" side of eighteenth-century Enlightenment rediscovered in recent years. Cf. G. Clive, *The Romantic Enlightenment—Ambiguity and Paradox in the Western Mind 1750–1920* (New York, 1960); J. Starobinski, *J. J. Rousseau—la transparence et l'obstacle* (Paris, 1957); L. G. Crocker, *An Age of Crisis: Man and World in Eighteenth-Century French Thought* (Baltimore: Johns Hopkins University, 1959); *Rastushchii vinograd*, I (April, 1785), 8, and II (November, 1785), 1.

8. *Sobesednik liubitelei rossiiskogo slova*, IV, No. 7 (1783), 172–73. Also *Rastushchii vinograd*, II (December, 1785), 1–8; II (January, 1786), 6–13; III (July, 1786), 2–4.

9. The reader should keep in mind the Russian Church's relatively weak intellectual tradition, the impact of the Schism, etc. One may speculate that the absence of a powerful theological tradition and scholastic intellectual framework facilitated the early and extreme radicalization of the secular and rational ideas taken over from the West.

10. See a sample listing of eighteenth-century moral literature in Demkov, *Istoriia russkoi pedagogiki* (Saint Petersburg, 1897), II, 580–655. Bolotov provides a nice illustration of

the impact that the discovery of Western moral philosophy
had on a Russian serviceman (Bolotov, II, *passim*).

11. On the literary manifestations of Utopianism, cf. Sipovskii,
Ocherki iz istorii Russkogo romana (2 vols.; Saint
Petersburg, 1910); the literature on Shcherbatov in Raeff,
"State and Nobility in the Ideology of M. M. Shcherbatov,"
loc. cit.; Gukovskii, *Ocherki po istorii russkoi literatury
XVIII v.* (Moscow-Leningrad, 1936); for a most suggestive
comment on the relationship between moralizing and Utopian
didacticism and style, see A. Tertz, *On Socialist Realism*
(New York, 1960). For the Western models, Georges May,
Le dilemme du roman au XVIIIe siècle (New Haven: Yale
University Press, 1963).

12. This transformation culminated in the generation of the Decembrists. Cf. also N. F. Chulkov, "Krechetov—zabytyi radi-
kal'nyi publitsist," *Literaturnoe Nasledstvo*, Nos. 9–10 (Moscow, 1933), pp. 453–70; V. Orlov, *Russkie prosvetiteli 1790–
1800kh godov* (Moscow, 1950). Soviet historians are actively
interested in this generation, and in spite of some tendency to
exaggerate the radicalism and originality of these Russian
followers of Radishchev, they have unearthed much interesting information. Cf. Orlov, ed., *Poety radishchevtsy* (Leningrad, 1961); Iu. M. Lotman, *Puti razvitiia preddekabristskoi
obshchestvenno-politicheskoi mysli* (Unpublished dissertation, University of Leningrad, 1961); V. V. Pugachev, *Iz
istorii preddekabristskoi obshchestvenno-politicheskoi mysli*
(Unpublished dissertation, University of Leningrad, 1962).

13. The stimulating distinction between "positive" and "negative" liberty made by Sir Isaiah Berlin comes to mind (I.
Berlin, *Two Concepts of Liberty* [Oxford, 1958]).

14. W. Stieda, "Deutsche Gelehrte als Professoren an der Universität Moskau," *Abhandlungen der Sächsischen Akad. der
Wissenschaften*, XI, No. 4 (1930); E. Winter, *Halle als der
Ausgangspunkt der deutschen Russlandkunde im 18. Jahrhundert* (Berlin, 1953); E. Amburger, *Beiträge zur Geschichte der deutsch-russischen kulturellen Beziehungen*
(Giessen, 1961).

15. Among the writers most widely read were Strube de Piermont, V. Zolotnitskii, and S. Desnitskii. Besides the classics

of natural law like Pufendorf and Grotius, the Russians read
in translation Bielfeld, Chr. Wolf, and Baumeister. Cf. also
A. Fateev, "K istorii iuridicheskoi obrazovannosti v Rossii,"
*Uchenye Zapiski osnovannye Russkoi uchebnoi kollegiei v
Prage*, I, No. 3 (1924), 129–256; G. S. Fel'dshtein, *Glavnye
techeniia v istorii nauki ugolovnogo prava v Rossii* (Iaroslavl',
1909); A. S. Lappo-Danilevskii, "Sobranie i svod zakonov
Rossiiskoi imperii, sostavlennye v tsarstvovanie Ekateriny II,"
Zh. M. N. Pr., CCCIX, CCCX, CCCXI, CCCXIV (January,
March, May, December, 1897); G. Shershenevich, *Nauka
grazhdanskogo prava v Rossii* (Kazan, 1893).

16. H. M. Wolff, *Die Weltanschauung der deutschen Aufklärung
in geschichtlicher Entwicklung* (Bern, 1949); E. Wolf,
Grosse Rechtsdenker (2nd ed.; Tübingen, 1943); G. Gur-
vitch, *L'Idée du droit social* (Paris, 1931); W. Dilthey,
"Das allgemeine Landrecht," *Gesammelte Schriften* (2nd
ed.; Stuttgart, 1960), III, 131–204; F. Valjevec, *Geschichte
der abendländischen Aufklärung* (Wien-Münschen, 1961).

17. Pekarskii, *Nauka i literatura v Rossii pri Petre Velikom* (2
vols., Saint Petersburg, 1862); B. Syromiatnikov, *"Reguli-
arnoe" gosudarstvo Petra Velikogo i ego ideologiia* (Moscow-
Leningrad, 1943), I; G. Gurvich, *"Pravda voli monarshei"
Feofana Prokovicha i ee zapadno-evropeiskie istochniki*
(Iur'ev, 1915). Also *Pravda voli monarshei* (Saint Petersburg, 1726) itself and Tatishchev, "Razgovor dvukh priatelei
o pol'ze nauk i uchilishch (1733)," *Chteniia*, 1887, Part I,
pp. 1-171.

18. With Catherine the Great's Nakaz we have in addition a
sharper turn to notions and arguments based on considerations of the "welfare of the people." This came out even more
clearly in the *Nakaz glavnoi politsii* (*UK 1767*, XLIII, 296–
362) and the *Ustav blagochiniia* (*PSZ*, #15 379). On the relationship between natural-law doctrines and the assumptions
of the "well-regulated police state" of the eighteenth century,
cf. K. Wolzendorf, *Der Polizeigedanke des modernes Staates*
(Breslau, 1918) (Abhandlungen aus dem Staates und Verwaltungsrecht mit Einschluss des Kolonial- und Völkerrechts,
Heft 35). See also the remarks and literature in N. I.
Pavlenko, "Idei absoliutizma v zakonodatel'stve XVIII," and

N. M. Druzhinin, "Prosveshchennyi absoliutizm v Rossii" in *Absoliutizm v Rossii (XVII–XVIII vv.)* (Moscow, 1964), pp. 389–460.

19. The parallel with Stoicism is quite striking, of course.

20. See works cited in note 15.

21. Soviet writers have argued that this point of view was first expressed by Tatishchev. Everyone will agree, however, that it provides the ideological inspiration and background of Radishchev's famous book of protest, *Journey from Saint Petersburg to Moscow,* and the writings of Kozel'skii and Pnin.

22. Cf. the works by Fateev and Lappo-Danilevskii cited in note 15. Also, see V. N. Latkin, *Zakonodatel'nye kommissii v Rossii v XVIII st.* (Saint Petersburg, 1887).

23. Many of the instructions given to deputies of the nobility make direct reference to, or implicitly acknowledge, natural-law concepts as their starting point. In contrast see the complaint of one deputy in *UK 1767,* VIII, 152.

24. Valjavec, *op. cit.;* W. Dilthey, "Das achtzehnte Jahrhundert und die geschichtliche Welt," *Gesammelte Schriften,* III, 210–68; F. Meinecke, *Die Entstehung des Historismus* (2nd ed.; München, 1946); E. Cassirer, *Die Philosophie der Aufklärung* (Tübingen, 1932); H. Trevor-Roper, "The Historical Philosophy of the Enlightenment," *Studies on Voltaire and the Eighteenth Century* (Geneva, 1963), XXVII, 1667–88.

25. The histories of Russian historiography do not touch on the question of the sense of history that the nonprofessional educated layman had in the eighteenth century. Some passing references to this sense may be gleaned in a few memoirs, for example Bolotov's. On Russian historiography, cf. P. Miliukov, *Glavnye techeniia russkoi istoricheskoi mysli* (2nd ed.; Moscow, 1898), I; N. L. Rubinshtein, *Russkaia istoriografiia* (Moscow, 1941); S. L. Peshtich, *Russkaia istoriografiia XVIII veka* (Leningrad, 1961–1965), I–II. See also N. A. Belozerskaia, "Istoricheskii zhurnal XVIII v. (*Rossiiskii Magazin sent. 1792-mart 1794, 3 chasti*)," *Zh. M. N. Pr.,* CCCXV (January, 1898), 61–84.

26. V. N. Karazin, "Pokazanie o sebe," *Sochineniia, pis'ma i bumagi*, D. I. Bagalei, ed. (Khar'kov, 1910), p. 613.

27. Is this not the underlying reason for the growing popularity and revival of "universal history" in the West, particularly the United States?

28. H. Rogger, *National Consciousness in Eighteenth-Century Russia* (Cambridge, Mass.: Harvard University Press, 1960), Chap. 5.

29. For many this happened in fact only in 1812, but for the genuine élite of the educated nobility it occurred even before 1789 (Radishchev, Pnin, and, in his own way, Karamzin).

30. André Mazon, *Deux russes écrivains français* (Paris, 1964 [Etudes de littérature étrangère et comparée, LI]).

31. Cf. Cherniavsky, *op. cit.*, the chapter on "Holy Russia," and H. Rogger, *op. cit.*, Chap. 4.

32. This craving also explains the popularity of Polish literary models and romances of chivalry in the seventeenth and throughout most of the eighteenth centuries. Sipovskii, *op. cit.*; D. Čiževskii, *History of Russian Literature from the XIth Century to the End of the Baroque* (The Hague, 1960) (Slavistic Printings and Reprintings, XII), Chap. 7. Also L. R. Lewitter, "Peter the Great, Poland and the Westernization of Russia," *Journal of History of Ideas*, XIX, No. 4 (October, 1958), 493–506; *idem*, "Poland, the Ukraine, and Russia in the seventeenth century," *Slavonic and East European Review*, XXVII, Nos. 68 and 69.

33. This provoked Catherine's literary attacks on the Freemasons. Cf. also V. Narezhnyi, *Rossiiskii Zhil'blaz* (Moscow, 1938); N. Kurganov, *op. cit.*, II, 97–98.

34. A. N. Pypin, *Russkoe masonstvo—XVIII i pervaia chetvert' XIX v.* (Petrograd, 1916); G. V. Vernadskii, *Russkoe masonstvo XVIII v.* (Petrograd, 1917); S. Mel'gunov & N. Sidorov, *Masonstvo v ego proshlom i nastoiashchem* (2 vols.; Moscow, 1914–1915); Ia. L. Barskov, *Perepiska moskovskikh masonov XVIII v.* (Saint Petersburg, 1915); T. Sokolovskaia, *Russkoe masanstvo i ego znachenie v istorii obshchestvennogo dvizheniia* (Saint Petersburg, 1908). Also T. A. Bakounine, *Le répertoire biographique des francs-maçons russes* (*XVIIIe*

et XIXe siècles) (Bruxelles, 1940); T. A. Bakunina, *Russkie vol'nye kamenshchiki* (Paris, 1934).

35. The long and interesting relationship between Bolotov and Novikov, for example, which was reported in full by the former. Cf. also the memoirs of Tuchkov and Dobrynin.

36. Thus Novikov's orthodoxy was confirmed by the Metropolitan of Moscow, who examined him at the order of Catherine the Great. The lives of Labzin and Prince Lopukhin are good illustrations of the religious element in Masonry.

37. Charity through alms giving, of course, does not count in this context. Boyar Rtishchev, so well described by Kliuchevskii (*Kurs russkoi istorii,* lecture LVI) was a striking exception.

38. Best known were the activities of Schwartz and Novikov in Moscow, cf. Bogoliubov, *N. I. Novikov i ego vremia* (Moscow, 1916). The pietistic Protestant influence is unmistakable in Schwartz. Cf. collection of Masonic songs, *Pesni* (n.d., n.pl.) in Library of Congress (T. Fessenko, *Eighteenth-Century Russian Publications in the Library of Congress* [No. 791 (Washington, D.C., 1961)]).

39. Chiefly Novikov's efforts, cf. V. Semennikov, *Knigoizdatel'skaia deiatel'nost' N. I. Novikova i typograficheskoi kompanii* (Saint Petersburg, 1913); *idem,* "Literaturnaia i knigopechatnaia deiatel'nost v provintsii v kontse XVIII i v nachale XIX vv.," *Russkii Bibliofil,* 1911, Bk. V; N. K. Piksanov, *Oblastnye kul'turnye gnezda* (Moscow-Leningrad, 1928). Cf. also V. Semennikov, "Bibiograficheskii spisok knig, napechatannykh v provintsii so vremeni vozniknoveniia grazhdanskikh tipografii po 1807 g.," *Russkii Bibliofil* (1912), II, 47–77, and III, 36–58; and *idem,* "Dopoeonitel'nye materialy dlia istorii provintsial'nykh tipografii XVIII i nachala XIX v.," *Russkii Bibliofil* (1913), VII, 58–83; V. V. Shangin, *Sel'skie tipografii v poslednei chetverti XVIII v. i ruzaevskie izdaniia Struiskogo* (Saint Petersburg, 1903); N. P. Smirnov-Sokol'skii, *Russkie literaturnye almanakhi i sborniki XVIII–XIX vv.* (Moscow, 1965).

40. V. V. Zen'kovskii, "Pravoslavie i russkaia kul'tura," *Problemy russkogo religioznogo soznaniia* (Berlin, 1924), p. 243.

41. One has to think of the parallel achievement of Renaissance Humanism in the West in secularizing the Christian notions of dignity and worth of the individual.

42. Besides the information on the circles around 1801 adduced above, see Bazanov, *Obshchestvo liubitelei i sobesednikov rossiiskogo prosveshcheniia* (Petrozavodsk, 1949); M. Raeff *The Decembrist Movement* (Englewood Cliffs, N.J.: Prentice-Hall, 1966), Introduction; A. Fomin, *K istorii voprosa o razvitii v Rossii obshchestvennykh idei v nachale XIX veka* (Petrograd, n.d.).

43. G. Fedotov, "Tragediia intelligentsii," *op. cit.*, Chap. 1, p. 13.

44. Natural-law precepts, stressing the moral equality of all human beings, provided the intellectual component of this "populist" orientation. Strube de Piermont, *Ebauche des loix naturelles et du droit primitif* (nouv. éd.: Amsterdam, 1744), pp. 150 (§260), 153–54 (§263); *O dolzhnostiakh cheloveka*, p. 83; H. Rogger, *op. cit.* Also Iu. Ia. Kogan, *Prosvetitel' XVIII veka Ia. P. Kozel'skii* (Moscow, 1958) and the vast Soviet literature on Radishchev.

45. C. Hinrichs, "Der Hallische Pietismus als politisch-soziale Reformbewegung des 18. Jahrhunderts," *Preussen als historisches Problem* ("Veröffentlichungen der historischen Kommission zu Berlin"—X [Berlin, 1964]), pp. 171–84.

46. Cf. the interesting material in E. Winter, *op. cit.*

47. Bolotov's readings illustrate this, as does the intellectual development of Karamzin, Labzin, etc. I. Galakhov, "Obzor misticheskoi literatury v tsarstvovanie Aleksandra I," *Zh. M. N. Pr.*, CLXXXII (November, 1875) is relevant for the eighteenth century also. Filaret (Gumilevskii), *Obzor russkoi dukhovnoi literatury* (3rd ed.; Saint Petersburg, 1884).

48. I. Pnin, *Sochineniia*, I. K. Luppol, ed. (Moscow, 1934), pp. 66–68 (the poem entitled "Chelovek").

49. The best source on this generation is the *Arkhiv brat'ev Turgenevykh* (5 vols.; Saint Petersburg, 1911); cf. also the literature cited in notes 12 and 42 (cf. also Chapter 4, note 64). Naturally, the vast documentation on the Decembrists contains much of interest and relevance; for a guide see N. M. Chentsov, *Vosstanie Dekabristov—Bibliografiia* (Moscow-Leningrad, 1929) and M. V. Nechkina,

ed., and R. G. Eimontova, compiler, *Dvizhenie Dekabristov —Ukazatel' literatury 1928–1959* (Moscow, 1960).

50. In some respects they had forerunners in M. M. Shcherbatov, N. Panin, and the Vorontsov brothers.

51. The help extended by Alexander I in establishing constitutional settlements in Prussia, France, and Poland only raised the expectations of the Russians and increased their disappointment at Russia's failure to follow suit.

52. In a critical mood, this feature has been well noted by M. O. Gershenzon (*Istoricheskie zapiski* [Moscow, 1910], pp. 153–54):

When . . . we consider an average member of the Russian intelligentsia, a characteristic trait immediately catches our eye: more than anything else he is a man who, from youth, lives in the literal sense *outside himself, i.e.* he recognizes as an object worthy of his interest and participation only something lying outside his own personality—the people, society, the state. Nowhere in the world does public opinion rule as despotically as with us, and for two-thirds of a century already our public opinion rests immovably on the acceptance of the [following] supreme principle: to think of one's own personality is egoistic and indecent; only he who thinks of social problems, is interested in social questions, works for the common good, is truly a person. The number of those among the intelligentsia who realized this program in practice was, of course, insignificant; but everybody acknowledged the sanctity of the banner, and those who did not act, platonically still recognized this activity alone as salutary and were thereby freed from the necessity of doing anything else.

Index